Classical Sub

Well-Ordered Language

TEACHER'S EDITION

Level 1A

The Curious Child's Guide to Grammar

REVISED EDITION

Tammy Peters and Daniel Coupland, PhD

Well-Ordered Language:
The Curious Child's Guide to Grammar
Level 1A Teacher's Edition: REVISED EDITION

Version 2.0

ISBN: 978-1-60051-444-9

Classical Academic Press
515 S. 32nd Street
Camp Hill, PA 17011

www.ClassicalAcademicPress.com

Content editor: Marie Kramb Campbell, PhD
Illustrator: Katharina Drees
Series editor and book designer: Lauraine Gustafson

PGP.04.24

Acknowledgments

Tammy Peters

I am deeply indebted to Mars Hill Academy in Cincinnati, Ohio. I give a sincere thanks to the students, families, and teachers who have supported me and contributed to this work over the last twenty years. A special thanks to Sharon Peterson, Ellen Liebing, and Traci DeBra for their constant encouragement.

With a grateful heart, I thank Dr. Dan Coupland for his insights and love of language. It has been a privilege to coauthor Well-Ordered Language with him. I also thank Dr. Marie Campbell, our content editor, for her expertise and precision in the English language. She is a joy and a friend. I greatly appreciate Dr. Chris Perrin, Laurie Gustafson, and the whole Classical Academic Press staff for their vision and professionalism.

There are not enough words to express my gratitude to my family for their constant support. My heartfelt appreciation is to the love of my life, Hud Peters, who has prayerfully supported me through it all.

Daniel Coupland, PhD

I am grateful for the *grammarphiles* in my life: Mrs. Linda Tiarks, my elementary school teacher who showed me how to study and love the English language; Dr. Bryan Coupland, my father, who appreciates a well-crafted sentence; and Mrs. Tammy Peters, my coauthor, who is the most talented (and most energetic) grammar teacher I have ever seen. I am also thankful for Marie, our talented content editor, who has helped to make the Well-Ordered Language program even better. And of course, I appreciate Chris, Laurie, and the entire Classical Academic Press team for their tireless effort to get this program in print.

Well-Ordered Language Level 1

At a Glance

Book A

Chapter	Main Topic	Supplemental Topics
1	Four Kinds of Sentences	Eight parts of speech; end punctuation; interjections and punctuation
2	Principal Elements, Part 1—Subject and Predicate	Singular and plural nouns as subjects; suffixes and parts of speech
3	Principal Elements, Part 2—Subject and Predicate Verb	Helping verbs; verb tense; subject-verb agreement; singular and plural subjects with helping verbs
4	Adverbs	*Not* and *never* as negative adverbs; placement of adverbs in sentence order
5	Adjectives	Article adjectives; correct usage of articles *a* and *an*
6	Direct Objects	Transitive and intransitive verbs; word order in sentences
7	Subject Pronouns	Agreement in person and number: subject pronouns and antecedents; subject pronouns and verbs
8	Interrogative Sentences—Subject Pronouns and Helping Verbs	Contractions: subject pronouns and helping verbs; verbs and the adverb *not*

Table of Contents

Well-Ordered Language
A Classical Approach to English Grammar Instruction

Why Study Grammar?

We study grammar because we wish to master language, and language cannot be easily mastered without grammar. Grammar is the study of what makes language work—the way letters form words, the way words form sentences, the way sentences express human thought.

An educated person wants to understand the rich variety of human thought enshrined in language of all sorts—books from yesterday and the last millennium, books in English and books in other languages as well. An educated person also yearns to express himself clearly, accurately, and completely. It is the study of grammar that yields the capacity to do this, and the student who sees the connection between the study of grammar and the mastery of language will study grammar with zeal.

Learning Grammar, Teaching Grammar

We have designed Well-Ordered Language (WOL) with the understanding that many teachers who will use this book don't know grammar as well as they would like. Therefore, we have created a rich teacher's edition that will enable teachers to review and deepen their own understanding of grammar even as they teach students.

We have also worked to provide a clear, incremental presentation of grammar in this series that includes plenty of illustrations, practice, and review. For example, in each chapter, students will memorize through song clear definitions of relevant grammatical concepts. Helpful analogies and attractive graphical illustrations at the beginning of each chapter introduce and complement the concepts in the chapter. Students also will discover a story emerging from the sentence exercises, featuring characters who appear throughout the text and in the graphical illustrations.

Effective Teaching Methods

The series employs an innovative choral analysis method that makes learning enjoyable and permanent. With clear guidance from the teacher's edition, instructors will easily be able to lead students through the choral analysis of grammar, and through this analysis, students will see grammar embodied in the sentences they study. In *Well-Ordered Language Level 2* and beyond, the students also learn to diagram, visualizing the grammatical relationships within sentences. The program has been layered concept on concept, an approach that aids students in seeing and experiencing how a well-ordered language works. As their mastery of grammar develops, students also understand poems and stories more thoroughly and enjoy them more deeply.

Learning with Delight

We think that the right study of grammar should lead to delight. The traditional study of grammar should be more than mere rote memorization of rules; it must also include opportunities for students to engage language in works of literature and human expression. As students acquire a greater capacity to understand language and use it effectively themselves, they will experience joy and delight. This is one reason we have included for grammatical study beautiful poetry and excerpts from great literature. Students will see that their ongoing study of grammar will open up a deeper understanding of beautiful literature that both instructs and delights.

Compelling Need

In this cultural moment, there is a desperate need for language that is well ordered. Today's discourse is often filled with ambiguity, equivocation, and crudeness. Those who have mastered a well-ordered language not only will stand out as eloquent and clear but also will be able to say well what they mean and to say what others will heed. It will be those with a command of language who will be able to mine the wisdom of the past and to produce eloquence in the future.

Ongoing Support

We have created not only a series of texts but a constellation of products that will help teachers to use WOL effectively. Visit our website at ClassicalAcademicPress.com for additional support for using WOL, including video training featuring author Tammy Peters (available at http://capress.link/wol1att), downloadable PDF documents (available for purchase), and other resources.

Thank you for joining us in this most important work of restoring a well-ordered language for the next generation!

Lesson-Planning Options

The Well-Ordered Language series is designed to be flexible, adaptable, and practical. Depending on the needs of the teacher, lessons can be modified to meet particular classroom expectations. The following options for teaching each chapter assume a 30–40 minute period.

	Option A (4 times per week)	**Option B** (3 times per week)	**Option C** (5 times, one week)
Week One	**Day One** ◇ Ideas to Understand ◇ Terms to Remember ◇ Sentences to Analyze ◇ Lesson to Learn A	**Day One** ◇ Ideas to Understand ◇ Terms to Remember ◇ Sentences to Analyze ◇ Lesson to Learn A	**Day One** ◇ Ideas to Understand ◇ Terms to Remember ◇ Sentences to Analyze ◇ Lesson to Learn A
	Day Two ◇ Lesson to Learn B	**Day Two** ◇ Lesson to Learn B	**Day Two** ◇ Lesson to Learn B
	Day Three ◇ Lesson to Learn C	**Day Three** ◇ Lesson to Learn C	**Day Three** ◇ Lesson to Learn C
	Day Four ◇ Lesson to Enjoy—Poem ***or*** ◇ Sentences for Practice		**Day Four** ◇ Lesson to Learn D
			Day Five ◇ Quiz (PDF)
Week Two	**Day Five** ◇ Lesson to Learn D	**Day Four** ◇ Lesson to Learn D ***or*** ◇ Review (PDF)	
	Day Six ◇ Review (PDF)	**Day Five** ◇ Review (PDF) ***or*** ◇ Lesson to Enjoy—Poem or Fable* ◇ Sentences for Practice	
	Day Seven ◇ Lesson to Enjoy—Fable* ◇ Sentences for Practice—Fable (PDF)	**Day Six** ◇ Quiz (PDF)	
	Day Eight ◇ Quiz (PDF)		

From the Sideline:
Option C is an accelerated plan for *WOL1A* and *WOL1B*.

You could consider this option in tandem with a writing curriculum, such as Classical Academic Press's Writing & Rhetoric series, alternating weeks between grammar and writing

*The fables for chapters 1, 3, 5, 6, 7, and 8 can be found in the downloadable PDF. The poems for chapters 2 and 4 can be found in the PDF.

Introduction to Students

Do you have a favorite word? Most people have favorite words just as they have favorite numbers or colors. So, what is yours?

Maybe it is an extremely long word that your friends don't know. Maybe you just like the way its sound rolls off your tongue. Maybe you use it as often as you can, or maybe you save it for special occasions.

We want to share one of our favorite words with you. You probably know what it means already, but you may not have thought of it as an exceptional word. Probably few people would name it as a favorite because it seems so ordinary. It is far from ordinary though. The word is . . . *analyze.*

One reason we love the word *analyze* is because it has interesting grandparents. Its roots are Greek: *ana* meaning "up, throughout" and *lusis* meaning "unloose, release, set free." When you *analyze* something, you break it up into its parts and set them free!

Great thinkers are great analyzers.

Scientists who study bugs are called entomologists. They analyze insects by dissecting them. Sports analysts watch freeze-frames of each motion of a single play in football to make sure the referee applied the rules correctly. Detectives analyze every inch of a crime scene, inspecting it for clues. These great thinkers are curious about what is inside an insect, a play, or even a crime.

Great thinkers are always curious. For them, analysis is an adventure.

You are a curious child, and your adventure in this book will be learning how to *analyze* sentences. You will take them apart, unloose their knots, and set them free. Step-by-step you will learn the special function of each part of language.

Understanding the parts of something—whether you are a student, scientist, sports analyst, or detective—leads to appreciating the whole thing even more. Once you break something apart, it is natural and right that you should put it back together again. If you take apart a clock to see how it works, you will want to reassemble it so you don't miss dinnertime. Learning how to *analyze* sentences makes you more skilled at *constructing* them too, both in your writing and in your speaking.

The parts of language are words, and words are wonderful.

Introduction to Teachers

In the Well-Ordered Language (WOL) series, grammar instruction is focused, practical, and lively. The curriculum is designed so that teachers and students actively engage with grammar concepts through physical movement and song. Students will use all four language skills—reading, writing, listening, and speaking—to develop a better understanding of English grammar. Your students will find that the thirty to forty minutes devoted to grammar instruction are among the most dynamic of the school day.

The WOL Marking System—Analyze, Analyze, Analyze

Analysis is the heart and soul of the WOL method. Each chapter includes multiple sentences for students to analyze aloud and on paper, as a class and individually. Just as children naturally enjoy taking things apart and putting them back together, your students will learn that understanding how words in a sentence work together to convey meaning is intriguing and enjoyable. Students will see analysis as a stimulating activity of a curious mind.

The unique WOL marking system will help students identify the function of words and the relationship between words in a sentence. In Level 2 and above, WOL teaches classical diagramming alongside this analysis, but the analytic approach in all the levels is extraordinary:

- ◇ The teacher explains the concept to students through active engagement with specific, carefully selected sentences.
- ◇ The teacher models the structural analysis on the board while the students participate by speaking the analysis in chorus. Scripts are provided for you in the teachers' pages in each chapter.
- ◇ The structural analysis uses an innovative marking system that builds incrementally, chapter by chapter, preparing the students for sentence diagramming.
- ◇ The students begin to analyze the sentences themselves, starting with choral analysis and moving to individual analysis.

To emphasize the importance of analysis to the method and to illustrate WOL's marking system, here are sample sentences with complete markings, one taken from early in *WOL Level 1* and one from the end:

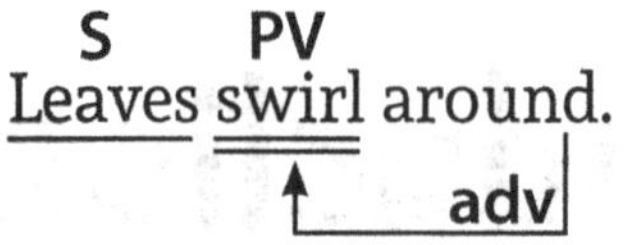

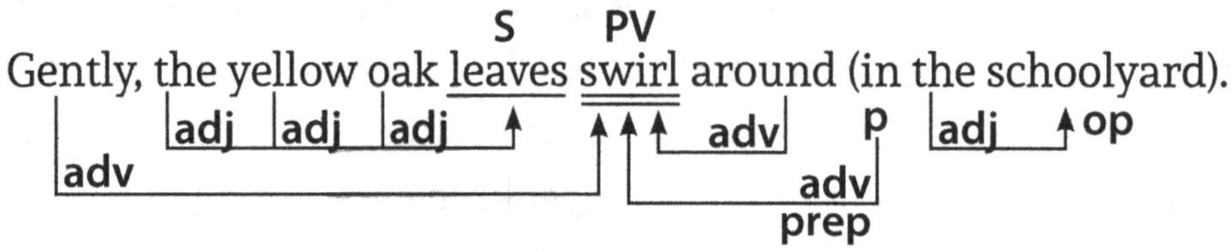

These samples illustrate what would appear on the student's paper during a lesson. But more important than this end product is the lively, unfolding *process*, the progression of markings as the students chorally analyze the grammar. In addition, before analyzing sentences in each lesson, the students already will have enjoyed singing or chanting the definitions of key terms and practicing the grammatical concepts with short activities and exercises.

How to Use This Book: Learn, Memorize, Review

Well-Ordered Language offers you a wealth of material—perhaps more than some teachers will need. When teaching students to analyze and mark sentences with enthusiastic competence, teachers can creatively modify the curriculum, adapting it to meet the needs of particular students. The following pages explain the book's structure and suggest a possible daily approach. The Lesson-Planning Options chart on page viii shows a variety of ways to fit the curriculum into your weekly plan. To assist your lesson planning, we have organized each chapter into three main sections:

Introducing the Chapter (first day)

The opening text of each chapter acquaints students with the grammatical concepts and important terms covered in the chapter. Then, the students will be ready to participate in a choral analysis of a sentence.

- ◇ **Ideas to Understand:** The opening paragraphs introduce the chapter's main focus, using as an example an excerpt from poetry or fiction. (For enrichment beyond the scope of the grammar lessons, WOL includes a literary appendix containing the complete poems and longer passages from the fiction. Appendices containing brief biographical sketches of the authors and bibliographic information for the sources are also included.)

- **Terms to Remember:** Each chapter introduces new terms and reviews previously encountered terms. Students learn important terms by reciting short, inviting songs or chants. Adding movement and hand gestures helps keep the lesson lighthearted and captivating. The book's glossary includes pertinent definitions of terms found throughout the book. For quick reference, the Song Lyrics section, which starts on page 191, provides in verse form all of the songs and chants, which are also available as a CD or downloadable audio files at ClassicalAcademicPress.com.

- **Moment for Mechanics (or Pause for Punctuation):** Each chapter has a brief section highlighting a particular rule of mechanics or punctuation. This rule is then reinforced in the lessons. Foundational mechanics lead to the punctuation rules in subsequent WOL levels.

- **Sentences to Analyze:** This section shows teachers how to guide the students through an initial sentence analysis and to explain what happens in each step. At this point in the lesson, students recite together the analysis as the teacher marks the sentence with WOL's unique marking system.

Teaching the Lessons (daily)

Each chapter includes four lessons to reinforce and practice the main grammar principle of that chapter. They are called Lesson to Learn A, B, C, and D. In the teacher's edition, each of these lessons is preceded by corresponding Well-Ordered Notes, which help the teacher introduce each lesson.

- **Well-Ordered Notes:** These fifteen-minute, teacher-directed lessons consist of three parts. They employ a variety of instructional methods and often include interactive activities.

    - **Review It:** To start the lesson, the teacher leads review of the grammar terms. The students sing or chant the definitions along with the CD/audio files. Teachers can lead students in physical movement (e.g., hand motions, marching, bending, and reaching) during the songs to help students absorb and memorize the definitions.

    - **Practice It:** Next, the teacher warms up the class for the main task—sentence analysis—with a short activity. This section is provided in the teacher's edition only to give the students the opportunity to use the new concept in an oral exercise. The exercises are designed to be lighthearted and quick.

    - **Analyze It:** Finally, the lesson climaxes with the students demonstrating the analysis of the grammatical concept, using WOL's unique marking system. The teacher models the analysis of the first sentence in the lesson, for which the markings and an analytic script are provided in the teacher's pages. Teachers should expect full participation from the students during choral analysis. The class should complete the analysis vigorously, never allowing it to become monotone or dull.

◇ **Lesson to Learn:** After the teacher-directed lesson, the teacher will help the students with the remaining practice sentences on the lesson worksheets. These guided practice sheets should be done as a class, with the choral analysis completed in unison. The teacher guides the class through the sentences that comprise the first part of the worksheet while the rest is done independently. The optional Sentences for Practice worksheets, found in the Extra Practice and Assessments PDF, have ten sentences for analysis and can be used as additional practice, a classroom lesson, or enrichment.

Extending the Lessons (weekly options)

In each chapter, a number of options are offered for additional practice and application.

◇ **Lesson to Enjoy:** This section provides a poem and a fable to read and to discuss as enrichment activities beyond the daily lessons. These activities usually require thirty minutes or a whole class period to complete. If the student edition contains a poem, then both the downloadable PDF and the teacher's edition include a tale as an alternative, and vice versa. The material that accompanies the literary excerpt not only draws attention to grammar in action, but also provides a range of activity suggestions to help foster the students' love of language. Each poem itself exemplifies the grammatical principle covered in the chapter, while the fables are accompanied by a practice sheet that provides the grammatical connection. Sentences for Practice—Fable is a synopsis of the narrative written as ten sentences for analysis. Teachers may use these practice sentences either to introduce the tale or to conclude the discussion of it. (Note: Many of the fables included in this book can also be found in Writing & Rhetoric, Classical Academic Press's writing curriculum.)

◇ **Extra Practice & Assessments PDF:** The downloadable PDF (available for purchase at ClassicalAcademicPress.com) provides all the extra fables, poems, and sentences for practice in a convenient printable format. In addition, the PDF includes a review lesson and a quiz for each chapter, which match exactly the format of the answer key that is included in the printed teacher's edition.

◇ **Sentence Bank:** Analysis scripts for extra sentences are located at the end of each chapter in the teacher's edition. Teachers can use these sentences for extra guided practice if more practice is needed for individual students or the entire class.

◇ **Side Panels:** The side panels furnish both the student and the teacher with additional information to stimulate further discussion and learning. There are four types of panels: two for the student (To the Source and Off the Shelf) and two for the teacher that do not appear in the student edition (From the Sideline and Fewer than Five).

- **To the Source** helps the students understand the etymology of various grammar terms.
- **Off the Shelf** provides more information to the students about books mentioned in the chapters and should pique the interest of curious readers.
- **From the Sideline** offers pedagogical tips for teachers from teachers.
- **Fewer than Five** provides alternative activities for class sizes smaller than five students, such as homeschool classrooms, tutoring situations, and co-op learning environments.

Pedagogical Principles and Guidance

The classical tradition has passed down a rich collection of teaching methods that have been successfully used for generations to teach children well. We encourage teachers of WOL to become familiar with and employ these methods while teaching grammar. Below is a list of some key pedagogical principles that come to us from the classical tradition of education. A video overview of the principles of classical pedagogy is available at http://capress.link/prpd. A subscription to ClassicalU.com will grant you access not only to additional videos that cover the nine essential principles in more detail, but also to scores of other online training videos for classical educators.

- *Festina Lente* (Make Haste Slowly)
- *Multum Non Multa* (Much Not Many)
- *Repetitio Mater Memoriae* (Repetition Is the Mother of Memory)
- Embodied Learning
- Songs, Chants, and Jingles
- Wonder and Curiosity
- Educational Virtues
- *Scholé*, Contemplation, Leisure
- *Docendo Discimus* (By Teaching We Learn)

adjectives
CONJUNCTIONS
prepositions
verbs
interjections
adverbs

From the Sideline: Command the class. Remind students that learning is orderly and civil. Start each day by standing and greeting your class: "Good morning, students." Expect them to greet you: "Good morning, Mrs. Wordsmith."

Chapter 1

Four Kinds of Sentences[A]

[A]Bring in eight books, each with an attached note card labeled with one of the eight parts of speech. Line them up to represent how the entire English language is made up of these few, simple building blocks.

Since you have grown up hearing and speaking English, you already know a good bit about how our language■ works—after all, you can speak it. You probably also know something about bugs, but aren't you curious about that long, green, six-legged creature you just found? It looks like a living stick! If you had a field guide to insects, you could look it up and learn about it.

To the Source: ■ language
Our word *language* comes from the Latin word *lingua*, which means "tongue."

Just as you might need an insect field guide to identify that fascinating bug, you will need *Well-Ordered Language*, which is a sort of field guide to English, to help you learn about the language you speak. Like all field guides, this one starts with identifying the most basic characteristics of its subject: words.

All words in English can be sorted into eight different groups. The words that fall into each of those groups have the same kind of meaning and use. Think of it this way: If you could take a book off your shelf and literally spill all the words on the floor, you would have a mess. To organize them, you could put all the words that are alike together. Some words name things, some show action, and others just describe things. Once you sorted them, you would discover that you had eight piles, or groups, of words. These groups are called the **eight parts of speech** and they are nouns, verbs, adjectives, adverbs, prepositions, pronouns, conjunctions, and interjections. You may not know what all these strange terms mean yet, but soon they will become your friends! All the books written in English on all the shelves in all the libraries in the world are filled with only these eight kinds of words. The eight parts of speech are the foundation of our English grammar,■ and we will study each one in turn, chapter by chapter.

To the Source: ■ grammar
Our word *grammar* comes from the Greek word *gramma*, which means "letter."

To the Source: ■ sentence
The term *sentence* comes from the Latin word *sententia*, which means "opinion" or "judgment."

Fortunately, we don't usually organize random words into piles. We organize them into **sentences.**■ Words make up sentences. We use sentences to express our thoughts, ideas, and opinions. To communicate well, we choose particular kinds of sentences to make statements, ask questions, give commands, or express strong feelings. Learning the different types of sentences is a good place to begin.

From the Sideline: For each chapter's grammar lesson, write on the board the literary example highlighted in the Ideas to Understand section. In this chapter, the four lines from "What O'Clock" illustrate the four kinds of sentences. To lead a literary discussion, see the full poem in The Curious Child's Literary Appendix. Tips for teaching poetry are included in the teacher's edition.

Ideas to Understand

There are only four kinds of sentences. Later you will learn that every sentence has a subject and predicate, which make the thought of the sentence complete, but there's no need to worry about subjects and predicates yet. In this lesson, we focus on the four different kinds of sentences: declarative, interrogative, imperative, and exclamatory. Their names tell exactly what each one of them does.

Do you think it is fun to blow a cloud of seeds off a dandelion? That's what happens in one stanza of a poem called "What O'Clock?" by Edith Nesbit. You can find the whole poem in the back of this book in The Curious Child's Literary Appendix, but for now let's look at how Nesbit uses all four kinds of sentences in a few verses about dandelions:

What o'clock is it, children dear?
Ask of the dandelions here!
Blow, blow, blow, and away they go—
But they do not tell us the time you know[.][1]

To the Source: ■ declarative
The word *declarative* comes from the Latin word *declarare*, meaning "make clear, reveal, disclose," from *de-*, "totally," and *clarare*, "to clarify."

To the Source: ■ interrogative
The word *interrogative* comes from the Latin word *interrogare*, from *inter*, meaning "between," and *rogare*, meaning "to ask, to question."

A **declarative■ sentence** declares something or states that something is a fact. A declarative sentence makes something clear or known. In her poem, Nesbit makes known something about dandelions and time: "But they do not tell us the time you know[.]" A declarative sentence ends with a period.

An **interrogative■ sentence** is also known as a question. To interrogate is to ask questions. The poet asks the question of the reader, "What o'clock is it, children dear?" She does not expect an actual answer, but

1. E. Nesbit and Saretta Nesbit (aka Caris Brooke), *All Round the Year* (London: Von Portheim & Co.), last modified January 20, 2007, http://tinyurl.com/ocao7gy.

she is asking her readers to stop and think about what time it is. When you look at the whole poem, you will see that the author also asks about the time of year and even about the time of a child's life. An interrogative sentence is easy to identify because it ends with a question mark.

An **imperative**■ **sentence** expresses a command or a request. An imperative is something that is necessary or unavoidable. The subject of imperative sentences is always "you" even though the word *you* usually does not appear in them. When the subject *you* is invisible because it is indirectly expressed or just suggested, it is called an **implied subject**. Nesbit uses an invisible, implied subject in this imperative sentence: "Blow, blow, blow, and away they go." Although she does not use the word *you*, she suggests it. She calls out a command to the readers, which we could rewrite like this: "Children, you blow, blow, and away the seeds go!" An imperative sentence sometimes ends with an exclamation point and sometimes with a period.

An **exclamatory**■ **sentence** is a sentence that expresses strong feelings. Exclamatory sentences are written to show emotion. They exclaim something, and they end with an exclamation point (!). When the poet writes, "Ask of the dandelions here!" she wants her readers to see how senseless it is to ask dandelions the time since they are here and gone so quickly. It is as if she is saying, "Humph, the silly dandelions don't seem to know!" Pay attention to the difference between an exclamatory sentence and an imperative sentence since they both can end with an exclamation point. Remember, an exclamatory sentence expresses strong feelings and an imperative sentence gives a command. Sometimes a sentence can be both exclamatory and imperative: "Ask of the dandelions here!"

To the Source:
■ imperative
The word *imperative* comes from the Latin word *imperare*, meaning "to command, to requisition," from *in*, "into, in," and *parare*, "prepare, order, arrange."

To the Source:
■ exclamatory
The word *exclamatory* comes from the Latin word *exclamare*, which means "cry out loud," from *ex*, "out," and *clamare*, "to cry, shout, call."

From the Sideline: While interjections are introduced in this chapter, they are not covered in depth until *WOL Level 2*. Each level in WOL incrementally builds on the previous, providing layers of learning.

II Pause for Punctuation

An **interjection** is a part of speech that is a word, such as "oops" or "argh," expressing strong emotion. The word *interjection* is from the Latin word *interjicere*, meaning "to throw between" (*inter* means "between" and *jacere* means "throw"). Usually followed by a comma or an exclamation point, interjections are often thrown into or between exclamatory sentences.

Comma: Aha, some people call fluffy dandelions *clocks*!
Exclamation Point: Aha! some people call fluffy dandelions *clocks*!

We will cover interjections in more depth in *WOL2B*, but for now try to spot them, like dandelions in a field, in your reading. Hey, let's start collecting a bouquet of interjections!

[B]For the lyrics to all of the songs, please see the Song Lyrics section on page 191. Play the appropriate audio tracks and have students sing/chant along. Make sure to keep it lively. Whether you have the students stand and jump or sit and clap, they will memorize the definitions more quickly.

To the Source: ■ definition

The word *definition* comes from the Latin words *de*, meaning "about, from," and *finis*, meaning "boundary, limit." A definition gives us the limits of what a word can mean.

To the Source: ■ analyze

The word *analyze* comes from the Greek word *analusis*—*ana* means "up, throughout" and *lusis* means "unloose, release, set free."

To the Source: ■ dissect

Our word *dissect* comes from the Latin words *dis*, which means "apart," and *secare*, which means "to cut." Our word *section* can mean something that has been cut, divided, or set apart.

We have pointed out that all the books in the world that are written in English contain only eight kinds of words. Well, now you see that they also contain only four kinds of sentences.

Terms to Remember[B]

A field guide for insects is organized according to characteristics that you can see and inspect, such as the parts, shapes, and colors of the insect. Knowing vocabulary for talking about insects—words such as *mandible* (jaw), *thorax* (middle section), and *abdomen* (end part of the insect)—helps you understand that strange and fascinating bug you found earlier.

Similarly, knowing the language, or vocabulary, of grammar is the first step in understanding how grammar works. This book includes many new words and definitions.■ Be sure to memorize the definitions in each lesson as you go.

NEW! **Eight Parts of Speech** *(1–1)*

NEW! **Sentence** *(1–2)*

Sentences to Analyze

Learning how to analyze■ a sentence is your most important goal in completing this whole book. To analyze something is to take it apart or unloosen its parts to understand it better. We will start out slowly identifying the kinds of sentences, and later we will identify all the parts of a sentence. Each chapter will introduce another part of the analysis, building on what we know.

Think of analyzing a sentence like dissecting■ a big insect, dividing it into separate parts in order to study it. Each layer of the dissection is another layer of learning. To begin, we make two observations: 1) identify the words as a sentence, and 2) identify what kind of sentence it is.

The following examples show how to analyze the four kinds of sentences. The words in black are for the teacher to say. The words in gray are to be said aloud together. Think about the words as you say them, and follow these three steps for each sentence:

- Read the sentence out loud.
- Review the definition of a sentence and then identify the sentence as a sentence.
- State what kind of sentence it is and explain why it is that kind of sentence.

Declarative Sentence: Winston reads a great deal.

a. (First, read the sentence aloud.) "Winston reads a great deal."

b. "This is a *sentence* because it is a group of words that expresses a complete thought."

c. "It is a *declarative sentence* because it makes a statement."

Interrogative Sentence: Does Fritz like to read too?

a. (First, read the sentence aloud.) "Does Fritz like to read too?"

b. "This is a *sentence* because it is a group of words that expresses a complete thought."

c. "It is an *interrogative sentence* because it asks a question."

Imperative Sentence: Read your book silently.

a. (First, read the sentence aloud.) "Read your book silently."

b. "This is a *sentence* because it is a group of words that expresses a complete thought."

c. "It is an *imperative sentence* because it gives a command."

Exclamatory Sentence: Wow, you read the whole book!

a. (Read the sentence aloud.) "Wow, you read the whole book!"

b. "This is a *sentence* because it is a group of words that expresses a complete thought."

c. "It is an *exclamatory sentence* because it expresses strong feelings."

From the Sideline: We use *analysis* and *analyze* throughout WOL to refer to a system of grammatical classification that includes choral analysis. It is a precursor to diagramming, which is introduced in WOL Level 2. The Sentences to Analyze section in this first chapter is your students' first step into a new world of grammatical study. Do not gloss over this section or skip any steps.

Each chapter adds more steps in the analysis of increasingly sophisticated sentences. Starting in chapter 2, a set of written marks is added, which students record on sentences as they recite the analysis. In the WOL series, analysis is systematic; it is both choral and written; it is dynamic in its call and response rhythm; and it is at the heart of our approach to grammar. We encourage you to visit ClassicalAcademicPress.com for a video demonstration of this analysis.

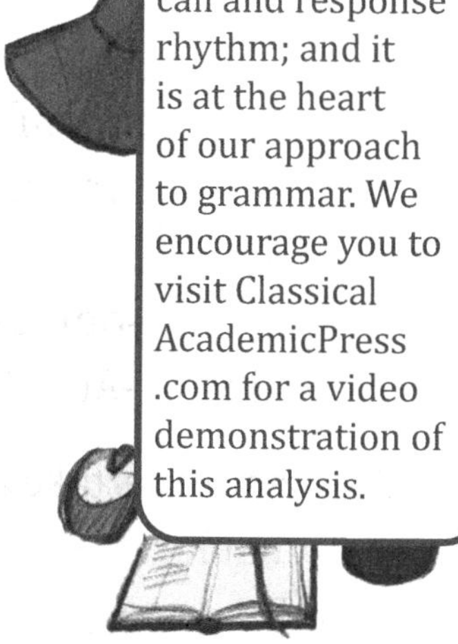

If analyzing a sentence is like dissecting a big bug, then you have just finished the first part of the dissection. The first thing an entomologist would do is identify the creature's genus, or the family of bugs that it belongs to. It is an insect. The next step is to identify its species, or the specific kind of bug it is. It is a praying mantis. Similarly, you have just identified the group of words as a complete sentence, and then you named what kind of sentence it is. Now it's time to turn the pages of your field guide and practice identifying all sorts of insects—that is, sentences—until you become an expert.

At the beginning of every chapter, you'll see an illustration that features members of the Clark family: Mom, Dad, Winston, Heidi, Fritz, and their mischievous dog, Rex. In the sentences you'll be studying throughout the book, you'll read about some of their adventures as a family and also meet some of their extended family as well, including their cousins—Theo and Lucy—Aunt Gabby, Uncle Ulysses, Grandma, and Grandpa.

In the meantime, take a look at the illustration at the beginning of this chapter. Did you notice what Rex (the dog) is up to? Can you find books labeled with some of the eight parts of speech? Do you ever pull out stacks of books and spread them out on the floor?

Notes

adjectives
CONJUNCTIONS
prepositions
verbs
interjections

Well-Ordered Notes A

From the Sideline: Please note that the teacher's edition includes a quiz and other extras at the end of each chapter. The Extra Practice & Assessments PDF, available for purchase at ClassicalAcademicPress.com, that accompanies the textbook contains this material in reproducible form.

Review It

Start each lesson by singing/chanting the definitions in Terms to Remember along with the audio tracks. Review with the students what they have learned today.

What is a sentence?
What are the four kinds of sentences?
What are the eight parts of speech?

Practice It

Lead the students in the activity What Kind Is It? Have the students stand next to their desks and be seated after they each answer. Read or say a sentence to the first student and have him identify the kind of sentence (declarative, interrogative, imperative, or exclamatory) and the reason for his answer (definition). If needed, prompt the student for the definition. Continue around the room, giving time for the students to think of their answers.

Variation: Create a sentence jar together with the students. Each student writes three or four examples of each of the four kinds of sentences (declarative, interrogative, imperative, or exclamatory) on separate index cards. Put the cards in a jar. Use these sentences as a sentence bank for activities such as What Kind Is It?

Example:

Teacher: "What kind of sentence is this: 'When was the first official baseball game played in the US?'"
Student 1: "That is an interrogative sentence."
Teacher: "Why is it an interrogative sentence?"
Student 2: "That sentence is an *interrogative* sentence because it asks a question."

Suggested sentences:

1. "See if Dad bought tickets for the game." (This sentence is an *imperative* sentence because it gives a command.)
2. "Where was the first baseball game played?" (This sentence is an *interrogative* sentence because it asks a question.)
3. "One of the first African American players in the major leagues was Jackie Robinson." (This sentence is a *declarative* sentence because it makes a statement.)
4. "Do you have my mitt and ball?" (This sentence is an *interrogative* sentence because it asks a question.)
5. "Grab my baseball cap from the closet, please." (This sentence is an *imperative* sentence because it gives a command.)

6. "Wow, the shortest game in the major league history was fifty-one minutes!" (This sentence is an *exclamatory* sentence because it expresses strong feelings.)
7. "I thought he said there were five bases." (This sentence is a *declarative* sentence because it makes a statement.)
8. "What a fantastic sport baseball is!" (This sentence is an *exclamatory* sentence because it expresses strong feelings.)

Analyze It

From the Sideline: Throughout the book, the Analyze It section is the most important part of each lesson. Choral recitation is fundamental to the curriculum, so even though it may start out seeming elementary, you should guide the students through each line of the script. The analysis becomes increasingly sophisticated with each chapter, so don't skip any of the steps. In all succeeding chapters, the analysis will be both spoken and written. Keep the analysis lively and not monotone. Visit http://capress.link/wol1att for video demonstrations of analysis for each chapter.

Now, as a class, analyze the ten sentences in the lesson. Here is the script for the first one to help you lead the choral analysis. The words in parentheses are like stage directions to guide you and are not to be spoken. The words in gray and enclosed in quotation marks are for you and the students to speak in chorus.

The sun is shining in the afternoon.

i. (First, read the sentence aloud.) "The sun is shining in the afternoon."

j. "This is a sentence because it is a group of words that expresses a complete thought."

k. "It is a declarative sentence because it makes a statement."

From the Sideline: For extra guided practice, refer to the Sentence Bank at the end of this chapter.

Lesson to Learn
Four Kinds of Sentences

A

1. Analyze the following sentences with your teacher. Then, on the lines provided, write *Dec* for a declarative sentence, *Int* for an interrogative sentence, *Imp* for an imperative sentence, or *Ex* for an exclamatory sentence.

   a. The sun is shining in the afternoon. Dec

   b. What a perfect day to play baseball! Ex

   c. Are you planning to play ball with us? Int

   d. Get the bases from the garage. Imp

   e. Baseball is my favorite sport. Dec

   f. Oh no, Rex ran off with the ball! Ex

   g. How many outs do we have? Int

   h. Is it your turn to bat? Int

   i. Stand back while she swings the bat. Imp

   j. It is time to head home for dinner. Dec

From the Sideline: Remember that to *analyze* means you should guide the students in reciting the analysis aloud, which is important preparation for more complicated sentences in later chapters.

2. All sentences begin with a capital letter and end with an end mark. In the following sentences, add the missing end mark: a period (.), a question mark (?), or an exclamation point (!).

   a. How are hot dogs made (?)

   b. Hot dogs can also be called frankfurters (.)

   c. Where was the first hot dog sold in the US (?)

   d. Yick, Fritz put orange marmalade on his hot dog (!)

   e. Give me some sweet potato fries, please (.)

   f. Heidi just gobbled five chili dogs by herself (!)

3. Imagine you're talking with your friend about playing a backyard baseball game, and then write the following kinds of sentences about it. **Answers will vary.**

a. Write a declarative sentence. **I like baseball more than football.**

b. Write an interrogative sentence. **What is your favorite position to play?**

c. Write an imperative sentence. **Bring your bat to the game.**

d. Write an exclamatory sentence. **Rats, we lost the ball again!**

Well-Ordered Notes B

Review It

Using the songs/chants, help the students memorize the definitions from Terms to Remember. Keep review fresh by varying your approach each day. Today, have them sing slowly and softly. Tomorrow, quickly and loudly.

What is a sentence?
What are the four kinds of sentences?
What are the eight parts of speech?

Practice It

Lead the students in Change It, which requires students to change a sentence into another kind of sentence. Ask the first student to construct a declarative sentence and then to change it into an interrogative one. Each student has five seconds to think of an example or say "pass." If a student says "pass," the next student can either choose to change that sentence or to request a new sentence. Be sure to mix it up so that the class gets the opportunity to construct all four types of sentences. It will be helpful for the students if you suggest a context from which they can create their sentences, such as playing soccer, swimming in a pool, building forts, or practicing piano.

Example:

Teacher: "Rex is up to some mischief again. State a *declarative* sentence about what Rex is doing."
Student 1: "I think Rex ran off with my shoe."
Teacher: "Change it and make it into an *interrogative* sentence."
Student 1: "Did Rex really run off with my shoe?"

Analyze It

From the Sideline: Visit http://capress.link/wol1att for a video demonstration of analysis.

Now, as a class, analyze the ten sentences in the lesson. The script for the first one has been provided to help you lead the choral analysis. The words in parentheses are like stage directions to guide you and are not to be spoken. The words in gray and enclosed in quotation marks are for you and the students to speak in chorus.

Listen to the sound of the noisy katydids.

a. (First, read the sentence aloud.) "Listen to the sound of the noisy katydids."

b. "This is a sentence because it is a group of words that expresses a complete thought."

c. "It is an imperative sentence because it gives a command."

From the Sideline: For extra guided practice, refer to the Sentence Bank at the end of this chapter.

Lesson to Learn
Four Kinds of Sentences

B

1. Analyze the following sentences with your teacher. Then, on the lines provided, write *Dec* for a declarative sentence, *Int* for an interrogative sentence, *Imp* for an imperative sentence, or *Ex* for an exclamatory sentence.

   a. Listen to the sound of the noisy katydids. ___Imp___

   b. Grasshoppers and crickets are insects. ___Dec___

   c. Are all grasshoppers green? ___Int___

   d. Wow! that little critter jumped high! ___Ex___

   e. Is a katydid a grasshopper too? ___Int___

   f. Give me that butterfly net. ___Imp___

   g. I love catching grasshoppers. ___Dec___

   h. Do crickets really rub their legs together? ___Int___

   i. My, that cricket is chirping loudly! ___Ex___

   j. Grasshoppers are bigger than crickets. ___Dec___

From the Sideline:
Remember that to *analyze* means you should guide the students in reciting the analysis aloud, which is important preparation for more complicated sentences in later chapters.

2. Remember that every sentence begins with a capital letter and ends with an end mark. In the following sentences, add the missing end mark: a period (.), a question mark (?), or an exclamation point (!).

   a. Ugh, Rex ate that big orange beetle ___(!)___

   b. You can catch moths with a butterfly net ___(.)___

   c. Who said that some moths are tasty ___(?)___

   d. My dad once ate a cricket at Boy Scout camp ___(.)___

   e. What a crazy thing to do ___(!)___

   f. Are certain insects really healthy to eat ___(?)___

3. Imagine that you're at the library looking for insect books and are taking books off the bookshelves, and then write the following kinds of sentences about it. **Answers will vary.**

   a. Write a declarative sentence. **I would like a book about katydids.**

   b. Write an interrogative sentence. **What book are you reading?**

   c. Write an imperative sentence. **Select a book from the shelf.**

   d. Write an exclamatory sentence. **Icky! that book is so sticky!**

From the Sideline: Remind the students that interjections can be followed by either a comma or an exclamation point, as illustrated in Pause for Punctuation, page 5.

Well-Ordered Notes C

Review It

Sing/chant and review the definitions as a class. You can vary your approach, but be sure the students are memorizing the terms.

What is a sentence?
What are the four kinds of sentences?
What are the eight parts of speech?

Practice It

Lead the students in Tell Me the Definition, an activity that can be either oral or written. Divide the students into pairs to quiz one another. Each student asks her partner to define and give examples of each kind of sentence.

1. A **declarative sentence** is a sentence that makes a statement.
   Example: I love reading about inventors.
2. An **interrogative sentence** is a sentence that asks a question.
   Example: Who invented the microwave?
3. An **imperative sentence** is a sentence that expresses a command or a request.
   Example: Remove the popcorn bag carefully from the microwave.
4. An **exclamatory sentence** is a sentence that expresses strong feelings or emotions.
   Example: Wow, microwave ovens channel heat energy directly to the food molecules!

Analyze It

From the Sideline: Visit http://capress.link/wol1att for a video demonstration of analysis.

Now, as a class, analyze the ten sentences in the lesson. The script for the first one has been provided to help you lead the choral analysis. The words in parentheses are like stage directions to guide you and are not to be spoken. The words in gray and enclosed in quotation marks are for you and the students to speak in chorus.

Do you want to make oatmeal cookies?

e. (First, read the sentence aloud.) “Do you want to make oatmeal cookies?”

f. “This is a sentence because it is a group of words that expresses a complete thought.”

g. “It is an interrogative sentence because it asks a question.”

From the Sideline: For extra guided practice, refer to the Sentence Bank at the end of this chapter.

Lesson to Learn

Four Kinds of Sentences

1. Analyze the following sentences with your teacher. Then, on the lines provided, write *Dec* for a declarative sentence, *Int* for an interrogative sentence, *Imp* for an imperative sentence, or *Ex* for an exclamatory sentence.

   a. Do you want to make oatmeal cookies? **Int**

   b. I do not know how to bake them. **Dec**

   c. Follow the directions in the cookbook. **Imp**

   d. Will we put raisins and walnuts in them? **Int**

   e. Turn on the oven to 350 degrees. **Imp**

   f. Oops, I sure am clumsy! **Ex**

   g. Get a sponge and clean up the mess. **Imp**

   h. I will stir in the butter with a spoon. **Dec**

   i. Have you put in all the ingredients yet? **Int**

   j. Yummy, these cookies are delicious! **Ex**

From the Sideline:
Remember that to *analyze* means you should guide the students in reciting the analysis aloud, which is important preparation for more complicated sentences in later chapters.

2. Imagine that you're going to watch a cooking show, and then write the following kinds of sentences about it.

   a. Write a *declarative* sentence. **The chef on the show made shepherd's pie.**

   b. Write an *interrogative* sentence. **Do you think it tastes as good as it looks?**

   c. Write an *imperative* sentence. **Turn the channel to the other station.**

   d. Write an *exclamatory* sentence. **Ugh, we missed our favorite cooking show again!**

3. In the poem "Mix a Pancake," the poet Christina Rossetti strings together six imperative sentences that tell her readers how to make pancakes. Rewrite each sentence as an interrogative sentence. Don't forget your capital letters and end marks.

Mix a pancake,
Stir a pancake,
Pop it in the pan;
Fry the pancake,
Toss the pancake—
Catch it if you can.

Answers will vary.

a. Mix a pancake. **Can you mix a pancake?**

b. Stir a pancake. **Will you stir a pancake?**

c. Pop it in the pan. **Did you pop it in the pan?**

d. Fry the pancake. **Should you fry the pancake?**

e. Toss the pancake. **Can you toss that pancake?**

f. Catch it if you can. **Do you think you can catch it?**

Well-Ordered Notes D

Review It

Review the following using the song/chants on the audio tracks:

What is a declarative sentence?
What is an imperative sentence?
What is an interrogative sentence?
What is an exclamatory sentence?

Practice It

Lead the students in Lightning, which is an activity of quick thinking. Have the students stand next to their desks. Call on the first student and name one of the four kinds of sentences (declarative, interrogative, imperative, or exclamatory). That student has five seconds to think of an example of that type of sentence. Once she answers, she is seated. If the student cannot think of a sentence, she says, "Pass," and remains standing until you can circle back to her. To make this activity easier and more enjoyable for students, provide them with a context or theme on which they can base their sentences, such as things that have to do with vacations.

Fewer than Five: This activity is perfect for either a small group or an individual student. Call on the first student and name one of the four kinds of sentences. If he answers correctly, he can sit down. When the students have answered correctly and are seated, call on the first student again in the same way, except if he answers correctly, he stands up. The activity continues with students standing and then sitting with correct answers.

Example:

Teacher: "Give an example of a *declarative* sentence that has to do with a family vacation."
Student 1: "Last summer, our family went on an airplane."
Teacher: "Give an example of an *interrogative* sentence." (Or "Ask a question.")
Student 2: "Where did you go that you needed to fly?"

Analyze It

From the Sideline: Visit http://capress.link/wol1att for a video demonstration of analysis.

Now, as a class, analyze the ten sentences in the lesson. The script for the first one has been provided to help you lead the choral analysis. The words in parentheses are like stage directions to guide you and are not to be spoken. The words in gray and enclosed in quotation marks are for you and the students to speak in chorus.

No way! volcanoes are vents in the earth!

a. (First, read the sentence aloud.) "No way, volcanoes are vents in the earth!"

b. "This is a sentence because it is a group of words that expresses a complete thought."

c. "It is an exclamatory sentence because it expresses strong feeling."

From the Sideline: For extra guided practice, refer to the Sentence Bank at the end of this chapter.

Lesson to Learn
Four Kinds of Sentences

1. Analyze the following sentences with your teacher. Then, on the lines provided, write *Dec* for a declarative sentence, *Int* for an interrogative sentence, *Imp* for an imperative sentence, or *Ex* for an exclamatory sentence.

   a. No way! volcanoes are vents in the earth! Ex

   b. What is the definition of a volcano? Int

   c. Today, we are studying volcanoes. Dec

   d. Don't touch the lava. Imp

   e. Can you name some famous volcanoes? Int

   f. Mt. Vesuvius erupted thirty times! Ex

   g. Open your textbooks to page 25. Imp

   h. Using papier-mâché, we will make them. Dec

   i. Will the volcanoes actually erupt? Int

   j. What an incredible science project! Ex

From the Sideline:
Remember that to *analyze* means you should guide the students in reciting the analysis aloud, which is important preparation for more complicated sentences in later chapters.

2. For each of the following sentences, write a sentence that identifies what kind of sentence it is and what makes it that kind of sentence. Don't forget capital letters and end marks in your responses.

   a. Show me the picture of Mauna Kea, the highest point in the state of Hawaii.

   This sentence is an *imperative* sentence because it gives a command.

   b. Mt. Mauna Kea is one of our National Natural Landmarks.

   This sentence is a *declarative* sentence because it makes a statement.

   c. When did your neighbors hike to the top? This sentence is an *interrogative* sentence because it asks a question.

   d. Wait, Aunt Gabby really did climb a 11,000-foot mountain! This sentence is an *exclamatory* sentence because it expresses strong feelings.

3. Imagine that you're going on a family trip to the Hawaiian Islands, and then write the following kinds of sentences about it.

   a. Write a *declarative* sentence. **Next week, we are heading to Honolulu, Hawaii.**

   b. Write an *interrogative* sentence. **Will we be snorkeling in the ocean?**

   c. Write an *imperative* sentence. **Pack my swimsuit and goggles, please.**

   d. Write an *exclamatory* sentence. **Phew, the airplane trip will be nearly five hours from California!**

Sentences for Practice
Four Kinds of Sentences — ANSWERS

From the Sideline: In each chapter, an extra practice sheet provides more sentences for analysis to use as needed—perhaps for review as a class, for individual students requiring more practice, or even for a refresher for students later in the year.

Analyze the following sentences with your teacher. Then, on the lines provided, write *Dec* for a declarative sentence, *Int* for an interrogative sentence, *Imp* for an imperative sentence, or *Ex* for an exclamatory sentence.

1. Grandpa has several apple trees. Dec
2. Ugh, the cat is stuck in that tree! Ex
3. Please help me get her down. Imp
4. Who will bring the ladder? Int
5. An apple is a kind of fruit. Dec
6. Gosh, that is a huge one! Ex
7. Winston has the bushel basket. Dec
8. When can we pick them? Int
9. Put the ripe apples here. Imp
10. Will Grandma make a pie? Int

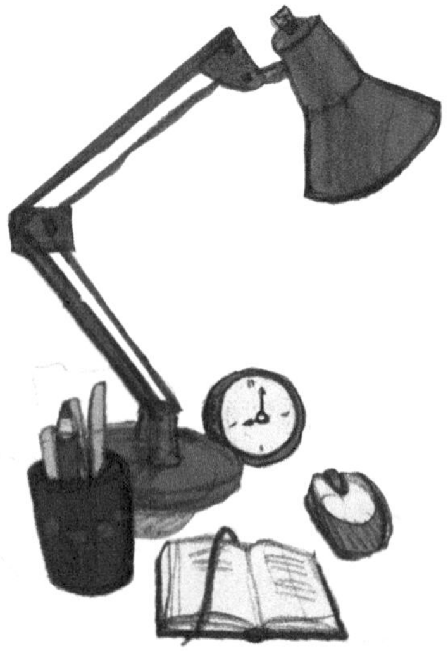

Notes

adjectives
CONJUNCTIONS
prepositions
verbs
interjections

Lessons to Enjoy—Poem

Four Kinds of Sentences

It is amazing how many profound ideas have been expressed, how many interesting stories have been told, and how many complex books have been written with just eight parts of speech and four kinds of sentences! Here is a poem called "Robin Redbreast" written by William Allingham more than a century ago. Like you, he says good-bye to summer every year as the seasons changed. He puts words together in a beautiful way to do it. See if you can find all four kinds of sentences in the poem. Which sentence best describes a robin?

From the Sideline: In Well-Ordered Notes, you'll find ideas for how to use poems in the classroom. The poems have been chosen to exemplify grammar in action, but you may want to touch on the basic elements of poetry as well: images, metaphor, sound, rhythm, and shape. For more guidance, see "Understanding Poetry" at the end of The Curious Child's Literary Appendix. Also consult *The Art of Poetry*, published by Classical Academic Press.

Robin Redbreast

by William Allingham (1824–1889)

Good-bye, good-bye to Summer!
For Summer's nearly done;
The garden smiling faintly,
Cool breezes in the sun;
Our Thrushes now are silent,
Our Swallows flown away—
But Robin's here, in coat of brown,
With ruddy breast-knot gay.
Robin, Robin Redbreast,
O Robin dear!
Robin singing sweetly
In the falling of the year.

ruddy: red or reddish

breast-knot: a necktie or scarf tied into a knot

gay: proud and merry

Bright yellow, red, and orange,
The leaves come down in hosts;
The trees are Indian Princes,
But soon they'll turn to Ghosts;
The scanty pears and apples
Hang russet on the bough,
It's Autumn, Autumn, Autumn late,
'Twill soon be Winter now.
Robin, Robin Redbreast,

host: multitude or a great number

scanty: barely enough

russet: reddish brown

O Robin dear!
And welaway! my Robin,
For pinching times are near.

The fireside for the Cricket,
The wheatstack for the Mouse,
When trembling night-winds whistle
And moan all round the house;
The frosty ways like iron,
The branches plumed with snow,—
Alas! in Winter, dead and dark,
Where can poor Robin go?
Robin, Robin Redbreast,
O Robin dear!
And a crumb of bread for Robin,
His little heart to cheer.[2]

welaway: alas

pinching times: the hard wintertime when food is scarce and must be conserved or "pinched"

plumed: feathered

Questions to Ponder

1. How are thrushes and swallows different from robins?
2. Where do crickets and mice go in winter?
3. What question does the poet ask at the end of the poem?

2. William Allingham, "Robin Redbreast," in *Anthology of Children's Literature*, ed. Edna Johnson, Carrie Scott, and Evelyn Sickels (Cambridge, MA: Houghton Mifflin Company, 1948), 908.

Well-Ordered Notes—Poem

The following are springboard ideas to help you stir your students to think beyond the poem. Those teachers who wish to study and teach poetry more in depth should consult *The Art of Poetry*, published by Classical Academic Press. See also the pages at the end of The Curious Child's Literary Appendix in this book.

Read

- Enjoy reading the poem aloud to the students, and then listen to a recording of the song of a robin, such as "American Robin Song and Call" (http://capress.link/wol1are0101).
- Divide the students into three groups and have each group read a stanza aloud (e.g., group 1—stanza 1; group 2—stanza 2; group 3—stanza 3).
- Have the students memorize the poem.

Retell

- Use the Questions to Ponder as discussion starters:

  1. **How are thrushes and swallows different from robins?**
     Thrushes and swallows are migratory birds, whereas not all robins migrate. As long as robins have enough food, they can withstand cold temperatures and will stay through the winter.

  2. **Where do crickets and mice go in winter?**
     Crickets go inside a house near a fire and mice go outside in the barn by the wheatstacks. They have cozy, protected homes during the hard times, but the robins must survive the elements.

  3. **What question does the poet ask at the end of the poem?**
     The poet asks where do Robins go in the winter? It is a rhetorical question. The speaker worries about the robins that have not migrated. How will they survive? Throwing breadcrumbs out for the robin will help.

- In this poem, Allingham makes declarations, asks questions, exclaims, and even at the end almost commands the reader to feed the robin. Draw your students' attention to this during your discussion by asking them to translate some of the poetic language into more everyday language, using all four kinds of sentences. Here are some examples:

  Declarative: The thrushes and swallows have left for the winter.
  Interrogative: How will the robins survive with scarce food?
  Exclamatory: Oh, the poor robins do not have enough to eat!
  Imperative: Throw some crumbs on the ground to help the robins.

Record

- Have the students copy the two lines that are repeated in each stanza of the poem or any of their favorite lines. Using colored pencils or crayons, students can draw pictures of robins in autumn or otherwise illustrate their chosen lines.

Review
Four Kinds of Sentences

ANSWERS

1. On the lines provided, write *Dec* for a declarative sentence, *Int* for an interrogative sentence, *Imp* for an imperative sentence, or *Ex* for an exclamatory sentence.

   a. Put on your green and gold jersey for the game. ___Imp___

   b. I have never been to the stadium before. ___Dec___

   c. How did Dad get tickets for this game? ___Int___

   d. Grab a program for me too. ___Imp___

   e. What an incredible pass! ___Ex___

   f. I think we have two timeouts left. ___Dec___

   g. Do they have twelve players on the field? ___Int___

   h. On no, he fumbled the ball! ___Ex___

   i. Dad said it was a five-yard penalty. ___Dec___

   j. Is it halftime yet? ___Int___

From the Sideline: The material on the following pages is not included in the student edition. You can find the Review lesson, the Quiz, the extra Sentences for Practice, and the second Lesson to Enjoy in reproducible form in the Extra Practice & Assessments PDF, available for purchase at ClassicalAcademicPress.com.

2. Every sentence begins with a capital letter and ends with an end mark. In the following sentences, add the missing end mark: a period (.), a question mark (?), or an exclamation point (!).

   a. How many games do you play with a ball ___(?)___

   b. Ah, I thought it was a baseball bat ___(!)___

   c. Volleyball is a team sport ___(.)___

   d. What a strange sport broomball is ___(!)___

   e. How did basketball get its name ___(?)___

   f. Throw that ball to me ___(.)___

3. Imagine that you're playing a football game in your front yard, and then write the following kinds of sentences about it.

   a. Write a declarative sentence. ___Theo plays football in the front yard.___

Review
Four Kinds of Sentences

b. Write an interrogative sentence. What position do you play?

c. Write an imperative sentence. Throw the ball to me.

d. Write an exclamatory sentence. Ugh, I dropped it again!

Quiz
Four Kinds of Sentences — ANSWERS

1. On the lines provided, write *Dec* for a declarative sentence, *Int* for an interrogative sentence, *Imp* for an imperative sentence, or *Ex* for an exclamatory sentence.

   a. Have you seen Rex lately? ____Int____

   b. Oh no, he has been rolling in the mud again! ____Ex____

   c. That silly dog often rolls in something. ____Dec____

   d. Get the garden hose and liquid soap. ____Imp____

   e. Who will wash Rex with me? ____Int____

   f. Some dogs like baths, but Rex doesn't. ____Dec____

   g. Ick, he's shaking the water everywhere! ____Ex____

   h. Use the dog leash to keep him still. ____Imp____

   i. I will get the towel ready. ____Dec____

   j. Where did he run off to now? ____Int____

2. Remember that every sentence begins with a capital letter and ends with an end mark. In the following sentences, add the missing end mark: a period (.), a question mark (?), or an exclamation point (!).

   a. Aunt Gabby was once a dog trainer ____(.)____

   b. Can your dog do any tricks ____(?)____

   c. Wow, most dogs cannot stand on two legs ____(!)____

   d. Shut the door after you leave ____(.)____

   e. What is the first rule in training dogs ____(?)____

3. Imagine that you were chasing the dog Rex, and then write the following kinds of sentences about it.

   a. Declarative: The garden hose is still on the driveway.

b. Interrogative: **Will you help me catch Rex?**

c. Imperative: **Grab his collar.**

d. Exclamatory: **Phew, I didn't think we were going to get him!**

Sentences for Practice—Fable
Four Kinds of Sentences ANSWERS

From the Sideline: These extra practice sentences are a synopsis of the fable "The Hunter and the Doves." The fable and the extended lesson notes are on the following pages.

Analyze the following sentences, which are based on the "The Hunter and the Doves." Then, on the lines provided, write *Dec* for a declarative sentence, *Int* for an interrogative sentence, *Imp* for an imperative sentence, or *Ex* for an exclamatory sentence.

1. A flock of Doves spotted some seeds. Dec
2. Who is hiding in the tree? Int
3. Drop the net on the birds. Imp
4. Oh no, the birds were trapped! Ex
5. Calmly, the King Dove gave a command. Dec

Sentences for Practice—Fable

ANSWERS

Four Kinds of Sentences

6. Lift a string of the net and flap. Imp
7. Did each Dove really lift a string? Int
8. The birds worked together. Dec
9. Hurray, the Doves escaped the Hunter! Ex
10. What is the moral of this fable? Int

Have you ever noticed that when you are with your family or with a group of friends, you can do so much more by working together? Aesop's fable "The Hunter and the Doves" is a clever tale of unity. Notice which of the four kinds of sentences are included. Which ones are missing?

The Hunter and the Doves

by Aesop

A flock of Doves spotted some seeds scattered on the ground. When they flew down to eat the seeds, a Hunter hiding in the tree above dropped a net upon them. The birds were trapped! Keeping his head, the King Dove told the other Doves to each lift up a string of the net and to flap her wings. By doing so, the Doves were able to lift the net together and carry it off as they escaped through the air.

Moral: In unity is strength.[1]

1. Aesop, "The Hunter and the Doves," taken from *Writing & Rhetoric Book 1: Fable* by Paul Kortepeter (Camp Hill, PA: Classical Academic Press, 2013), 22.

Questions to Ponder

1. Why do the Doves fly down to the field?
2. Where was the Hunter hiding?
3. What did the King of the Doves instruct the other Doves to do?
4. What lesson can be learned from this fable?

Well-Ordered Notes—Fable

Read

- Read the fable to your students slowly so they can imagine the flock of doves and their plight.
- Have students sing the definition of a fable (audio track 1–14; see page 194 for lyrics).

Retell

- Use the Questions to Ponder as discussion starters:
  1. **Why do the Doves fly down to the field?**
     They fly down to eat seeds that are scattered on the ground. Ask the students how they think the seeds got there. Did the wind blow them randomly or did the Hunter himself scatter them as part of the trap?
  2. **Where was the Hunter hiding?**
     He was hiding in the branches of the tree. He must have been so well hidden that the doves did not notice him as they flew down near him. They were the victims of a very clever trap.
  3. **What did the King of the Doves instruct the other Doves to do?**
     The King Dove tells them to work as one strong unit and fly away with the net. If they had panicked and flown around in individual directions, they could not have escaped this clever trap. Ask the students to imagine what the hunter was thinking as his net rose from the ground and flew away into the sky.
  4. **What lesson can be learned from this fable?**
     Have the students explain the moral using real-life examples. Have them consider examples from their life in school or at home, such as how much more efficiently cleanup happens when a group works as a unit. Consider examples from other stories, such as in the movie *Finding Nemo* when Nemo leads a school of fish caught in a net to swim downward all together, breaking the fishermen's line and freeing themselves.
- Have the students locate all four kinds of sentences on page q, which contains "The Hunter and the Doves." The fable itself includes only declarative sentences and one exclamatory sentence. Steer the students' attention to the introductory paragraph to locate a couple of interrogative sentences and one imperative sentence.

Record

- Have students copy the first three sentences of the fable into their copybooks.
- Have the students make origami doves and use them to act out the fable. Use other props (e.g., fisherman's net) to help retell the tale.

Origami Dove Instructions

Students must start with a square piece of paper. If they need to cut one from an 8 ½" by 11"-inch piece of paper, demonstrate how to do so. Fold the upper left corner down to the right side, creasing diagonally from the upper right corner. The rectangular strip at the bottom can be cut away, leaving a perfect square. As you guide students through the diagram for folding a dove, explain that the shaded parts of the diagram represent the side of the paper that was down in step 1. The dotted lines are fold lines. In the tricky Step 5, they will need to fold the point in an inside-out fashion to create the beak.

Make Your Own Origami Dove!

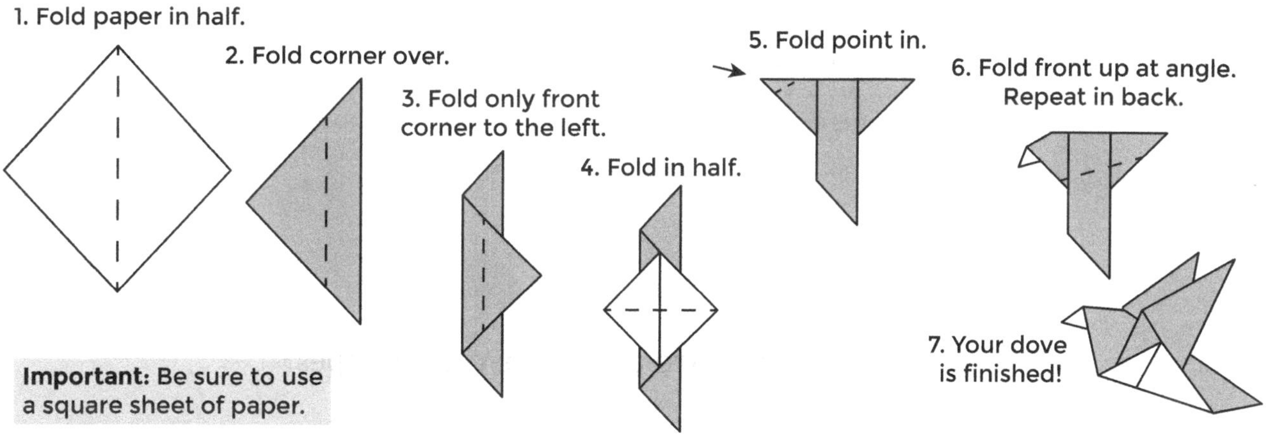

Sentence Bank

From the Sideline: Visit http://capress.link/wol1att for a video demonstration of analysis.

These eight additional sentences are for extra practice if needed. The scripts are provided for your reference as you and the students analyze the sentences aloud together.

We will be going to the apple farm next week.

a. (First, read the sentence aloud.) "We will be going to the apple farm next week."

b. "This is a sentence because it is a group of words that expresses a complete thought."

c. "It is a declarative sentence because it makes a statement."

Does your mom have any apple crisp recipes?

a. (First, read the sentence aloud.) "Does your mom have any apple crisp recipes?"

b. "This is a sentence because it is a group of words that expresses a complete thought."

c. "It is an interrogative sentence because it asks a question."

Ah, the baseball is lost forever!

a. (First, read the sentence aloud.) "Ah, the baseball is lost forever!"
b. "This is a sentence because it is a group of words that expresses a complete thought."
c. "It is an exclamatory sentence because it expresses strong feelings."

Tell a story to your brother.

a. (First, read the sentence aloud.) "Tell a story to your brother."
b. "This is a sentence because it is a group of words that expresses a complete thought."
c. "It is an imperative sentence because it gives a command."

Does September come after August?

a. (First, read the sentence aloud.) "Does September come after August?"

b. "This is a sentence because it is a group of words that expresses a complete thought."

c. "It is an interrogative sentence because it asks a question."

Autumn is a beautiful season.

a. (First, read the sentence aloud.) "Autumn is a beautiful season."

b. "This is a sentence because it is a group of words that expresses a complete thought."

c. "It is a declarative sentence because it makes a statement."

Rake the leaves in the backyard.

a. (First, read the sentence aloud.) "Rake the leaves in the backyard."

b. "This is a sentence because it is a group of words that expresses a complete thought."

c. "It is an imperative sentence because it gives a command."

Ouch, that ball hit my leg!

a. (First, read the sentence aloud.) "Ouch, that ball hit my leg!"

b. "This is a sentence because it is a group of words that expresses a complete thought."

c. "It is an exclamatory sentence because it expresses strong feelings."

From the Sideline: Delight in your work. Students will absorb your attitude toward the material. Teach with sincerity. We use the maxim, "Be earnest. Be entrusting. Be engaging."

[A]Bring in a miniature train engine and a coal car to visually represent the principal elements—subject and predicate. You can bring in other train cars as well to stand for other words in a sentence. Discuss how the subject and predicate are necessary to make the whole train move.

Chapter 2

Principal Elements, Part 1—Subject and Predicate[A]

Have you ever wondered why we can understand each other? Yes, we speak to one another, but how is the message of what we're saying passed on? The words you choose are important for meaning, but words alone are not enough to communicate■ ideas. The word order, or **syntax**,■ of a sentence determines meaning too. You can think of sentences as something like a steam-powered train. The engine of an old-fashioned steam train comes first, and the coal car, which carries the fuel for the train, comes second. You could add all sorts of passenger cars, a dining car, freight cars, hoppers, even more than one caboose, but without an engine and a coal car, your train would not go anywhere. Similarly, a sentence needs two essential parts—the **subject** and the **predicate**—or it is not a sentence, no matter how many words it contains.

To the Source: ■ communicate
The term *communicate* comes from the Latin word *communicare,* meaning "to share" or "impart." Literally, the word in Latin means "to make common."

To the Source: ■ syntax
The word *syntax* comes from the Greek word *syntaxis,* meaning "putting together or arrangement" of words.

Ideas to Understand

In the previous chapter, we learned that a sentence expresses a complete thought. Now, we will study what makes a thought complete. In George MacDonald's tale *At the Back of the North Wind*, a little boy named Diamond makes friends with the North Wind, and she lets him ride on her back until he learns compassion for a little broom girl. The North Wind leaves Diamond in the streets of London as he befriends the girl. Together they don't know where to go. Finally, the little broom girl suggests that they just wander. The author uses the shortest form of an English sentence to show how Diamond responds to her idea:

Diamond obeyed.

From the Sideline: Write "Diamond obeyed" on the board to point to as you explain the principal elements, emphasizing that the subject is what the sentence is about. For a longer excerpt from MacDonald's novel, see The Curious Child's Literary Appendix.

Off the Shelf: For more than one hundred years, children and adults have loved the book *At the Back of the North Wind*. It's a classic. Diamond is a very poor little boy who gets to go on a great adventure, riding on the wind, which changes his life forever. Guess what? You can go along with him! All you have to do is take the book off the library shelf, open it up, and fly off on your journey.

MacDonald chooses only two words to tell his readers something about the main character. Diamond did something: he obeyed.

"Diamond obeyed" is a simple sentence, but we know that it is complete because MacDonald uses the two **principal elements** to make his sentence: a subject and a predicate. *Diamond* (the subject) is the focus of the sentence—it is what the sentence is about. The word *obeyed* (the predicate) tells us something about the subject. It tells us what Diamond (subject) did: obeyed (predicate).

Usually the subject of a sentence is a **noun**. A noun is a word that names a person, place, thing, quality, or idea. Subjects can be either **singular**, such as *train*, or **plural**, such as *trains*. In English, we usually add an *s* to the end of a noun to make it plural. There are some words that have a special form for their plural, such as *mice*.

The predicate can be simply a **verb**—a word that shows action. This chapter will focus primarily on the subject. Chapter 3 will discuss predicate verbs. A sentence cannot be constructed without both a subject and a predicate, just like a steam train needs both an engine and a coal car in order to move.

Moment for Mechanics

A **suffix** is a group of letters added to the end of a **root word** (the most basic form of a word) to make a different word. Suffixes help determine the part of speech of words. For example, if the suffix *-er* is added to a verb like *paint*, the new word is a noun, *painter*. When the suffix *-er*, *-tion*, or *-age* is added to a root word, the new word will probably be a noun. Observing the suffix can help identify how the word is behaving in the sentence.

Root Word	Noun	Example
paint	Paint**er**	The *painter* works.
imagine	Imagina**tion**	Her *imagination* soared.
pack	Pack**age**	The *package* was colorful.

Terms to Remember[B]

Now, you are ready to memorize three new grammar definitions and review one from the previous chapter. Do you see how they are all connected? The principal elements of a sentence are the subject■ and the predicate.■ The subject is often a noun. A noun is one of the eight parts of speech. Keep listening to the audio tracks to memorize the definitions and to review the eight parts of speech.

NEW! **Principal Elements** *(1–3)*

NEW! **Subject and Predicate** *(1–4)*

Eight Parts of Speech *(1–1)*

NEW! **Noun** *(1–5)*

[B]For the lyrics to all of the songs, please see the Song Lyrics section on page 191. Play the appropriate audio tracks and have students sing/chant along. Students should commit the songs to memory.

A Sentence to Analyze

Have you ever taken apart a clock or a wind-up toy out of curiosity to see how it works? That's analysis. Now you are going to take apart, or analyze, a sentence. You will already know how to do the first part of the analysis because you know the different kinds of sentences. Now, you will also add written marks to the sentence. Make sure you cover each step:

1. Read the sentence aloud.
2. Identify the sentence as a sentence because it fits the definition of a sentence.
3. State what kind of sentence it is and explain why it is that kind of sentence.
4. Identify the subject, tell how you know it is the subject, and mark it.
5. Identify the predicate, tell how you know it is the predicate, and mark it.

In the beginning of your study of grammar this year, it is important to understand the order of analysis because each step adds to the one before

To the Source:
■ subject

The word *subject* comes from the Latin word *subjectus*, which means "dependent upon or under the power of." The subject of a sentence is dependent on the predicate.

To the Source:
■ predicate

The word *predicate* comes from the Latin word *praedicare*, which means "to make known or public." The predicate "makes known" or tells us something about the subject.

From the Sideline: Here it is! Analysis—the centerpiece of the WOL method. Now, during the choral analysis, written markings are added to the sentence. Model marking sentences on the board, so students see how to do it in their books during subsequent lessons.

it, like adding freight cars to a train. Each chapter of this book will add more steps to the analysis, so take care to master these five basic steps now.

With your teacher, use these steps to analyze the sentence "Heidi paints." The words in parentheses are there to guide you and should not be spoken. Speak the words in gray along with your teacher. As you say the analysis, use a lively, energetic voice. Also, be sure to pay close attention to what your teacher is writing on the board. Later, you will mark sentences in your book as you analyze them aloud.

S P
Heidi paints.

a. (First, read the sentence aloud.) "Heidi paints."

b. "This is a sentence because it is a group of words that expresses a complete thought."

c. "It is a declarative sentence because it makes a statement."

d. "This sentence is about *Heidi*." (Underline the subject.) "So, *Heidi* is the subject because it is what the sentence is about." (Since *Heidi* is the subject, place a capital letter *S* above it to show that it is the subject of the sentence.)

e. "This sentence tells us that Heidi *paints*." (Double underline the predicate.) "So, *paints* is the predicate because it is what the sentence tells us about *Heidi*." (Since *paints* tells something about *Heidi*, place a capital letter *P* above it to show that it is the predicate.)

If sentences are like steam trains, then *Heidi* is the engine and *paints* is the coal car of our little sentence "Heidi paints." It may be a short train, but it does have everything it needs to chug along the track. It has a subject and a predicate. Understanding that means you understand the most essential parts of sentences.

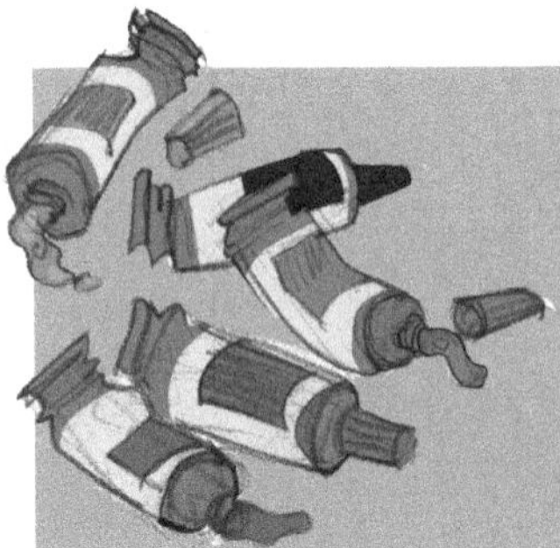

Study the illustration at the beginning of this chapter. How many tubes of paint are on Heidi's table? What color do you think she is painting the engine and coal car? If you were painting a train, what colors would you use?

Notes

Well-Ordered Notes A

From the Sideline: Please note that the teacher's edition includes a quiz and other extras at the end of each chapter. The Extra Practice & Assessments PDF, available for purchase at ClassicalAcademicPress.com, that accompanies the textbook contains this material in reproducible form.

Review It

Start each lesson by singing/chanting the definitions in Terms to Remember along with the audio tracks. Keep your review regular but seasoned with something fresh.

What is a sentence?
What are the four kinds of sentences?
What are the eight parts of speech?
What are the principal elements?

Practice It

Lead the students in the activity What Is This Sentence About? Write the following predicates on the board and ask the students to create complete sentences by suggesting subjects for the predicates. Ask different students to write a subject for each predicate on the board. Have them underline the subjects and read the resulting sentences aloud. We have provided some suggested subjects for each of the predicates.

Example: surge <u>Waters</u> **surge.**

1. _______________ dive. **(Sample subjects: penguins, otters, whales)**
2. _______________ squawk. **(Sample subjects: crows, seagulls, parrots)**
3. _______________ flash. **(Sample subjects: flashlights, cameras, sparks)**
4. _______________ pop. **(Sample subjects: balloons, firecrackers, bubbles)**
5. _______________ sink. **(Sample subjects: rocks, pebbles, anchors)**
6. _______________ prowl. **(Sample subjects: panthers, tigers, cats)**
7. _______________ fall. **(Sample subjects: raindrops, leaves, temperatures)**
8. _______________ honk. **(Sample subjects: cars, geese, horns)**

Prowl: to move about quietly or secretly

Analyze It

From the Sideline: The Analyze It section is the climax of each lesson. It is where your young grammarians apply their newfound analytic skill. In this chapter, they combine the two parts of the method—the oral analysis and the written markings—for the first time. During the choral analysis, you model how to mark the sentences on the board while the students mark them in their books. Don't skip any steps. Later on it will pay off as the sentences get more difficult. Visit http://capress.link/wol1att for video demonstrations of analysis for each chapter.

Now, as a class, analyze the four sentences in the lesson. Here is the script for the first one to help you lead the choral analysis and model the markings on the board. The words in parentheses are like stage directions to guide you and are not to be spoken. The words in gray and enclosed in quotation marks are for you and the students to speak in chorus.

S P
Heidi screams.

a. (First, read the sentence aloud.) "Heidi screams."

b. "This is a sentence because it is a group of words that expresses a complete thought."

c. "It is a declarative sentence because it makes a statement."

d. "This sentence is about *Heidi*." (Underline the subject.) "So, *Heidi* is the subject because it is what the sentence is about." (Place a capital letter *S* above the subject.)

e. "This sentence tells us that Heidi *screams*." (Double underline the predicate.) "So *screams* is the predicate because it is what the sentence tells us about *Heidi*." (Place a capital letter *P* above the predicate.)

From the Sideline: For extra guided practice, refer to the Sentence Bank at the end of this chapter.

Lesson to Learn
Principal Elements, Part 1

A

1. Analyze the following sentences.

   a. S: Heidi P: screams.

   b. S: Centipedes P: scatter.

   c. S: Rex P: barks.

   d. S: Winston P: laughs.

From the Sideline: For each of the four sentences, lead the students through the choral analysis as you mark it on the board so the students learn both the script and the markings.

2. Subjects are one of the principal elements that make up the core of a sentence. In the following sentences, underline the subject.

   a. Clocks tick.

   b. Fingers tap.

   c. Lucy fidgets.

   d. Theo waits.

   e. Mom comes.

   f. Cousins leave.

3. The subject of a sentence is usually a noun, which can be either singular or plural. For each of the following sentences, from the word bank choose a subject that would make sense with the provided verb. You may add the word *the* before the subject if it sounds better. **Answers may vary.**

Word Bank: cousins, friends, farmer, crows, pumpkins, wagon, scarecrow

a. **The scarecrow** stands.

b. **Crows** caw.

c. **The farmer** invites.

d. **The wagon** stops.

e. **Pumpkins** roll.

f. **Cousins** shout.

4. Imagine that you were at a pumpkin farm and your pumpkin rolled off the wagon, and then write the following kinds of sentences about it.

a. Write an exclamatory sentence. **Ah, my pumpkin just smashed on the ground!**

b. Write an interrogative sentence. **What should I do now with seeds everywhere?**

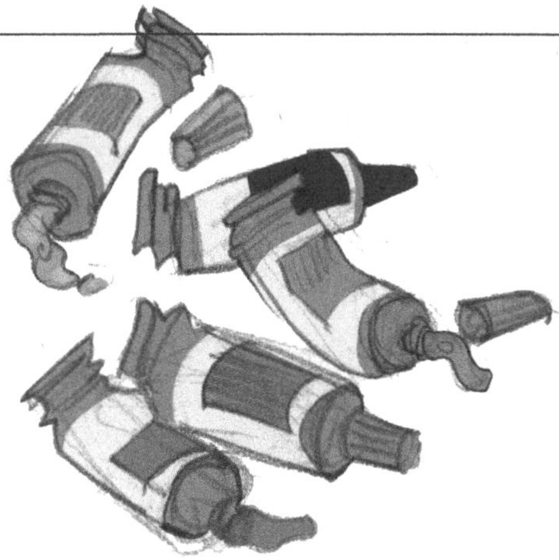

Well-Ordered Notes B

Review It

Memory work requires practice. Sing/chant the definitions with your class.

What is a sentence?
What are the eight parts of speech?
What is a noun?

Practice It

Lead the students in the activity Make It Make Sense, in which the students will construct sentences using a subject and a predicate. Make a set of 3 x 5 word cards or index cards. Write one word per card using the following six subjects (e.g., *Squirrels, Rex, Parents, Winston, Doorbell, Neighbors*) and six predicates (*chatter, barks, rake, helps, rings,* and *visit*). Distribute the twelve cards to twelve volunteers. Have the volunteers hold the cards for all to see. Then have the volunteers arrange themselves into six sentences, each with a subject and predicate.

Fewer than Five: Adapt this activity using the 3 x 5 word cards or index cards. Instead of distributing one card each to twelve volunteers, give the whole set of twelve cards to your student(s) to arrange into sentences.

Example:
Student 1 holds the subject card: *Squirrels*
Student 2 holds the predicate card: *chatter*
The sentence is formed when they stand together: *Squirrels chatter.*

Suggested sentences:

1. Squirrels chatter.
2. Rex barks.
3. Parents rake.
4. Winston helps.
5. Doorbell rings.
6. Neighbors visit.

Analyze It

From the Sideline: Visit http://capress.link/wol1att for a video demonstration of analysis.

Now, as a class, analyze the four sentences in the lesson. Here is the script for the first one to help you lead the choral analysis and model the markings on the board. The words in parentheses are like stage directions to guide you and are not to be spoken. The words in gray and enclosed in quotation marks are for you and the students to speak in chorus.

S P
Fritz dashes.

g. (First, read the sentence aloud.) "Fritz dashes."

h. "This is a sentence because it is a group of words that expresses a complete thought."

i. "It is a declarative sentence because it makes a statement."

j. "This sentence is about *Fritz*." (Underline the subject.) "So, *Fritz* is the subject because it is what the sentence is about." (Place a capital letter *S* above the subject.)

k. "This sentence tells us that Fritz *dashes*." (Double underline the predicate.) "So, *dashes* is the predicate because it is what the sentence tells us about *Fritz*." (Place a capital letter *P* above the predicate.)

From the Sideline: For extra guided practice, refer to the Sentence Bank at the end of this chapter.

Lesson to Learn

Principal Elements, Part 1

B

1. Analyze the following sentences.

   a. Fritz (S) dashes (P).

   b. Heidi (S) gallops (P).

   c. Winston (S) sprints (P).

   d. Rex (S) wins (P).

From the Sideline: For each of the four sentences, lead the students through the choral analysis as you mark it on the board so the students learn both the script and the markings.

2. Subjects are one of the principal elements that make up the core of a sentence. In the following sentences, underline the subject.

   a. Dad barbecues.

   b. Kids play.

   c. Tail swishes.

   d. Tables overturn.

   e. Lemonade cascades.

   f. Grandpa grumbles.

3. The subject of a sentence is usually a noun, which can be either singular or plural. For each of the following sentences, from the word bank choose a subject that would make sense with the provided verb. You may add the word *the* before the subject if it sounds better. **Answers may vary.**

Word Bank: Theo, flies, Winston, hamburgers, Dad, hot dogs, Mom

a. ______**Hamburgers**______ sizzle.

b. ______**Flies**______ buzz.

c. ______**Mom**______ swats.

d. ______**Dad**______ serves.

e. ______**Theo**______ munches.

f. ______**Winston**______ devours.

4. Imagine that you are at a cookout, and then write the following kinds of sentences about it.

a. Write an declarative sentence. **I love going to the annual cookout.**

b. Write an exclamatory sentence. **Ick, that hot dog has pineapple mustard on it!**

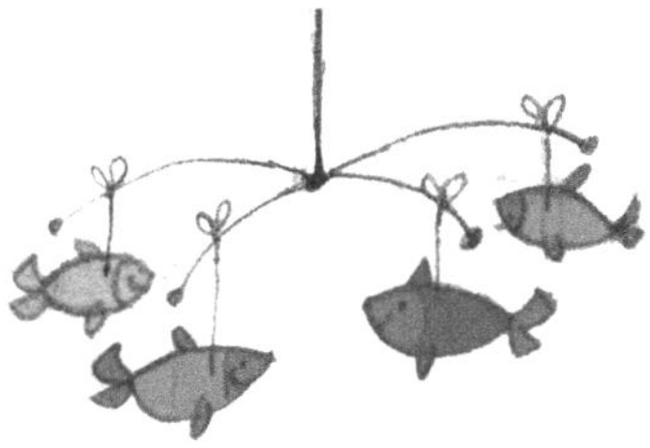

Well-Ordered Notes C

Review It

Review the definitions as a class. Add variety by having the students march while singing or chanting.

What is a noun?
What are the principal elements?
What are the eight parts of speech?

Practice It

Lead the class in the activity Write on White using mini whiteboards. As you read the following sentences, saying "blank" for the subject, have the students write an appropriate subject on their boards and hold up their answers. You can quickly see if the answers are nouns and if the students have chosen the correct plural or singular form. Note: Allow the students to add *the* or *a/an* before the subject if it sounds better that way. These article adjectives will be covered in chapter 5.

From the Sideline: If you don't have mini whiteboards, you can make them by laminating card stock. Use whiteboard markers to write on them and tissues to clean them off.

Example:

__________ howls.
A wolf howls.
The whirlwind howls.

1. __________ cracks. (a window, a bone)
2. __________ whistle. (people, tea kettle)
3. __________ hums. (an insect, a motor)
4. __________ whisper. (friends, winds)
5. __________ growls. (a dog, an animal)
6. __________ croak. (frogs, ravens)

Analyze It

From the Sideline: Visit http://capress.link/wol1att for a video demonstration of analysis.

Now, as a class, analyze the four sentences in the lesson. Here is the script for the first one to help you lead the choral analysis and model the markings on the board. The words in parentheses are like stage directions to guide you and are not to be spoken. The words in gray and enclosed in quotation marks are for you and the students to speak in chorus.

S P
Geese migrate.

g. (First, read the sentence aloud.) "Geese migrate."

h. "This is a sentence because it is a group of words that expresses a complete thought."

i. "It is a declarative sentence because it makes a statement."

j. "This sentence is about *geese*." (Underline the subject.) "So, *geese* is the subject because it is what the sentence is about." (Place a capital letter *S* above the subject.)

k. "This sentence tells us that geese *migrate*." (Double underline the predicate.) "So, *migrate* is the predicate because it is what the sentence tells us about *geese*." (Place a capital letter *P* above the predicate.)

From the Sideline: For extra guided practice, refer to the Sentence Bank at the end of this chapter.

Lesson to Learn
Principal Elements, Part 1

C

1. Analyze the following sentences.

   a. Geese (S) migrate (P).

   b. Colors (S) change (P).

   c. Leaves (S) dance (P).

   d. Theo (S) rakes (P).

From the Sideline: For each of the four sentences, lead the students through the choral analysis as you mark it on the board so the students learn both the script and the markings.

2. Subjects are one of the principal elements that make up the core of a sentence. In the following sentences, underline the subject.

   a. Autumn begins.

   b. Sun shines.

   c. Clouds form.

   d. Winds change.

   e. Skies darken.

   f. Rain falls.

3. The subject of a sentence is usually a noun, which can be either singular or plural. For each of the following sentences, from the word bank choose a subject that would make sense with the provided verb. You may add the word *the* before the subject if it sounds better. **Answers may vary.**

Word Bank: fire, kids, branch, marshmallows, leaves, chocolate, trees

a. **Trees** rustle.

b. **The branch** snaps.

c. **Fire** crackles.

d. **Marshmallows** toast.

e. **Chocolate** melts.

f. **Kids** gobble.

4. Imagine that you are making s'mores around a firepit, and then write the following kinds of sentences about it.

a. Write an imperative sentence. **Hand me another marshmallow.**

b. Write an interrogative sentence. **Who invented s'mores, anyway?**

Well-Ordered Notes D

Review It

Start each lesson by singing/chanting the definitions as a class.

What are the principal elements?
What is a noun?
What are the four kinds of sentences?

Practice It

Lead the class in the activity Construction Zone. Write the following chart on the board or generate your own subjects and predicates. Divide the students into pairs and have them construct as many sentences as they can in five minutes using the list of subjects and predicates you write on the board. Some of the sentences may be humorous (such as "Birds gallop") and may make for some interesting mental pictures. You may want to have the students choose their favorite sentence and then draw a picture based on it.

Example: subject (Birds) + predicate (chirp) = Birds chirp.

Subject	Predicate
Birds	hum(s).
Rabbits	gallop(s).
Snakes	whine(s).
Centipedes	race(s).
Ponies	grunt(s).
Hogs	squeak(s).
Bees	yodel(s).
Bicycles	chirp(s).
Scouts	sway(s).
Branches	hop(s).
Hikers	babble(s).
Puppy	buzz(es).
Stream	crawl(s).
Mosquitoes	hike(s).
Hinges	hiss(es).

Analyze It

From the Sideline: Visit http://capress.link/wol1att for a video demonstration of analysis.

Now, as a class, analyze the four sentences in the lesson. Here is the script for the first one to help you lead the choral analysis and model the markings on the board. The words in parentheses are like stage directions to guide you and are not to be spoken. The words in gray and enclosed in quotation marks are for you and the students to speak in chorus.

S P
Winston bikes.

a. (First, read the sentence aloud.) "Winston bikes."

b. "This is a sentence because it is a group of words that expresses a complete thought."

c. "It is a declarative sentence because it makes a statement."

d. "This sentence is about *Winston*." (Underline the subject.) "So, *Winston* is the subject because it is what the sentence is about." (Place a capital letter *S* above the subject.)

e. "This sentence tells us that Winston *bikes*." (Double underline the predicate.) "So, *bikes* is the predicate because it is what the sentence tells us about *Winston*." (Place a capital letter *P* above the predicate.)

From the Sideline: For extra guided practice, refer to the Sentence Bank at the end of this chapter.

Lesson to Learn
Principal Elements, Part 1

1. Analyze the following sentences.

   a. Winston (S) bikes (P).

   b. Pedals (S) move (P).

   c. Wheels (S) turn (P).

   d. Time (S) flies (P).

From the Sideline: For each of the four sentences, lead the students through the choral analysis as you mark it on the board so the students learn both the script and the markings.

2. Suffixes help define the roles of words. In the following sentences, underline the word with the suffix *-er*, *-tion*, or *-age* and write its root word on the line.

   a. The sender gave a clue. **Root word:** send

   b. The invitation was mysterious. **Root word:** invite

   c. The biker left the house. **Root word:** bike

   d. The coverage was a helmet. **Root word:** cover

   e. The passage was the bike trail. **Root word:** pass

   f. The direction was uncharted. **Root word:** direct

3. The subject of a sentence is usually a noun, which can be either singular or plural. For each of the following sentences, from the word bank choose a subject that would make sense with the provided verb. You may add the word *the* before the subject if it sounds better. **Answers may vary.**

Word Bank: lady, sirens, newscaster, biker, police, vehicles, windshield

a. **The biker** swerves.

b. **Vehicles** collide.

c. **The windshield** shatters.

d. **Sirens** wail.

e. **Police** appear.

f. **The newscaster** reports.

4. Imagine that you saw the bike accident, and then write the following kinds of sentences about it.

a. Write an exclamatory sentence. **Yikes, that biker just caused that accident!**

b. Write an interrogative sentence. **Did anyone get hurt?**

Sentences for Practice—Fable
Principal Elements, Part 1 ANSWERS

Analyze the following sentences, which are based on "The Jay and the Peacock."

From the Sideline: These extra practice sentences are a synopsis of the fable "The Jay and the Peacock." The fable and the extended lesson notes are on the following pages.

1. Peacocks (S) strut (P).

2. Feathers (S) fall (P).

3. Jay (S) ventures (P).

4. Plumes (S) flutter (P).

5. Feathers (S) adorn (P).

adorn: decorate; make attractive

Sentences for Practice—Fable

Principal Elements, Part 1

6. Jay (S) paraded (P).

7. Peacocks (S) pecked (P).

8. Birds (S) plucked (P).

9. Feathers (S) fly (P).

10. Jay (S) sobbed (P).

Lessons to Enjoy—Fable
Principal Elements, Part 1

Admired since ancient times for their beauty, peacocks make colorful characters in stories because of their plumage, or feathers. In this tale, which is one of Aesop's fables, a common Jay bird envies the Peacocks' beautiful feathers and tries to be something that he is not. Have you ever been tempted to pretend to be someone you are not?

The Jay and the Peacock

by Aesop

A Jay, venturing into a yard where Peacocks used to walk, found there a number of feathers which had fallen from the Peacocks when they were molting. He tied them all to his tail, and strutted down towards the Peacocks. When he came near them they soon discovered the cheat, and striding up to him pecked at him and plucked away his borrowed plumes. So the Jay could do no better than go back to the other Jays, who had watched his behavior from a distance; but they were equally annoyed with him and told him:

"It is not only fine feathers that make fine birds."[1]

venturing: going ahead in spite of danger
molting: shedding feathers so that new ones can grow in
strutted: walked in an overly proud way, with head held high and chest thrown out
the cheat: the trick
plumes: beautiful feathers

From the Sideline: Fables are included as an enrichment activity. The goal is for students to delight in language. The ten Sentences for Practice on the preceding pages reinforce the grammar lesson of the chapter as students enjoy the tale.

1. Aesop, "The Jay and the Peacock," taken from *The Fables of Aesop* by Joseph Jacobs (London and New York: Macmillan and Company, 1917), 55.

Questions to Ponder

1. Where did the Jay find the Peacock feathers?
2. Why do you think the Jay wanted to tie Peacock feathers to himself?
3. What did the Peacocks do when they met the Jay?
4. What lesson can be learned from this fable?

Well-Ordered Notes—Fable

Read

- Enjoy reading the fable aloud with the students. Bring in bird feathers, such as peacock and blue jay feathers, to show their differences.
- Have students sing the definition of a fable (audio track 1–14; see page 194 for lyrics).

Retell

- Use the Questions to Ponder as discussion starters:
  1. **Where did the Jay find the Peacock feathers?**
     He found the feathers in the yard where the Peacocks walk.
  2. **Why do you think the Jay wanted to tie Peacock feathers to himself?**
     Answers may vary. The common Jay admires the gorgeous plumes of the Peacocks and wants them for himself. Some students may think he seems dissatisfied with his lot in life and would rather be a Peacock than a Jay. Others may say he is just playing, or even making fun of the proud Peacocks. Encourage the students to support their opinion by referring to specific details in the fable.
  3. **What did the Peacocks do when they met the Jay?**
     When the Peacocks meet the Jay, they peck away the feathers that don't belong to him.
  4. **What lesson can be learned from this fable?**
     When people put on airs, or act like they are something they are not, others are not fooled.
- Have the students research the structure of bird feathers and the molting process, especially for blue jays and peacocks.

Record

- Have the students copy the fable into their copybooks.
- Have the students design a poster illustrating the moral of the fable. They can use craft feathers to decorate the poster.

Notes

Review
Principal Elements, Part 1 — ANSWERS

1. Analyze the following sentences.

   a. Stripes (S) leaped (P).

   b. Rex (S) barked (P).

   c. Fritz (S) chased (P).

   d. Twins (S) laughed (P).

From the Sideline: The material on the following pages is not included in the student edition. You can find the Review lesson, the Quiz, the extra Sentences for Practice, and the second Lesson to Enjoy in reproducible form in the Extra Practice & Assessments PDF, available for purchase at ClassicalAcademicPress.com.

2. Subjects are one of the principal elements that make up the core of a sentence. In the following sentences, underline the subject.

   a. Pets frolic.

   b. Noises rise.

   c. Kids shout.

   d. Music plays.

   e. Doors shut.

   f. Silence begins.

3. The subject of a sentence is usually a noun, which can be either singular or plural. For each of the following sentences, from the word bank choose a subject that would make sense with the provided verb. You may add the word *the* before the subject if it sounds better. **Answers may vary.**

Word Bank: artist, children, musician, architect, singers, poets, authors

a. **The architect** draws.

b. **Authors** write.

c. **The musician** composes.

d. **Singers** sing.

e. **The artist** sketches.

f. **Children** wonder.

4. Imagine that you have a new set of colored pencils, and then write the following kinds of sentences about it.

a. Write a declarative sentence. **I like drawing pictures.**

b. Write an imperative sentence. **Hand me another piece of paper, please.**

Quiz
Principal Elements, Part 1 ANSWERS

1. Analyze the following sentences.

> If you choose not to give a quiz, these sentences could be used for choral analysis. But as a quiz, the sheet is designed for silent, individual work.

a. Mom (S) bakes (P).

b. Bread (S) rises (P).

c. Timer (S) buzzes (P).

d. Fritz (S) devours (P).

2. Subjects are one of the principal elements that make up the core of a sentence. In the following sentences, underline the subject.

a. Morning dawns.

b. Alarm rings.

c. Eyes open.

d. Water runs.

e. Faucet drips.

3. The subject of a sentence is usually a noun, which can be either singular or plural. For each of the following sentences, from the word bank choose a subject that would make sense with the provided verb. You may add the word *the* before the subject if it sounds better. **Answers may vary.**

Word Bank: Rex, Mom, teapot, Dad, family, Stripes, kids

a. **The family** sleeps.

b. **Rex** woofs.

c. **Stripes** meows.

d. **The teapot** whistles.

e. **Kids** rise.

f. **Mom** calls.

4. Imagine that you cannot wake up one morning because you are so sleepy. Write the following kinds of sentences about it.

a. Write an interrogative sentence. **Why is it so hard to wake up?**

b. Write an exclamatory sentence. **Bah, let me sleep longer!**

Sentences for Practice
Principal Elements, Part 1 — ANSWERS

Analyze the following sentences.

S P
1. Wind gusts.

S P
2. Kites soar.

S P
3. Children play.

S P
4. Leaves swirl.

S P
5. Acorns fall.

Sentences for Practice

ANSWERS

Principal Elements, Part 1

6. Geese (S) honk (P).

7. Rex (S) howls (P).

8. Chipmunks (S) scurry (P).

9. Monarchs (S) fly (P).

10. September (S) begins (P).

Lesson to Enjoy—Poem

Principal Elements, Part 1

Do hardwood trees, such as chestnuts, oaks, and maples, grow in your state? If so, you get to see a wonderful display of colors every autumn when the leaves change. If not, you've probably seen pictures. Over a hundred years ago, a poet named George Cooper imagined that the leaves turning color and then falling seemed like a party thrown by October. Well, October seems to have numerous friends, and they are definitely ready for dressing up, making music, dancing, and playing a game. That's why the poet has chosen to use many colorful action verbs. Can you find them?

From the Sideline: The goal of Lesson to Enjoy is for the students to delight in language and grammar. Lightly introduce the elements of poetry, such as image, metaphor, and rhythm. To study and teach poetry in depth, we suggest visiting the Understanding Poetry section in the appendix or reviewing *The Art of Poetry*, published by Classical Academic Press.

October's Party

by George Cooper (1840–1927)

October gave a party;
The leaves by hundreds came—
The Chestnuts, Oaks, and Maples,
And leaves of every name.
The Sunshine spread a carpet,
And everything was grand,
Miss Weather led the dancing,
Professor Wind the band.

The Chestnuts came in yellow,
The Oaks in crimson dressed;
The lovely Misses Maple
In scarlet looked their best;
All balanced to their partners,
And gaily fluttered by;
The sight was like a rainbow
New fallen from the sky.

Then, in the rustic hollow,
At hide-and-seek they played,
The party closed at sundown,
And everybody stayed.
Professor Wind played louder;
They flew along the ground;
And then the party ended
In jolly "hands around."[1]

Questions to Ponder

1. Who came to October's party and what did they look like?
2. What did Professor Wind do at the beginning and end of the party?
3. Name some words that rhyme in this poem. Which rhyming words are your favorites?

1. George Cooper, "October's Party," in *The Home Book of Verse: American and English 1580–1912*, ed. Burton Egbert Stevenson (New York: Henry Holt and Company, 1915), 144.

Well-Ordered Notes—Poem

Read

- Enjoy reading the poem aloud while listening to a classical piece of music, such as Gustav Holst's *St. Paul's Suite* (available at http://capress.link/wol1arev0201). Consider making or buying leaf-shaped sugar cookies to bring for the students to enjoy while they read the poem.
- Have the students memorize the whole poem or divide the stanzas among the students, assigning each student one stanza to memorize.

Retell

- Use the Questions to Ponder as discussion starters:

1. **Who came to October's party and what did they look like?**
   The second line of the poem tells us that the leaves came. The second stanza tells us how they looked: the chestnut leaves dressed in yellow; the oak leaves dressed in crimson (red); and the maple leaves dressed in scarlet (red). Encourage the students to notice and appreciate the subtle difference in the colors of autumn leaves; for example, crimson is a deep, purplish red while scarlet is a bright red. The poet makes the visual description of the leaves especially vivid by giving them human qualities. They are dressed like people would be, and they also dance and play games. This literary device is called personification.
2. **What did Professor Wind do at the beginning and end of the party?**
   Professor Wind leads the band at the beginning of the party. In other words, the sound of the wind blowing accompanies the leaves turning color and beginning to fall in the autumn weather. At the end of the party, Professor Wind plays louder, as the increasingly gusty autumn winds send all the leaves to settle on the ground.
3. **Name some words that rhyme in this poem. Which rhyming words are your favorites?**
   Rhyming words include came/name, grand/band, dressed/best, by/sky, played/stayed, ground/around. Answers to the second question will vary.

- To highlight grammatical concepts within the poem, write on the board the following sentences (without the underlining) that are embedded in the poem. This exercise will help the students see the beauty of language. Even though most of the sentences contain other grammatical elements, such as a direct object or a prepositional phrase, each one has a clear subject followed immediately by an action verb. Ask various students to come up to the board and underline the subject and double underline the action verb predicate. Remind them that the subject is what the sentence is about and the predicate is what the subject is doing.

  - October gave a party.
  - The Sunshine spread a carpet.
  - The Chestnuts came in yellow.
  - They played.
  - The party closed at sundown.
  - Everybody stayed.
  - Professor Wind played louder.
  - They flew along the ground.
  - The party ended.

Record

- The night before you do the poem lesson, ask the students to collect a few leaves from their yard or the park and bring them to class. Show students how to make leaf rubbings using the collected leaves, crayons, and white paper. Gently rub the crayons over the paper with the leaf underneath.
- Have the students neatly copy the second stanza of the poem. Then have them decorate the copy work. They can use their leaf rubbings or cut out leaf shapes of the trees mentioned in the poem (chestnut, oak, and maple) to adorn the poem.

Sentence Bank

From the Sideline: Visit http://capress.link/wol1att for a video demonstration of analysis.

In this chapter's lessons, students combine the two parts of the method—the oral analysis and the written markings—for the first time. These four additional sentences are for extra practice if needed. The scripts are provided for your reference as you model the marking on the board while the students analyze the sentences aloud. Keep the analysis moving along with energy to establish a lively precedent for all the succeeding choral analyses during the year.

S P
Trains pull.

a. (First, read the sentence aloud.) "Trains pull."

b. "This is a sentence because it is a group of words that expresses a complete thought."

c. "It is a declarative sentence because it makes a statement."

d. "This sentence is about *trains*." (Underline the subject.) "So, *trains* is the subject because it is what the sentence is about." (Place a capital letter *S* above the subject.)

e. "This sentence tells us that trains *pull*." (Double underline the predicate.) "So, *pull* is the predicate because it is what the sentence tells us about *trains*." (Place a capital letter *P* above the predicate.)

S P
Gymnasts flip.

a. (First, read the sentence aloud.) "Gymnasts flip."

b. "This is a sentence because it is a group of words that expresses a complete thought."

c. "It is a declarative sentence because it makes a statement."

d. "This sentence is about *gymnasts*." (Underline the subject.) "So, *gymnasts* is the *subject* because it is what the sentence is about." (Place a capital letter *S* above the subject.)

e. "This sentence tells us that gymnasts *flip*." (Double underline the predicate.) "So, *flip* is the *predicate* because it is what the sentence tells us about *gymnasts*." (Place a capital letter *P* above the predicate.)

S P
Fire burns.

a. (First, read the sentence aloud.) "Fire burns."

b. "This is a sentence because it is a group of words that expresses a complete thought."

c. "It is a declarative sentence because it makes a statement."

d. "This sentence is about *fire*." (Underline the subject.) "So, *fire* is the *subject* because it is what the sentence is about." (Place a capital letter *S* above the subject.)

e. "This sentence tells us that fire *burns*." (Double underline the predicate.) "So, *burns* is the *predicate* because it is what the sentence tells us about *fire*." (Place a capital letter *P* above the predicate.)

S P
Heidi pours.

a. (First, read the sentence aloud.) "Heidi pours."

b. "This is a sentence because it is a group of words that expresses a complete thought."

c. "It is a declarative sentence because it makes a statement."

d. "This sentence is about *Heidi*." (Underline the subject.) "So, *Heidi* is the *subject* because it is what the sentence is about." (Place a capital letter *S* above the subject.)

e. "This sentence tells us that Heidi *pours*." (Double underline the predicate.) "So, *pours* is the *predicate* because it is what the sentence tells us about *Heidi*." (Place a capital letter *P* above the predicate.)

From the Sideline: Know your material and know your students. Remember the motto: "Be prepared."

[A]Bring in an apple and cut it into two equal parts. Use the apple to explain principal elements: one half represents the *subject* and the other half represents the *predicate*. Hold up each apple part as you generate short sentences: One half (e.g., *Winston*); the other half (e.g., *cuts*).

Chapter 3

Principal Elements, Part 2—Subject and Predicate Verb[A]

You may have heard the expression "Two halves make a whole." Think of an apple—the first, sweet, crisp apple of September, picked fresh by your own hand from a tree in an orchard. Now, imagine cutting that apple exactly in half. Would you want only half of it? If you love apples, you would want the whole thing. One half is as delicious as the other half, so you would want to eat and enjoy both parts of the apple—the whole apple! That is a good way to explain a sentence because a sentence has two equal parts that make a whole. When those two equal parts—the subject and the predicate—work together, they express one complete thought. In other words, principal■ elements—subject and predicate—express a complete thought, therefore forming the most basic of sentences. It is as if you ate half the apple in the last chapter when you learned about subjects; now, let us bite into predicates.

To the Source:
■ principal
The word *principal* comes from the Latin word *principalis*, meaning "first in importance, original." This is where the word *prince* comes from too. A sentence is like a kingdom with two important princes, the subject and the verb. The word *element* comes from the Latin word *elementum*, meaning "the simplest part of a larger whole."

Ideas to Understand

You should remember from the last chapter that a sentence has a subject and a predicate, and that the predicate tells us something about the subject. In this chapter we will study how verbs in a sentence tell us something about the subject. For example, in the sentence "Winston cuts," the verb *cuts* tells us something about Winston—that he is cutting! We can call these kinds of verbs **predicate verbs**■ because they show action (what verbs do) and also tell us something about the subject (what a predicate does). There are more kinds of verbs, such as **helping verbs**, which "help" other verbs. Also, there are **linking verbs**, but we will cover them in *Well-Ordered Language Level 2*, so you don't need to worry about them yet. For now we will just focus on predicate verbs.

To the Source:
■ verb
The word *verb* comes from the Latin word *verbum*, which simply means "word." We get our word *verbal* (having to do with words) from *verbum*.

To the Source:
■ stanza
The word *stanza* is the Italian word for "room." Think of sections of poem lines as gathered in their own little room.

From the Sideline: Write the first line of Tennyson's poem on the board, double underlining each action verb: *slip*, *slide*, *gloom*, and *glance*. Emphasize that the subject *I* tells what the sentence is about, and the verbs *tell* what the subject is doing. To appreciate the whole poem, see the complete poem in The Curious Child's Literary Appendix.

Predicate verbs show action, so they are also called **action verbs**. Predicate verbs show what the subject does. In the poem called "Song of the Brook," Alfred, Lord Tennyson chooses some unusual predicate verbs to make something known about a stream. Because all the words in the poem are spoken by the brook itself, the subject in almost every sentence is "I." Imagine sitting down beside a stream and having a conversation with it. What would it tell you about itself? In one **stanza**■ (or group of lines in a poem), the brook uses four vivid verbs to show its action. Let's take a look at that stanza:

> I slip, I slide, I gloom, I glance,
> Among my skimming swallows;
> I make the netted sunbeam dance
> Against my sandy shallows.[1]

Slip, *slide*, *gloom*, and *glance* all show the action of the brook. They are the predicate verbs for the subject "I." You know what slipping and sliding mean because you have done so yourself. Have you ever seen a stream slip and slide over rocks and around bends? This is what the stream *does*. This is how it *acts*. Tennyson is creative in his choice of verbs to help you see the bubbling brook in your imagination. What do you think *gloom* and *glance* mean as actions for a brook? In more ordinary speech, you might say "I frown" instead of "I gloom" and "I flash" or "I sparkle" instead of "I glance." All of these two-word pairs are complete sentences because they have a subject—*I*—and a predicate verb.

To the Source:
■ auxiliary
Our word *auxiliary* comes from the Latin word *auxilium*, which means "help, assistance!"

A predicate verb may be one word, such as *slip*. This action verb may also have one or more helping verbs with it in order to complete its meaning. There are twenty-three helping verbs (also known as **auxiliary**■ **verbs**, or auxiliaries): *am, is, are, was, were, be, being, been, has, have, had, do, does, did, may, might, must, should, could, would, shall, will, can.*

---

1. Alfred, Lord Tennyson, "Song of the Brook," in *Anthology of Children's Literature*, ed. Edna Johnson, Carrie E. Scott, and Evelyn R. Sickels (Cambridge, Massachusetts: Houghton Mifflin Company, 1948), 924–925.

A helping verb and an action verb together are known as a **verb phrase**.

Without **a Helping Verb**	***With*** **a Helping Verb**
I slip.	I am slipping.
I slipped.	I have slipped.

Note that when a helping verb appears in a sentence, the action verb might be in the *-ing* form, as in *slipping*.

Including a helping verb affects the predicate verb's **tense**, or the time when the action occurs—past, present, or future. For example, notice how the tense changes when we add helping verbs to Tennyson's "I slip" or to "I slipped": *I am slipping, was slipping, have slipped, had slipped, have been slipping, had been slipping, will slip, will be slipping, will have slipped, will have been slipping*. When you slip a helping verb into your sentence, you can indicate if the action is continuing right now or if the action was or will be completed at the moment the sentence was written or spoken.

From the Sideline: It might be helpful to note that a few words can function as different kinds of verbs. For instance, forms of *have* and *do* might be used as predicate verbs in some sentences—*Rex* ***has*** *a bone; Rex* ***does*** *a trick*—and helping verbs in others—*Rex* ***has barked*** *all night; Rex* ***did*** *not* ***sleep***. Later in *WOL Level 2*, your students will notice that some helping verbs—the forms of *be*—can also be linking verbs. Other verbs usually function only as helping verbs: *may, might, must, should, could, would, shall, will, can*.

Moment for Mechanics

If the subject of a sentence is singular, then the verb must also be singular. If the subject is plural, then the verb must also be plural. That is called **subject-verb agreement**. Singular verbs usually end in *s*, while plural verbs do not. Some helping verbs have special forms for their plural, such as *are* and *were* (plural forms of *is* and *was*), *have* (plural form of *has*), and *do* (plural form of *does*).

	Singular Subject & Verb	Plural Subject & Verb
Verb w/o helping verb	Sun shines.	Clouds float.
Verb w/ helping verb	Sun *is* shining. Sun *was* shining.	Clouds *are* floating. Clouds *were* floating.

Terms to Remember[B]

It is important to memorize the twenty-three helping verbs and the definition of a verb because the predicate is an essential part of every sentence. Being able to identify and analyze the verb and its helpers is like understanding the most fundamental plays in a sport. Players always take the time needed to memorize the plays. It is worth doing.

Principal Elements *(1–3)*

Subject and Predicate *(1–4)*

Eight Parts of Speech *(1–1)*

Noun *(1–5)*

NEW! **Verb and Helping Verb** *(1–6)*

[B]For the lyrics to all of the songs, please see the Song Lyrics section on page 191. Play the appropriate audio tracks and have students sing/chant along. Students should commit the songs to memory.

Sentences to Analyze

Keep in mind that each time you analyze a sentence you learn to do it better and learn to see how the parts of a sentence work together to form a whole. With regular practice, your eyes will be trained to see these parts and how they work, just as a coach can quickly recognize the opposing team's plays. In this section, you will focus on both the subject and the predicate verb. Since you already know the first part of the analysis, the next step in analyzing a sentence is to identify the *kind* of predicate and to say how you know what kind it is.

With your teacher's guidance, use the following steps to analyze the sentence. Speak the words in gray along with your teacher and pay close attention to what she is writing. When your teacher is finished, the sentence will look like this:

From the Sideline: The two example sentences in the Sentences to Analyze section are meant to be analyzed aloud by the students and teacher in chorus. Model on the board how to mark each sentence while the students use the scripts to recite the analysis aloud with you. The spoken lines should flow without interruption and without sounding singsong or expressionless. The words in parentheses, like stage directions telling you what to write, should not be spoken. The repetition inherent in this method is important for the students to learn the relationships among the parts of the sentence.

S PV
Bees hum.

a. (First, read the sentence aloud.) "Bees hum."

b. "This is a sentence because it is a group of words that expresses a complete thought."

c. "It is a declarative sentence because it makes a statement."

d. "This sentence is about *bees*. So, *bees* is the subject because it is what the sentence is about." (Since *bees* is the subject, underline it and place a capital letter *S* above it.)

e. "This sentence tells us that bees *hum*. So, *hum* is the predicate because it is what the sentence tells us about *bees*." (Since *hum* tells something about *bees*, it is the predicate. Double underline the predicate and place a capital letter *P* above it.)

f. "It is a *predicate verb* because it shows action. There is no linking verb because predicate verbs do not need linking verbs." (Since *hum* shows action, place a capital letter *V* to the right of the letter *P* above the predicate.)

Here's a sentence to analyze that includes a helping verb and a predicate verb. Notice that during the analysis, the whole verb phrase is double underlined. When the analysis is finished, the sentence will look like this, with the capital letters *PV* above the predicate verb and the lowercase letters *hv* above the helping verb.

S hv PV
Bees are humming.

a. (First, read the sentence aloud.) "Bees are humming."

b. "This is a sentence because it is a group of words that expresses a complete thought."

c. "It is a declarative sentence because it makes a statement."

d. "This sentence is about *bees*. So, *bees* is the subject because it is what the sentence is about." (Since *bees* is the subject, underline it and place a capital letter *S* above it.)

From the Sideline: Even though students will not analyze linking verbs until *WOL Level 2*, the scripts still mention them from the beginning: "predicate verbs do not need linking verbs." Students do not need a full understanding of linking verbs to know that using an action verb excludes them. We find that planting this seed here helps students later analyze sentences that do include linking verbs. In Chapter 6 (see page 103) we do include a basic definition of linking verbs as one of the four classes of verbs.

e. "This sentence tells us that bees *are humming*. So, *are humming* is the predicate because it is what the sentence tells us about *bees*." (Since *humming* tells something about *bees*, double underline the predicate, including the helping verb, and place a capital letter *P* above the action verb.)

f. "It is a *predicate verb* because it shows action. There is no linking verb because predicate verbs do not need linking verbs." (Since *humming* shows action, place a capital letter *V* to the right of the letter *P* above the action verb.)

g. "*Are* is the helping verb because it helps the verb." (Place the lowercase letters *hv* above the helping verb.)

From the Sideline: At the moment you say "It is a predicate verb" during the choral analysis, add the capital letter *V* to the right of the capital *P* above the action verb.

From the Sideline: Saying that a helping verb helps the verb seems like a circular definition, but it also avoids over-complication. You can even make this part of the script playful, throwing in a shrug as you say "it helps the verb."

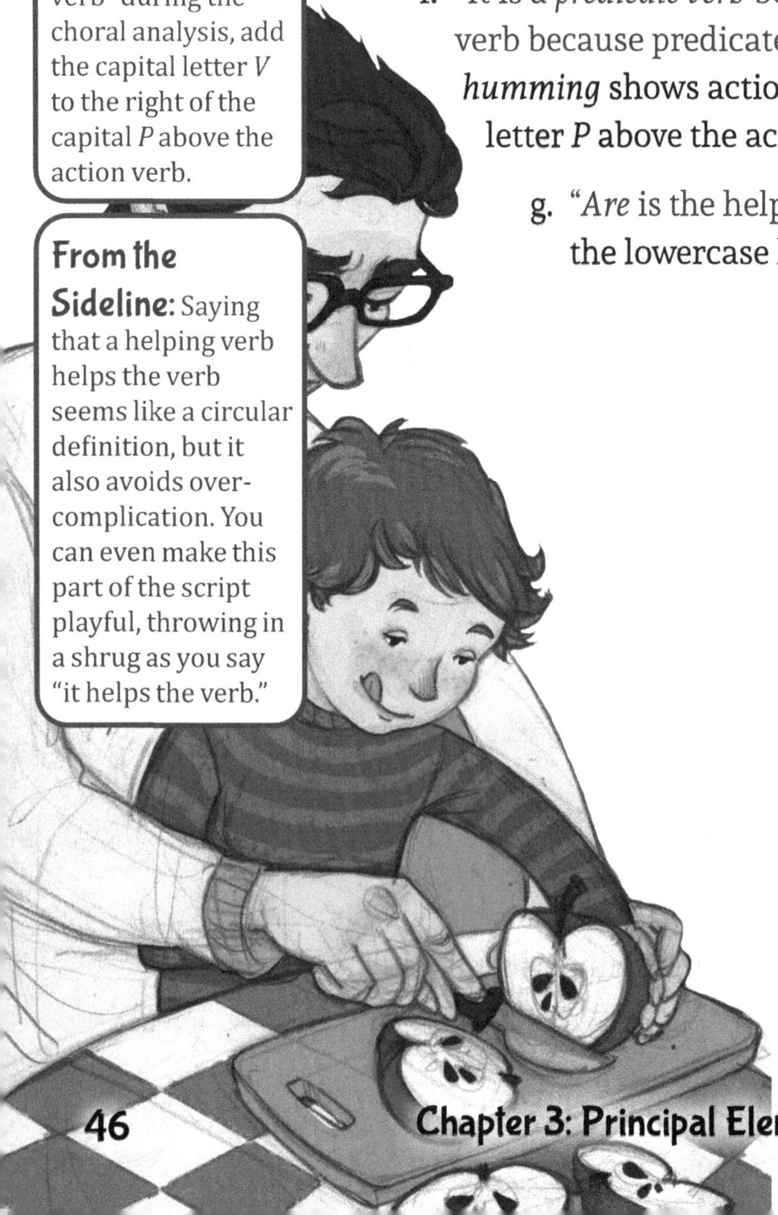

Step-by-step you are learning to analyze language, untying its knots in order to understand its basic parts. Did you ever get a big knot in your shoestrings? It may look complicated at first, but once you loosen it, you see there are only two strands. Now that you have untied the structure of sentences, you see that there are two principal elements: the subject and the predicate.

Flip back to the illustration at the beginning of this chapter. Do you see the apples on the table? How many apples are there? What is your favorite kind of apple?

Well-Ordered Notes A

From the Sideline: Please note that the teacher's edition includes a quiz and other extras at the end of each chapter. The Extra Practice & Assessments PDF, available for purchase at ClassicalAcademicPress .com, that accompanies the textbook contains this material in reproducible form.

Review It

Review the following:

What are the eight parts of speech?
What are the principal elements?
What is a noun?

Practice It

Lead your students in the activity Write on White using mini whiteboards. Write the following subjects on the board. Read each sentence aloud, saying "blank" in place of the verb, as in "Frogs *blank*." Have the students write on their mini whiteboards an appropriate verb for the sentence—in the singular form for a singular subject or in the plural form for a plural subject. Having students hold up their answers on whiteboards allows you to quickly see if all the students understand subject-verb agreement. After the students have shown their answers for each sentence, ask a few students to share their answers aloud.

From the Sideline: If you don't have mini whiteboards, you can make them by laminating card stock. Use whiteboard markers to write on them and tissues to clean them off.

Example: Frogs ______________. (croak, hop, leap)

1. Waves ______________. (ripple, flow, lap)
2. Ducks ______________. (quack, waddle, fly)
3. Fish ______________. (jump, swim, hide)
4. Fritz ______________. (laughs, squeals, runs)
5. Heidi ______________. (splashes, wades, dives)

Analyze It

From the Sideline: During the choral analysis, model on the board how to mark the sentences while the students mark them in their books. Don't skip any steps. Later on it will pay off as the sentences will get more difficult. Visit http://capress.link/wol1att for video demonstrations of analysis for each chapter.

Now, as a class, analyze the four sentences in the lesson. Here is the script for the first one to help you lead the choral analysis and model the markings on the board. The words in parentheses are like stage directions to guide you and are not to be spoken. The words in gray and enclosed in quotation marks are for you and the students to speak in chorus.

S PV
Worms wriggle.

a. (First, read the sentence aloud.) "Worms wriggle."
b. "This is a sentence because it is a group of words that expresses a complete thought."
c. "It is a declarative sentence because it makes a statement."
d. "This sentence is about *worms*." (Underline the subject.) "So, *worms* is the subject because it is what the sentence is about." (Place a capital letter *S* above the subject.)
e. "This sentence tells us that worms *wriggle*." (Double underline the predicate.) "So, *wriggle* is the predicate because it is what the sentence tells us about *worms*." (Place a capital letter *P* above the action verb.)
f. "It is a predicate verb because it shows action. There is no linking verb because predicate verbs do not need linking verbs." (Place a capital letter *V* to the right of the *P*.)

From the Sideline: For extra guided practice, refer to the Sentence Bank at the end of this chapter.

Lesson to Learn
Principal Elements, Part 2

A

1. Analyze the following sentences.

   a. Worms (S) wriggle (PV).

   b. Fishermen (S) cast (PV).

   c. Fish (S) nibble (PV).

   d. Boats (S) tip (PV).

From the Sideline: Remember that when you see the word *analyze* in instructions throughout this book, we mean both choral analysis and written notations. The two go hand in hand as a prediagramming system.

2. The principal elements are the core of the sentence. In the following sentences, underline the subject and double underline the predicate verb.

   a. Fireflies blink.

   b. Mosquitoes buzz.

   c. Gnats annoy.

   d. Bees hum.

   e. Spiders crawl.

   f. Critters scatter.

3. Construct complete sentences by choosing a predicate verb from the word bank and adding it to each of the following subjects. Remember, singular subjects should have singular verbs and plural subjects should have plural verbs. **Answers may vary.**

Word Bank: dives, annoy, swim, laugh, sprays, bite, splashes

a. The flies **bite**.

b. Winston **sprays**.

c. The kids **swim**.

d. Fritz **splashes**.

e. Heidi **dives**.

f. The campers **laugh**.

4. Imagine that you are talking about bugs with a friend, and then write the following kinds of sentences about it.

a. Write an interrogative sentence. **Do you have a bug collection?**

b. Write an imperative sentence. **Don't open that ant farm.**

Well-Ordered Notes B

Review It

Review the following:

What are the eight parts of speech?
What are the principal elements?
What is a verb?
What are the twenty-three helping verbs?

Practice It

Lead your students in the fast-paced activity Which Is Right? Read the following sentences aloud, including the two options for the verb. The students will use their hands to show which word correctly indicates subject-verb agreement. If the first option is correct, the students should raise their index fingers. If the second option is correct, then they should each raise two fingers. A quick glance around the room will let you determine if the students understand that singular subjects take singular verbs and plural subjects take plural verbs. As you go through the activity, point out to students that the helping verbs in the sentences show the time relations in the mini-narrative that unfolds in these sentences

Example:
Teacher: "Winston yawns/yawn daily at breakfast." (one finger)
Students: Raise one finger to indicate that "yawns" is the correct word. The sentence should be "Winston yawns daily at breakfast."

1. The two boys always sniffles/**sniffle** a lot. (two fingers)
2. Fritz **has**/have wheezed all day long. (one finger)
3. Winston **is**/are coughing again right now. (one finger)
4. The boys has/**have** hiccupped uncontrollably every day after lunch. (two fingers)
5. Now, the brothers is/**are** sneezing repeatedly. (two fingers)
6. Dad **is**/are wondering about these noises. (one finger)

Analyze It

From the Sideline: Visit http://capress.link/wol1att for a video demonstration of analysis.

Now, as a class, analyze the four sentences in the lesson. Here is the script for the first one to help you lead the choral analysis and model the markings on the board. The words in parentheses are like stage directions to guide you and are not to be spoken. The words in gray and enclosed in quotation marks are for you and the students to speak in chorus.

S hv PV
Dials have turned.

a. (First, read the sentence aloud.) "Dials have turned."

b. "This is a sentence because it is a group of words that expresses a complete thought."

c. "It is a declarative sentence because it makes a statement."

d. "This sentence is about *dials*." (Underline the subject.) "So, *dials* is the subject because it is what the sentence is about." (Place a capital letter *S* above the subject.)

e. "This sentence tells us that dials *have turned*." (Double underline the predicate.) "So, *have turned* is the predicate because it is what the sentence tells us about *dials*." (Place a capital letter *P* above the action verb.)

f. "It is a predicate verb because it shows action. There is no linking verb because predicate verbs do not need linking verbs." (Place a capital letter *V* to the right of the *P*.)

g. "*Have* is a helping verb because it helps the verb." (Place a lowercase *hv* above the helping verb.)

From the Sideline: For extra guided practice, refer to the Sentence Bank at the end of this chapter.

Lesson to Learn
Principal Elements, Part 2

B

1. Analyze the following sentences.

   a. S: Dials / hv: have / PV: turned.
   Dials have turned.

   b. S: Machines / hv: are / PV: rumbling.
   Machines are rumbling.

   c. S: Water / hv: is / PV: spraying.
   Water is spraying.

   d. S: Fritz / PV: snickers.
   Fritz snickers.

From the Sideline: Remember that when you see the word *analyze* in instructions throughout this book, we mean both choral analysis and written notations. The two go hand in hand as a prediagramming system.

2. Construct complete sentences by choosing a predicate verb from the word bank and adding it to each of the following subjects. Remember, singular subjects should have singular verbs and plural subjects should have plural verbs. **Answers may vary.**

Word Bank: barks, falls, blows, chatter, chases, floats, scatter

   a. The wind **blows**.
   b. A leaf **floats**.
   c. Seeds **scatter**.
   d. Squirrels **chatter**.
   e. Rex **barks**.
   f. Fritz **chases**.

3. Helping verbs show time relations. Rewrite the sentences from exercise 2 using the *-ing* form of the predicate verbs you supplied. Add a helping verb to show the action is happening right now. Use *is* for singular subjects and *are* for plural subjects.

   a. The wind **is blowing**.

   b. A leaf **is floating**.

   c. Seeds **are scattering**.

   d. Squirrels **are chattering**.

   e. Rex **is barking**.

   f. Fritz **is chasing**.

4. Imagine that you are talking to the city workers who have cleaned the streets, and then write the following kinds of sentences about it.

   a. Write an interrogative sentence. **Why do you clean the streets in the fall?**

   b. Write an exclamatory sentence. **Phew! The streets are sure dirty!**

Well-Ordered Notes C

Review It

Review the following:

What are the eight parts of speech?
What are the principal elements?
What is a noun?
What is a verb?

Practice It

Lead your students in the activity What Do They Do? to reinforce constructing sentences with appropriate action verbs. Write on the board a list of animals and insects (such as those provided here), and then ask, "What do *frogs* do?" The first student stands, answers the question with a complete sentence (e.g., "Frogs hop"), and then sits. Rephrase the same question for each student—"What else do *frogs* do?—but have the students provide different verbs as they stand to answer (e.g., Frogs *hop, croak, jump, dive, swim*). Or vary your questions with different animals from the list—"What do *snakes* do?"—continuing around the class until everyone has had a chance to answer a question.

Fewer than Five: Adapt the activity for an individual or a smaller group by asking the student(s) the question (e.g., "What do frogs do?"). She answers the question (e.g., "Frogs hop.") and then acts out the action (e.g., she hops around the room). Then ask the next question with the next animal on the list.

Example:
Teacher: "What do frogs do?"
Student 1: "Frogs hop."
Teacher: "What else do frogs do?"
Student 2: "Frogs croak."

Nouns (animals and insects):

- frogs
- snakes
- millipedes
- raccoons
- toads
- moths
- beetles
- mice
- ticks
- chipmunks

Analyze It

From the Sideline: Visit http://capress.link/wol1att for a video demonstration of analysis.

Now, as a class, analyze the four sentences in the lesson. Here is the script for the first one to help you lead the choral analysis and model the markings on the board. The words in parentheses are like stage directions to guide you and are not to be spoken. The words in gray and enclosed in quotation marks are for you and the students to speak in chorus.

S hv hv PV
Time has been passing.

a. (First, read the sentence aloud.) "Time has been passing."

b. "This is a sentence because it is a group of words that expresses a complete thought."

c. "It is a declarative sentence because it makes a statement."

d. "This sentence is about *time*." (Underline the subject.) "So, *time* is the subject because it is what the sentence is about." (Place a capital letter *S* above the subject.)

e. "This sentence tells us that time *has been passing*." (Double underline the predicate.) "So, *has been passing* is the predicate because it is what the sentence tells us about *time*." (Place a capital letter *P* above the action verb.)

f. "It is a predicate verb because it shows action. There is no linking verb because predicate verbs do not need linking verbs." (Place a capital letter *V* to the right of the *P*.)

g. "*Has been* are helping verbs because they help the verb." (Place a lowercase *hv* above each helping verb.)

From the Sideline: For extra guided practice, refer to the Sentence Bank at the end of this chapter.

Lesson to Learn
Principal Elements, Part 2

C

1. Analyze the following sentences.

   a. Time (S) has (hv) been (hv) passing (PV).

   b. Winston (S) should (hv) be (hv) studying (PV).

   c. Heidi (S) might (hv) be (hv) working (PV).

   d. Fritz (S) is (hv) bird-watching (PV).

From the Sideline: Remember that when you see the word *analyze* in instructions throughout this book, we mean both choral analysis and written notations. The two go hand in hand as a prediagramming system.

2. Construct complete sentences by choosing a predicate verb from the word bank and adding it to each of the following subjects. Remember, singular subjects should have singular verbs and plural subjects should have plural verbs. **Answers may vary.**

   Word Bank: swoop, hoot, squawk, chatter, hunt, peck, chirp

   a. Chickadees **chirp**.

   b. Woodpeckers **peck**.

   c. Blue jays **squawk**.

   d. Sparrows **swoop**.

   e. Owls **hoot**.

   f. Hawks **hunt**.

C

Lesson to Learn
Principal Elements, Part 2

3. Add the correct helping verb, either *is* or *are*, to make the verb phrase agree with the subject in each sentence. For a singular subject, use *is* with the action verb. For a plural subject, use *are* with the action verb.

   a. Winston ___is___ getting the heavy bags from the van.

   b. Heidi ___is___ dragging the birdseed bag along.

   c. The cousins ___are___ helping Grandpa outside.

   d. Grandpa ___is___ carrying the ladder.

   e. The boys ___are___ scooping cups of seed.

   f. Fritz ___is___ eating the sunflower seeds.

4. Imagine that you are looking for birds in your yard with your grandfather, and then write the following kinds of sentences about it.

   a. Write a declarative sentence. Grandpa loves bird-watching in the backyard.

   b. Write an interrogative sentence. Did Grandpa put more birdseed in the feeder?

Well-Ordered Notes D

Review It

Review the following:

What are the principal elements?
What is a noun?
What is a verb?
What are the twenty-three helping verbs?

Practice It

Lead your students in the activity What Am I Doing? as a way of reinforcing their understanding of action verbs. Write the following list of action verbs on cards and place the cards in a jar. (Be sure you have enough cards for each student to be able to participate at least once in the game. You may need to come up with some additional verbs to accommodate the size of your class.) Have each child select a card and pantomime the action while the other students guess the verb.

bending	lifting	dancing	leaping
drawing	boxing	wrestling	tidying
laughing	pointing	scratching	tripping
tossing	jogging	hopping	stomping

Analyze It

From the Sideline: Visit http://capress.link/wol1att for a video demonstration of analysis.

Now, as a class, analyze the four sentences in the lesson. Here is the script for the first one to help you lead the choral analysis and model the markings on the board. The words in parentheses are like stage directions to guide you and are not to be spoken. The words in gray and enclosed in quotation marks are for you and the students to speak in chorus.

S hv PV
Popcorn is popping.

a. (First, read the sentence aloud.) "Popcorn is popping."

b. "This is a sentence because it is a group of words that expresses a complete thought."

c. "It is a declarative sentence because it makes a statement."

d. "This sentence is about *popcorn*." (Underline the subject.) "So, *popcorn* is the subject because it is what the sentence is about." (Place a capital letter *S* above the subject.)

e. "This sentence tells us that popcorn *is popping*." (Double underline the predicate.) "So, *is popping* is the predicate because it is what the sentence tells us about *popcorn*." (Place a capital letter *P* above the action verb.)

f. "It is a predicate verb because it shows action. There is no linking verb because predicate verbs do not need linking verbs." (Place a capital letter *V* to the right of the *P*.)

g. "*Is* is a helping verb because it helps the verb." (Place a lowercase *hv* above the helping verb.)

From the Sideline: For extra guided practice, refer to the Sentence Bank at the end of this chapter.

Lesson to Learn
Principal Elements, Part 2

D

1. Analyze the following sentences.

   a. Popcorn (S) is (hv) popping (PV).

   b. Hot dogs (S) are (hv) sizzling (PV).

   c. Ice cubes (S) are (hv) melting (PV).

   d. Games (S) begin (PV).

From the Sideline: Remember that when you see the word *analyze* in instructions throughout this book, we mean both choral analysis and written notations. The two go hand in hand as a prediagramming system.

2. Construct complete sentences by choosing a predicate verb from the word bank and adding it to each of the following subjects. Remember, singular subjects should have singular verbs and plural subjects should have plural verbs. **Answers may vary.**

Word Bank: catches, run, scores, sprint, signals, compete, kicks

   a. Referee signals.

   b. Kicker kicks.

   c. Players run.

   d. Catcher catches.

   e. Athletes sprint.

   f. Team scores.

3. Add the correct helping verb, either *was* or *were*, to make the verb phrase agree with the subject in each sentence. For a singular subject, use *was* with the action verb. For a plural subject, use *were* with the action verb.

   a. The players ___were___ wearing new uniforms too.

   b. The cousins ___were___ excited for the game.

   c. Dad ___was___ taking the gang to the junior football game.

   d. Lucy ___was___ sitting with Heidi.

   e. The girls ___were___ telling jokes in the back of the van.

   f. Fritz ___was___ laughing at the jokes.

4. Imagine that you are going to a football game, and then write the following kinds of sentences about it.

   a. Write an exclamatory sentence. ___Hurray, I love football!___

   b. Write an interrogative sentence. ___What team are we playing this week?___

Sentences for Practice
Principal Elements, Part 2 — ANSWERS

Analyze the following sentences.

S PV
1. Stripes naps.

S hv PV
2. Rex is playing.

S hv PV
3. Lucy is singing.

S hv hv hv PV
4. Winston should have been watching.

S PV
5. Fritz hides.

From the Sideline: In each chapter, an extra practice sheet provides more sentences for analysis to use as needed—perhaps for review as a class, for individual students requiring more practice, or even for a refresher for students later in the year.

Sentences for Practice

ANSWERS

Principal Elements, Part 2

S hv hv PV
6. Dad will be calling.

S hv hv PV
7. Boys might be chasing.

S PV
8. Lucy runs.

S PV
9. Fritz trips.

S PV
10. Neighbors laugh.

Lesson to Enjoy—Poem
Principal Elements, Part 2

This poem tells a lesson of the busy honeybees. You can almost feel the beating of the honeybee's wings. The author has used many verbs in it. Which verb is your favorite?

To a Honey-Bee

by Alice Cary (1820–1871)

From the Sideline: In ordinary modern words, the lines of the first stanza would be, "Bee, wait a little bit, right there where you have landed, and explain to me why you are singing."

"Busy-body, busy-body,
Always on the wing,
Wait a bit, where you have lit,
And tell me why you sing."

lit: a poetic past-tense form of *alight* or *land*.

Up, and in the air again,
Flap, flap, flap!
And now she stops, and now she drops
Into the rose's lap.

"Come, just a minute come,
From your rose so red."
Hum, hum, hum, hum —
That was all she said.

Busy-body, busy-body,
Always light and gay,
It seems to me, for all I see,
Your work is only play.

And now the day is sinking to
The goldenest of eves,
And she doth creep for quiet sleep
Among the lily-leaves.

eves: a poetic form for the word *evenings*

doth: an old-fashioned word for *does*

"Come, just a moment come,
From your snowy bed."
Hum, hum, hum, hum—
That was all she said.

But, the while I mused, I learned
The secret of her way:
Do my part with cheerful heart,
And turn my work to play.[2]

mused: thought about something carefully

Questions to Ponder

1. What are the bee's various activities?
2. What does "the while I mused" mean?
3. What is the moral in the poem?

2. Alice Cary, "To a Honey-Bee," in *Ballads for Little Folks* (Boston and New York: Houghton Mifflin Co., 1873), 74. Available at https://books.google.com/books?id=D3dPAAAAYAAJ.

Well-Ordered Notes—Poem

Read

- Read the poem aloud to the students while listening to a classical piece of music, such as Rimsky-Korsakov's "Flight of the Bumblebee."
- Have the students take different parts as they read the poem aloud. Assign one student to read the "spoken" words in quotation marks, one to read the narrated parts, and the rest of the group to make buzzing sounds. Or divide the students into sections, having each group read in turn a different stanza.

Retell

- Use the Questions to Ponder as discussion starters:

  1. **What are the bee's various activities?**
     The bee sings (buzzes), flies, and alights, stops in midair and drops into the flower, hums, creeps, and sleeps. It is pollinating the flowers. What the bee does not do is come and rest when the poet calls it. Go through the poem stanza by stanza with the students and guide them in identifying all the action verbs, such as *wait, have lit, sing, flap, stops, drops, come, hum, said, seems, see, is sinking, doth creep, mused, learned, do, turn*. Point out the helping verbs *have, is*, and the archaic *doth* (does).

  2. **What does "the while I mused" mean?**
     "The while I mused" means "the whole time I watched the bee, I was trying to figure something out about the bee." Ask the students what the poet is pondering. Answers may include why the bee is so busy, why the bee doesn't pause and rest when asked to come, and why the bee is so cheerful while being so busy. Musing about how cheerful, light, and gay the bee is, the poet sees that the bee makes her ceaseless work seem playful.

  3. **What is the moral in the poem?**
     The moral of the poem is that, like the busy bee, humans can make work enjoyable by having a good attitude about it. Encourage the students to think about their own lives for examples of making unpleasant, difficult, or endless tasks seem fun. For instance, singing a cleanup song while doing work makes it fun. Having a race with siblings to finish chores makes them more enjoyable. Checking tasks off a chart feels rewarding.

- Help the students identify imperative structures (imperative sentences) that have an implied "you." Write the following sentences on the board to reinforce that imperative sentences give commands.

  - (You) Wait a bit where you have lit.
  - (You) Tell me why you sing.
  - (You) Come, just a minute come, from your rose so red.
  - (You) Do my part with cheerful heart.
  - (You) Turn my work to play.

Record

- Have students copy their favorite part of the poem in their copybooks.
- Have the students make thumbprint bees by following the directions below. (Keep the wet wipes handy!) You might have the students make their thumbprint bees in their copybooks as a border on a page where they have written their favorite part of the poem.

Make Fingerprint Bees!

1. Press your thumb in yellow paint.
2. Make one big stamp with your thumb on paper.
3. Dip the tip of another finger in black paint.
4. Make small black stamps with your finger for the head, the stripe and the stinger.
5. Press your finger in black paint again. Stamp your finger several times on a paper towel until most of the paint comes off.
6. Stamp wings on the top of the bee with the now gray paint.

Review
Principal Elements, Part 2 ANSWERS

1. Analyze the following sentences.

   a. Signal (S) is (hv) flashing (PV).

   b. Tires (S) are (hv) squealing (PV).

   c. Uncle Ulysses (S) should (hv) be (hv) braking (PV).

   d. Motorists (S) stop (PV).

From the Sideline: The material in the following pages is not included in the student edition. You can find the Review lesson, the Quiz, the extra Sentences for Practice, and the second Lesson to Enjoy in reproducible form in the Extra Practice & Assessments PDF, available for purchase at ClassicalAcademicPress.com.

2. Construct complete sentences by choosing a predicate verb from the word bank and adding it to each of the following subjects. Remember, singular subjects should have singular verbs and plural subjects should have plural verbs. **Answers may vary.**

Word Bank: comes, sound, directs, watches, stops, obey, stare

   a. The ambulance **comes**.
   b. A policeman **directs**.
   c. The drivers **obey**.
   d. Uncle Ulysses **watches**.
   e. Sirens **sound**.
   f. Onlookers **stare**.

Review
Principal Elements, Part 2
ANSWERS

3. Add the correct helping verb, either *was* or *were*, to make the verb phrase agree with the subject in each sentence. For a singular subject, use *was* with the action verb. For a plural subject, use *were* with the action verb.

   a. A man **was** driving to the auto repair shop.

   b. Two guys **were** standing in line.

   c. The owner **was** telling a story about his dog.

   d. The two friends **were** listening at the desk.

   e. A technician **was** checking the car parts.

   f. Three workers **were** busy with car engines.

4. Imagine that you were at a park when you saw an accident, and then write the following kinds of sentences about it.

   a. Write a exclamatory sentence. **Oh, I hope the people in that car are all right!**

   b. Write an interrogative sentence. **What caused the accident?**

Quiz
Principal Elements, Part 2 ANSWERS

1. Analyze the following sentences.

   a. Waves (S) are (hv) rolling (PV).

   b. Crabs (S) are (hv) scurrying (PV).

   c. Seagulls (S) soar (PV).

   d. Theo (S) is (hv) swimming (PV).

2. Construct complete sentences by choosing a predicate verb from the word bank and adding it to each of the following subjects. Remember, singular subjects should have singular verbs and plural subjects should have plural verbs. **Answers may vary.**

   Word Bank: fish, glides, wave, blasts, pull, grin, snaps

   a. The foghorn ______ blasts ______.

   b. Tugboats ______ pull ______.

   c. Fishermen ______ fish ______.

   d. The sailboat ______ glides ______.

   e. The photographer ______ snaps ______.

   f. Flags ______ wave ______.

Quiz
Principal Elements, Part 2

3. Add the correct helping verb, either *is* or *are*, to make the verb phrase agree with the subject in each sentence. For a singular subject, use *is* with the action verb. For a plural subject, use *are* with the action verb.

   a. The tourists __are__ sitting in beach chairs along the shore.

   b. The birds __are__ circling overhead.

   c. Heidi __is__ looking for driftwood.

   d. Fritz __is__ collecting shells along the beach.

   e. The minnows __are__ darting around in the water.

   f. Winston __is__ reading a book about marine animals.

4. Imagine that you are going to a beach with your family, and then write the following kinds of sentences about it.

   a. Write a declarative sentence. __We will be going to the beach next Saturday.__

   b. Write an interrogative sentence. __Who will come with us?__

Sentences for Practice—Fable

Principal Elements, Part 2 ANSWERS

Analyze the following sentences, which are based on "Two Travelers and the Bear."

From the Sideline: These extra practice sentences are a synopsis of the fable "Two Travelers and the Bear." The fable and the extended lesson notes are on the following pages.

S hv hv PV
1. Travelers will be walking.

S hv PV
2. Leaves were dancing.

S hv PV
3. Breezes are blowing.

S hv PV
4. Clouds are floating.

S hv hv PV
5. Bear has been growling.

Sentences for Practice—Fable

ANSWERS

Principal Elements, Part 2

S hv hv PV
6. Travelers will be climbing.

S hv hv PV
7. Branches had been quivering.

S hv PV
8. Man must rest.

S hv hv hv PV
9. Birds might have been trilling.

S PV
10. Companions continue.

Lesson to Enjoy—Fable
Principal Elements, Part 2

Some of Aesop's fables almost sound like a joke. Do you think this one is funny? Does it have a serious moral? You can think about it as you analyze the sentences that follow it on the next page.

Two Travelers and the Bear

by Aesop (adapted)

Two Travelers who were walking together through the woods agreed to stand by each other in any sort of dangers that might befall them. They had not gone far before a savage Bear rushed out upon them from the thicket.

One of the Travelers, a light, nimble fellow, climbed up into a tree and hid himself among the leaves. The other, seeing no help for it, threw himself flat down upon the ground with his face in the dust.

The Bear put his muzzle close to his ear and sniffed and sniffed. But at last with a growl, he shook his head, took him for dead, and lumbered back into the woods.

Then the fellow in the tree came down to his companion, and asked him, with a mischievous smile, "What was it that Master Bear whispered to you?"

"He told me," said the other, "never trust a friend who deserts you in a time of need."

Moral: Misfortune is the test of a true friendship.[1]

1. Aesop, 'Two Travelers and the Bear," in *The Book of Fables*, ed. Ernest Griset, Samuel Croxall, Jean de La Fontaine, and Roger L'Estrange (New York: American Book Exchange, 1880), 31. Available at https://books.google.com/books?id=msEqAAAAYAAJ.

Questions to Ponder

1. What did the two travelers agree to do while they traveled?
2. What does "put his muzzle close to his ear" mean?
3. What lesson can be learned from this fable?

Well-Ordered Notes—Fable

Read

- Read aloud the whole fable, or have a few students read sections of the fable to the others. Consider bringing in gummy bears for the students to enjoy while the fable is read.
- Have students sing the definition of a fable (audio track 1–14; see page 194 for lyrics).

Retell

- Use the Questions to Ponder as discussion starters:
  1. **What did the two travelers agree to do while they traveled?**
     The two travelers agreed to help each other out no matter what. Each agreed never to desert the other in a time of danger.
  2. **What does "put his muzzle close to his ear" mean?**
     A muzzle is the jaws, mouth, and nose of the bear. Emphasize to the students how terrifying it would be to have a bear's powerful teeth so close to your face. The bear is sniffing the traveler to figure out if he would make a good meal. But because the traveler doesn't move a muscle, the bear decides he's long dead and leaves. The other traveler tries to make a joke about how it appeared to him the bear was telling his friend a secret. He gets a sarcastic reply that indicates the traveler he abandoned to the bear is fully aware that his trust was betrayed.
  3. **What lesson can be learned from this fable?**
     It's easy to be a friend and to make promises when times are good. It's a true friend who sticks by you and helps during difficult times. Ask the students to name difficult things that they might help each other get through. Ask them to share times when they behaved like a true friend or when someone was a true friend to them. You might broaden the discussion to include pondering the virtue of trustworthiness.
- Have students act out the fable. You could have students use hat props, such as two hunting hats for the men and a bear hat for the bear.

Record

- Have students copy and illustrate the fable in their copybooks. Let them choose whether they will illustrate one scene or whether they will illustrate and copy it into frames with different pictures, like a graphic novel.
- Have the students write or tell their own fable, replacing the characters in "Two Travelers and the Bear" with new ones (e.g., two ducks and a wolf).

Notes

Sentence Bank

From the Sideline: Visit http://capress.link/wol1att for a video demonstration of analysis.

As in the previous chapter, students are now combining the two parts of the method—the oral analysis and the written markings. These four additional sentences are for extra practice if needed. The scripts are provided for your reference as you model the markings on the board while the students analyze the sentences aloud. Keep the analysis moving along with energy to establish a lively precedent for all the succeeding choral analyses during the year.

S PV
Sheep bleat.

a. (First, read the sentence aloud.) "Sheep bleat."

b. "This is a sentence because it is a group of words that expresses a complete thought."

c. "It is a declarative sentence because it makes a statement."

d. "This sentence is about *sheep*." (Underline the subject.) "So, *sheep* is the subject because it is what the sentence is about." (Place a capital letter *S* above the subject.)

e. "This sentence tells us that sheep *bleat*." (Double underline the predicate.) "So, *bleat* is the predicate because it is what the sentence tells us about *sheep*." (Place a capital letter *P* above the action verb.)

f. "It is a predicate verb because it shows action. There is no linking verb because predicate verbs do not need linking verbs." (Place a capital letter *V* to the right of the *P*.)

S hv PV
Dad is raking.

a. (First, read the sentence aloud.) "Dad is raking."

b. "This is a sentence because it is a group of words that expresses a complete thought."

c. "It is a declarative sentence because it makes a statement."

d. "This sentence is about *Dad*." (Underline the subject.) "So, *Dad* is the subject because it is what the sentence is about." (Place a capital letter *S* above the subject.)

e. "This sentence tells us that Dad *is raking*." (Double underline the predicate: *is* and *raking*.) "So, *is raking* is the predicate because it is what the sentence tells us about *Dad*." (Place a capital letter *P* above the action verb.)

f. "It is a predicate verb because it shows action. There is no linking verb because predicate verbs do not need linking verbs." (Place a capital letter *V* to the right of the *P*.)

g. "*Is* is a helping verb because it helps the verb." (Place a lowercase *hv* above the helping verb.)

S hv PV
Lightning is flashing.

a. (First, read the sentence aloud.) "Lightening is flashing."

b. "This is a sentence because it is a group of words that expresses a complete thought."

c. "It is a declarative sentence because it makes a statement."

d. "This sentence is about *lightning*." (Underline the subject.) "So, *lightning* is the subject because it is what the sentence is about." (Place a capital letter *S* above the subject.)

e. "This sentence tells us that lightning *is flashing*." (Double underline the predicate: *is* and *flashing*.) "So, *is flashing* is the predicate because it is what the sentence tells us about *lightning*." (Place a capital letter *P* above the action verb.)

f. "It is a predicate verb because it shows action. There is no linking verb because predicate verbs do not need linking verbs." (Place a capital letter *V* to the right of the *P*.)

g. "*Is* is a helping verb because it helps the verb." (Place a lowercase *hv* above the helping verb.)

S **hv** **PV**
Trumpets are blowing.

a. (First, read the sentence aloud.) "Trumpets are blowing."

b. "This is a sentence because it is a group of words that expresses a complete thought."

c. "It is a declarative sentence because it makes a statement."

d. "This sentence is about *trumpets*." (Underline the subject.) "So, *trumpets* is the subject because it is what the sentence is about." (Place a capital letter *S* above the subject.)

e. "This sentence tells us that trumpets *are blowing*." (Double underline the predicate: *are* and *blowing*.) "So, *are blowing* is the predicate because it is what the sentence tells us about *trumpets*." (Place a capital letter *P* above the action verb.)

f. "It is a predicate verb because it shows action. There is no linking verb because predicate verbs do not need linking verbs." (Place a capital letter *V* to the right of the *P*.)

g. "*Are* is a helping verb because it helps the verb." (Place a lowercase *hv* above the helping verb.)

From the Sideline: Expect full attention. Teach your students to give full attention to you with both eyes and hands. Don't ever teach without full attention. We say, "Eyes this way!" Then, "Hands on deck!" which means that students' hands are folded on the top of their desk.

[A]Use a table or a desk to demonstrate the lesson. Point to the legs and discuss how they function—as supports for the tabletop—and what would happen if they disappeared—the tabletop would fall over. Discuss how these legs (adverbs) support the tabletop (principal elements).

Chapter 4 Adverbs[A]

A sentence must have its principal elements. The **simple subject** (*S*) is just the noun that the sentence is about, and the **simple predicate** (*P*) is just the verb or verb phrase that tells us what the subject is doing or being. As you know, most sentences also have other words, **phrases**, or **clauses**. These are called **subordinate**■ **elements**. Their job in a sentence is to support the principal elements, to explain something about them.

Think of a table. You know the legs hold up the tabletop, but have you ever considered how the tabletop also holds the legs in their places? Well, think of a sentence as being a table. The principal elements (*S* and *P*) form the top of the table. The subordinate elements are like the legs of a table supporting its top. However, the reverse is true too. The legs (or subordinate elements) are able to stand only if the tabletop (or the principal elements) is already in place. The legs are "set in order" (*ordinare*) "under" (*sub*) the tabletop. Without the tabletop, the legs would fall like pick-up sticks. That would make a fine mess!

Subordinate elements are also called **modifiers**■ because they change or limit the meaning of principal elements. There are many kinds of modifiers, so we will focus on single-word modifiers first, learning in this chapter about **adverbs**■ that modify verbs, and in the next chapter about adjectives that modify nouns.

To the Source:
■ **subordinate**
Subordinate comes from the Latin word *subordinatus* (placed in a lower order), which comes from *sub*, meaning "under," and *ordinare*, meaning "arrange, set in order."

To the Source:
■ **modify**
The word *modify* comes from the Latin words *modus* for "change" or "limit" and *facio*, which means "make" or "do."

To the Source:
■ **adverb**
The word *adverb* comes from the Latin words *ad*, which means "to," and *verbum*, which means "word." The Latin word *adverbium* means "added to a verb."

Ideas to Understand

Adverbs tell how, when, or where the action takes place in the sentence. Adverbs are *added to* verbs, as the Latin root tells us. That's easy to remember since the word *verb* is in the word *adverb*. If you had a pet cat named

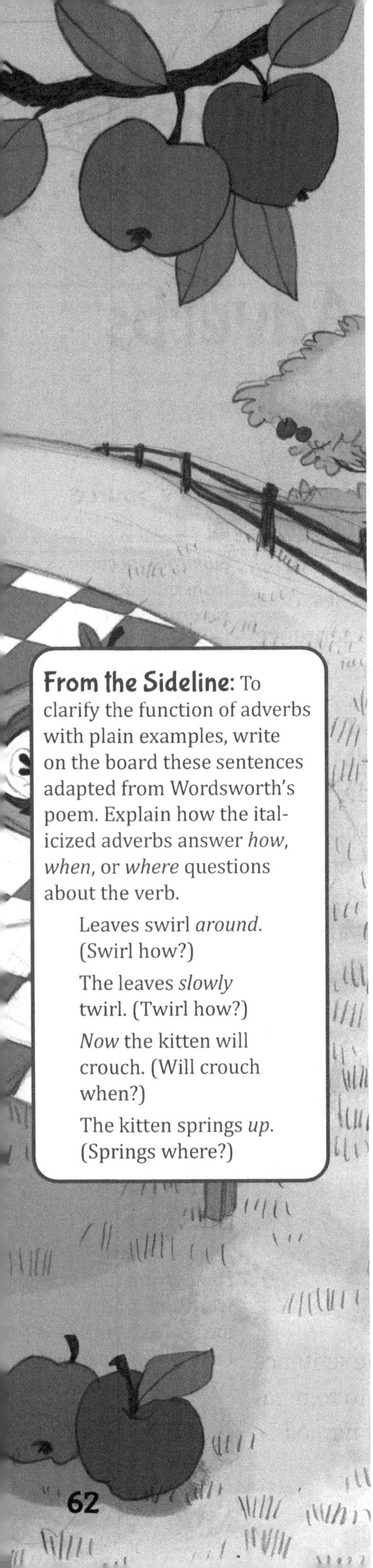

Stripes, you could write a simple sentence about her with only a subject and a predicate: "Stripes jumps." Imagine Stripes jumping. What happens if you add an adverb to the verb? *How* would she jump? Stripes jumps *playfully*. Stripes jumps *ferociously*. Stripes jumps *sleepily*. Stripes jumps *vertically*. All these different adverbs support or modify the jumping in different ways, making very different meanings and mental images.

A much-loved British poet named William Wordsworth wrote a poem in 1804 about a cat playing with a perfect cat toy—falling leaves in autumn. You can find the entire poem in The Curious Child's Literary Appendix. Before you look at the poem, can you guess how, when, or where Wordsworth's kitten plays? Can you guess how, when, or where the leaves fall? Those are questions that adverbs can answer.

From the Sideline: To clarify the function of adverbs with plain examples, write on the board these sentences adapted from Wordsworth's poem. Explain how the italicized adverbs answer *how*, *when*, or *where* questions about the verb.

> Leaves swirl *around*. (Swirl how?)
>
> The leaves *slowly* twirl. (Twirl how?)
>
> *Now* the kitten will crouch. (Will crouch when?)
>
> The kitten springs *up*. (Springs where?)

In these lines from the poem "The Kitten Playing with the Falling Leaves," Wordsworth uses the adverbs *softly* and *slowly* to describe how leaves twirl downward on an autumn day. He also uses the adverb *round* to tell how the leaves are moving as they sink:

> Through the calm and frosty air
> Of this morning bright and fair
> Eddying round and round they sink
> Softly, slowly.

When Wordsworth describes the kitten playing with the leaves, he chooses the words *first* and *then* to tell when the kitten pounces at them. Those words are adverbs too.

> —But the Kitten, how she starts!
> Crouches, stretches, paws, and darts:
> First at one, and then its fellow,
> Just as light, and just as yellow:
> There are many now—now one—
> Now they stop and there are none.[1]

---

1. William Wordsworth, "The Kitten Playing with the Falling Leaves," in *The Golden Treasury of Poetry*, ed. Louis Untermeyer (New York: Golden Press, 1998), 44.

The adverb *now* also tells when. You could ask, *When* are the falling leaves many and when is there only one? The answer is *now*. If the poet had also written, "The kitten springs up," he would have used the adverb *up* to tell *where* the kitten springs.

Wordsworth uses *softly*, *slowly*, and *round* to describe *how* an action happens. He uses *first*, *then*, and *now* to describe *when* an action happens. He could have used *up* to describe *where* an action happens. Telling how, when, or where is the way adverbs support action verbs—like the way table legs support a tabletop.

Notice that many adverbs (but not all) end with the letters *-ly*. If you find a word that ends in *-ly*, it is probably an adverb that tells you *how* an action happens (such as quickly, easily, stiffly, or carefully). Adverbs often come right after the verbs they modify, though they can be placed in different positions in the sentence. For example, sometimes they can appear before the verb like this: The kitten *softly* walks. When an adverb comes at the beginning of a sentence, it is often followed by a comma: *Softly*, the kitten walks.

Moment for Mechanics

Not and *never* are **negative adverbs**, which means they negate the verb or turn it into its opposite. Sometimes a negative adverb is placed between a helping verb and the action verb.

Adverbs	Sentence	Meaning
not	Acorns do *not* swirl.	The acorns are not doing the action of swirling.
never	Acorns *never* swirl.	The acorns will not ever do the action of swirling.

Terms to Remember[B]

You have a new term to deposit in your memory bank: *adverbs*. You should practice it along with the other terms you already know. *Where?* Here. *When?* Now, and later too. *How?* Well, cheerfully, actively, tunefully, persistently, and even loudly!

[B]For the lyrics to all of the songs, please see the Song Lyrics section on page 191. Play the appropriate audio tracks and have the students sing/chant along.

Principal Elements *(1–3)*

Subject and Predicate *(1–4)*

Noun *(1–5)*

Verb and Helping Verb *(1–6)*

NEW! **Adverb** *(1–7)*

Sentences to Analyze

From the Sideline: Remember to mark the sentence as you go without interrupting the choral analysis. The analysis script is becoming more streamlined as students' understanding evolves. You'll notice similar changes as you proceed through the curriculum. However, principal elements will always be marked above the sentences and modifiers below.

Remember that when you begin analyzing, you identify the words as a sentence, then you identify the kind of sentence it is, and then you identify the principal elements of the sentence. The next step of analysis is to systematically identify all of the modifiers, beginning at the far right of the sentence and moving from right to left. Later, when you analyze longer sentences, finding the modifiers from right to left helps you pay attention to every grammatical detail without missing anything.

As you know, the principal elements are marked with the capital letters *S* and *PV* above sentences. Now, you will mark adverbs with the lowercase letters *adv* below the sentences and then draw lines and arrows to the verbs they modify.

With your teacher's guidance, use the following steps to analyze the two example sentences. Speak with expression the words that are in gray, and pay attention as, at the same time, your teacher marks the sentence on the board according to the directions in parentheses. While the markings on these two sentences are already in your book, in the lessons section you will need to neatly mark the sentences yourself as you analyze them aloud with your classmates.

S PV
Leaves swirl around.
adv

a. (First, read the sentence aloud.) "Leaves swirl around."

b. "This is a sentence because it is a group of words that expresses a complete thought. It is a declarative sentence because it makes a statement."

c. "This sentence is about *leaves*. So, *leaves* is the subject because it is what the sentence is about." (Since *leaves* is the subject, underline it and place a capital letter *S* above it.)

d. "This sentence tells us that leaves *swirl*. So, *swirl* is the predicate because it is what the sentence tells us about *leaves*." (Since the predicate *swirl* tells us something about *leaves*, double underline it and place a capital letter *P* above it.) "It is a predicate verb because it shows action. There is no linking verb because predicate verbs do not need linking verbs." (Since *swirl* shows action, place a capital letter *V* to the right of the letter *P* above the action verb.)

e. "*Around* tells us *how* leaves swirl." (To mark adverbs, carefully draw a straight line down from the adverb, then a horizontal line toward the word that it modifies, and then a straight line with an arrow pointing to the word it modifies.)

f. "So, *around* is an **adverbial element** because it modifies a verb. It is an adverb." (Write *adv* in lowercase letters in the elbow opposite the line with the arrow.)

The following sentence to analyze includes a helping verb modified by two adverbs. Remember, once the principal elements are marked, the next step of the analysis is to begin at the far right of the sentence and move from right to left, identifying all modifiers. When you draw the lines from the adverbs to the verb, make sure the lines do not cross. In fact, they should be connected, becoming one line. The arrow points to the predicate verb and not the helping verb.

S hv PV
Leaves are swirling everywhere today.
adv adv

a. (Read the sentence first aloud.) "Leaves are swirling everywhere today."

b. "This is a sentence because it is a group of words that expresses a complete thought. It is a declarative sentence because it makes a statement."

c. "This sentence is about *leaves*. So, *leaves* is the subject because it is what the sentence is about." (Since *leaves* is the subject, underline it and place a capital letter *S* above the subject.)

d. "This sentence tells us that leaves *are swirling*. So, *are swirling* is the predicate because it is what the sentence tells us about *leaves*." (Since *swirling* tells something about *leaves*, double underline the predicate, including the helping verb, and place a capital letter *P* above the action verb.)

e. "It is a predicate verb because it shows action. There is no linking verb because predicate verbs do not need linking verbs." (Since *swirling* shows action, place a capital letter *V* to the right of the letter *P*.)

f. "*Are* is the helping verb because it helps the verb." (Place the lowercase letters *hv* above the helping verb.)

g. "*Today* tells us *when* leaves are swirling." (To mark an adverb, carefully draw a straight line down from the adverb, then a horizontal line toward the word that it modifies, and then a straight line with an arrow pointing to the word it modifies.)

h. "So, *today* is an adverbial element because it modifies a verb. It is an adverb." (Write *adv* in lowercase letters in the elbow opposite the line with the arrow.)

i. "*Everywhere* tells us *where* leaves are swirling." (To mark an adverb, carefully draw a straight line down from the adverb, then a horizontal line toward the word that it modifies. Connect this modifier line with the modifier line for *today* since both of the adjectival elements are modifying *swirling*.)

j. "So, *everywhere* is an adverbial element because it modifies a verb. It is an adverb." (Write *adv* in lowercase letters in the elbow opposite the line with the arrow.)

If a sentence has adverbs both before and after the verb, the modifier lines are distinct and separate. They are not to be joined even if they are both modifying the same verb.

From the Sideline: While the markings for this sentence are different from the previous sentence, the script would be identical because the order of the adverbs does not change the order of analysis.

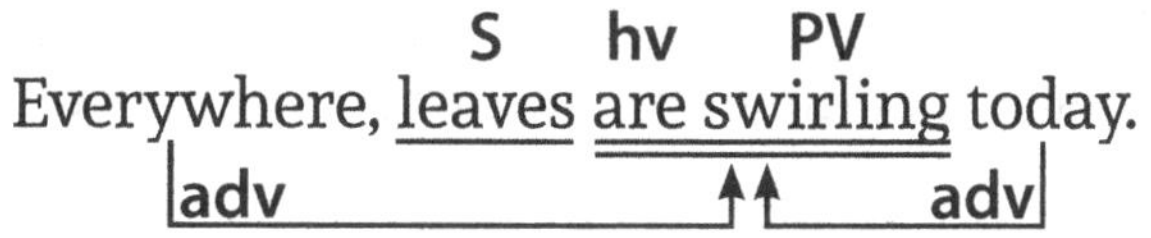

A carefully chosen adverb modifying a verb adds precision and color to your sentences. That is why learning to analyze adverbs is not only an important step in your training but also an enjoyable one. When you write about Stripes, you can make her jump in as many interesting ways as you choose. For you as a writer, Stripes will jump *obediently*!

Look again at the illustration at the beginning of this chapter. Why do you think Fritz is under the table? Why do you think Rex (the dog) is on top of the table? What do you think will happen next?

Well-Ordered Notes A

Review It

Review the following:

What are the eight parts of speech?
What is a noun?
What is a verb?
What are the twenty-three helping verbs?

Practice It

Lead the students in Tell Me More, an activity in which they will add adverbs to sentences using question prompts. Have the students stand next to their desks. Read a short sentence to the first student and ask her *how* the action happened. After she gives her response, she may be seated. Read the same sentence to the next student and ask *when* the action happened. Continue around the room with new subject-verb pairs.

Example: Travelers wait.
Teacher: "*How* do travelers wait?"
Student 1: "Travelers wait *anxiously*."
Teacher: "*When* do travelers wait?"
Student 2: "*Sometimes*, travelers wait."
Teacher: "*Where* do travelers wait?"
Student 3: "Travelers wait *around*."

Sentences	How	When	Where
Airplanes land.	*skillfully*	*now*	*there*
People are watching.	*eagerly*	*immediately*	*inside*
The lady announced.	*loudly*	*just*	*here*
Passengers were assembling.	*orderly*	*already*	*nearby*
Luggage wheels rolled.	*clumsily*	*next*	*forward*

Analyze It

From the Sideline: Visit http://capress.link/wol1att for a video demonstration of analysis.

Now, as a class, analyze the four sentences in the lesson. Here is the script for the first one to help you lead the choral analysis and model the markings on the board. The words in parentheses are like stage directions to guide you and are not to be spoken. The words in gray and enclosed in quotation marks are for you and the students to speak in chorus.

S hv PV
People were moving slowly.
adv

a. (First, read the sentence aloud.) "People were moving slowly."

b. "This is a sentence because it is a group of words that expresses a complete thought."

c. "It is a declarative sentence because it makes a statement."

d. "This sentence is about *people*." (Underline the subject.) "So, *people* is the subject because it is what the sentence is about." (Place a capital letter *S* above the subject.)

e. "This sentence tells us that people *were moving*." (Double underline the predicate.) "So, *were moving* is the predicate because it is what the sentence tells us about *people*." (Place a capital letter *P* above the action verb.)

f. "It is a predicate verb because it shows action. There is no linking verb because predicate verbs do not need linking verbs." (Place a capital letter *V* to the right of the *P*.)

g. "*Were* is the helping verb because it helps the verb." (Place a lowercase *hv* above the helping verb.)

h. (Continue the analysis of the sentence, starting at the far right and moving toward the left.) "*Slowly* tells us *how* people were moving." (Draw a straight line down from the adverb, then a horizontal line toward the word that it modifies, and then a straight line with an arrow pointing to the word it modifies.)

i. "So, *slowly* is an adverbial element because it modifies a verb. It is an adverb." (Write *adv* in lowercase letters in the elbow opposite the line with the arrow.)

From the Sideline: For extra guided practice, refer to the Sentence Bank at the end of this chapter.

Lesson to Learn
Adverbs

1. Analyze the following sentences.

   S hv PV
   a. People were moving slowly.
   adv

   S hv PV
   b. Fritz was impatiently standing.
   adv

   S PV
   c. Lines snake around.
   adv

   S hv PV
   d. Travelers are heading somewhere.
   adv

From the Sideline:
Remember that when you see the word *analyze* in instructions throughout this book, we mean both choral analysis and written notations. The two go hand in hand as a prediagramming system.

2. An adverb answers the questions *how, when,* or *where* in a sentence. On the lines provided, list the adverbs from the sentences in exercise 1.

   a. slowly

   b. impatiently

   c. around

   d. somewhere

3. Rewrite sentence *b* from exercise 1 by adding an adverb that tells *when* Fritz was impatiently standing. Earlier, Fritz was impatiently standing.

4. Fill in each blank below with an adverb that answers *how* the action is being done. You may choose an adverb from the word bank or think of your own.

Word Bank: gently, suddenly, loudly, eagerly, together, quietly

Answers may vary.

a. The family was flying **together**.

b. Passengers were **quietly** reading.

c. **Loudly**, a man snored.

d. The attendant spoke **gently**.

e. The gentleman **suddenly** awoke.

5. Imagine that your family was going on a trip, and then write a declarative sentence about your family waiting for an airplane. Include an adverb in your sentence.

My family waited forever.

Well-Ordered Notes B

Review It

Review the following:

What are the principal elements?
What is an adverb?
What is a verb?
What are the twenty-three helping verbs?

Practice It

Lead your students in Place the Adverb, an activity reinforcing the versatility of adverbs. Write the following sentences and accompanying adverbs (in parentheses) on the board. Point out that sometimes an adverb is placed directly after the verb, sometimes it is placed before the verb, and sometimes it sounds better at the beginning of the sentence. Where it is placed can create a different emphasis in the sentence. Read each sentence aloud as a class and discuss the possible placements of each adverb and how they might subtly affect the meaning of the sentence. There are no strictly right or wrong answers for this exercise; it demonstrates the versatility of adverbs.

Example: "Rabbits hop." (cautiously)
Option #1: "*Cautiously* rabbits hop."
Option #2: "Rabbits *cautiously* hop."
Option #3: "Rabbits hop *cautiously*."

1. Dad will be mowing. (soon)
2. Mom gardens. (thoughtfully)
3. Rex naps. (lazily)
4. Squirrels are scurrying. (excitedly)
5. Birds could be hunting. (hungrily)
6. Stripes is watching. (eagerly)

Analyze It

Now, as a class, analyze the four sentences in the lesson. Here is the script for the first one to help you lead the choral analysis and model the markings on the board. The words in parentheses are like stage directions to guide you and are not to be spoken. The words in gray and enclosed in quotation marks are for you and the students to speak in chorus.

S PV
Fritz yelled excitedly.
adv

a. (First, read the sentence aloud.) "Fritz yelled excitedly."

b. "This is a sentence because it is a group of words that expresses a complete thought."

c. "It is a declarative sentence because it makes a statement."

d. "This sentence is about *Fritz*." (Underline the subject.) "So, *Fritz* is the subject because it is what the sentence is about." (Place a capital letter *S* above the subject.)

e. "This sentence tells us that Fritz *yelled*." (Double underline the predicate.) "So, *yelled* is the predicate because it is what the sentence tells us about *Fritz*." (Place a capital letter *P* above the action verb.)

f. "It is a predicate verb because it shows action. There is no linking verb because predicate verbs do not need linking verbs." (Place a capital letter *V* to the right of the *P*.)

g. (Continue the analysis of the sentence, starting at the far right and moving toward the left.) "*Excitedly* tells us *how* Fritz yelled." (Draw a straight line down from the adverb, then a horizontal line toward the word that it modifies, and then a straight line with an arrow pointing to the word it modifies.)

h. "So, *excitedly* is an adverbial element because it modifies a verb. It is an adverb." (Write *adv* in lowercase letters in the elbow opposite the line with the arrow.)

Lesson to Learn B
Adverbs

1. Analyze the following sentences.

   a. Fritz (S) yelled (PV) excitedly (adv → yelled).

   b. Dad (S) was (hv) not (adv → listening) listening (PV).

   c. Suddenly (adv → hollered), Fritz (S) hollered (PV) loudly (adv → hollered).

   d. Stripes (S) was (hv) climbing (PV) higher (adv → was climbing).

2. An adverb answers the questions *how, when,* or *where* in a sentence. On the lines provided, list the adverbs from the sentences in exercise 1.

   a. excitedly

   b. not

   c. suddenly

   d. loudly

   e. higher

3. Rewrite sentence *b* from exercise 1 by adding an adverb that tells *how* Dad was not listening. Unfortunately, Dad was not listening.

4. Fill in each blank below with an adverb that answers *how* the action is being done. You may choose an adverb from the word bank or think of your own.

Word Bank: quickly, steadily, brightly, rapidly, nervously, frantically

Answers may vary.

a. ____**Rapidly**____, the clouds darkened.

b. Dad was ____**nervously**____ mowing.

c. The sky flashed ____**brightly**____.

d. Fritz was racing ____**frantically**____.

e. Doors ____**quickly**____ slammed.

5. Imagine that your family sees a thunderstorm coming, and then write a declarative sentence about your family's response to the storm. Include an adverb in your sentence.

Immediately, my family ran inside.

Well-Ordered Notes C

Review It

Review the following:

What is an adverb?
What are the principal elements?
What is a noun?
What is a verb?

Practice It

Lead the class in Toss It, an interactive activity to reinforce that *not* and *never* are negative adverbs. Read one of the following sentences, toss an object (e.g., a beanbag) to a student, and ask "How?" Have the student answer how by adding either *not* or *never* to the sentence. Remind the students that *not* and *never* are always adverbs and they negate a verb or turn it into its opposite. After a few tosses, choose one of the sentences and analyze it on the board.

Example: "Fishermen swim."
Toss 1: (How?) "*Not*: Fishermen do not swim."
Toss 2: (How?) "*Never*: Fishermen never swim."

1. Beachcombers are strolling.
   a. *Not*: Beachcombers are *not* strolling.
   b. *Never*: Beachcombers are *never* strolling.
2. Boats will sail.
   a. *Not*: Boats will *not* sail.
   b. *Never*: Boats will *never* sail.
3. Shopkeepers are selling.
   a. *Not*: Shopkeepers are *not* selling.
   b. *Never*: Shopkeepers are *never* selling.

Analyze It

Now, as a class, analyze the four sentences in the lesson. Here is the script for the first one to help you lead the choral analysis and model the markings on the board. The words in parentheses are like stage directions to guide you and are not to be spoken. The words in gray and enclosed in quotation marks are for you and the students to speak in chorus.

S hv PV
Waves were not rolling.
adv

a. (First, read the sentence aloud.) "Waves were not rolling."

b. "This is a sentence because it is a group of words that expresses a complete thought."

c. "It is a declarative sentence because it makes a statement."

d. "This sentence is about *waves*." (Underline the subject.) "So, *waves* is the subject because it is what the sentence is about." (Place a capital letter *S* above the subject.)

e. "This sentence tells us that waves *were rolling*." (Double underline the predicate.) "So, *were rolling* is the predicate because it is what the sentence tells us about *waves*." (Place a capital letter *P* above the action verb.)

f. "It is a predicate verb because it shows action. There is no linking verb because predicate verbs do not need linking verbs." (Place a capital letter *V* to the right of the *P*.)

g. "*Were* is the helping verb because it helps the verb." (Place a lowercase *hv* above the helping verb.)

h. (Continue the analysis of the sentence, starting at the far right and moving toward the left.) "*Not* tells us *how* waves were rolling." (Draw a straight line down from the adverb, then a horizontal line toward the word that it modifies, and then a straight line with an arrow pointing to the word it modifies.)

i. "So, *not* is an adverbial element because it modifies a verb. It is an adverb." (Write *adv* in lowercase letters in the elbow opposite the line with the arrow.)

Lesson to Learn
Adverbs

C

1. Analyze the following sentences.

a. Waves were not rolling. (S: Waves; hv: were; PV: rolling; adv: not)

b. Quietly, Theo watched. (S: Theo; PV: watched; adv: Quietly)

c. Seabirds were not circling together. (S: Seabirds; hv: were; PV: circling; adv: not; adv: together)

d. Gulls sometimes soar alone. (S: Gulls; PV: soar; adv: sometimes; adv: alone)

2. An adverb answers the questions *how*, *when*, or *where* in a sentence. On the lines provided, list the adverbs from the sentences in exercise 1.

a. not

b. quietly

c. not

d. together

e. sometimes

f. alone

3. Rewrite sentence *a* from exercise 1 by adding an adverb that tells *when* the waves were not rolling. Yesterday, waves were not rolling.

4. Fill in each blank below with an adverb that answers *how* the action is being done. You may choose an adverb from the word bank or think of your own.

Word Bank: slowly, tightly, freely, eagerly, slightly, cautiously

Answers may vary.

a. The barnacles were **tightly** closed.

b. **Slowly**, the tide returned.

c. Heidi was **eagerly** searching.

d. The boys waded **cautiously**.

e. Suddenly, a starfish moved **slightly**.

5. Remember, adverbs can negate a verb, or turn it into its opposite. Imagine a windy day on a beach. Rewrite the following sentences and add the adverb *not* to create the opposite meaning.

a. The kids are playing outside. **The kids are *not* playing outside.**

b. Theo will throw high. **Theo will *not* throw high.**

c. Now, Lucy will walk backward. **Now, Lucy will *not* walk backward.**

d. Heidi is hiding underneath. **Heidi is *not* hiding underneath.**

e. Fritz was reaching down. **Fritz was *not* reaching down.**

f. Grandpa will come afterward. **Grandpa will *not* come afterward.**

Well-Ordered Notes D

Review It

Review the following:

What is a sentence?
What are the four kinds of sentences?
What is an adverb?
What is a noun?

Practice It

Lead your students in the activity Show How It Is Done to reinforce adverbs that answer the question "how?" First, have the students create a list of adverbs on the board, or use the adverbs from the following table. Then write a sentence on the board that can be acted out (e.g., "One guy threw a Frisbee"). Have one student choose an adverb from the list and whisper it to you. Then, the student pantomimes or acts out the sentence as modified by her chosen adverb while the other students try to guess the adverb. Whoever guesses correctly gets the next turn to pantomime the sentence using a different adverb.

Fewer than Five: Adapt the activity by creating adverb cards. Together with your student(s), brainstorm adverbs and write one adverb per card. Have the student(s) read the sentence (e.g., "The boy threw the Frisbee"), select a card (e.g., *creatively*), and then act out the adverb in regard to the sentence (e.g., the student would pantomime doing something creative with an imaginary Frisbee). Let each student draw three cards to act out.

Example:

Sentence: "One guy threw a Frisbee."
Student 1 whispers her chosen adverb (e.g., *awkwardly*) to you and then acts out a guy throwing a Frisbee *in an awkward way*.
Student 2 guesses the adverb using the adverb chart.

Student 2 whispers his chosen adverb (e.g., *backward*) to you and then acts out a guy throwing a Frisbee *in a backward direction*.
Student 3 guesses the adverb using the adverb chart.

Adverb Chart

angrily	forward	sweetly	cautiously	sadly	patiently
bashfully	gingerly	backward	lately	boldly	slowly
awkwardly	calmly	hopelessly	woefully	joyfully	mournfully
together	heartily	willfully	never	bravely	sternly

Analyze It

Now, as a class, analyze the four sentences in the lesson. Here is the script for the first one to help you lead the choral analysis and model the markings on the board. The words in parentheses are like stage directions to guide you and are not to be spoken. The words in gray and enclosed in quotation marks are for you and the students to speak in chorus.

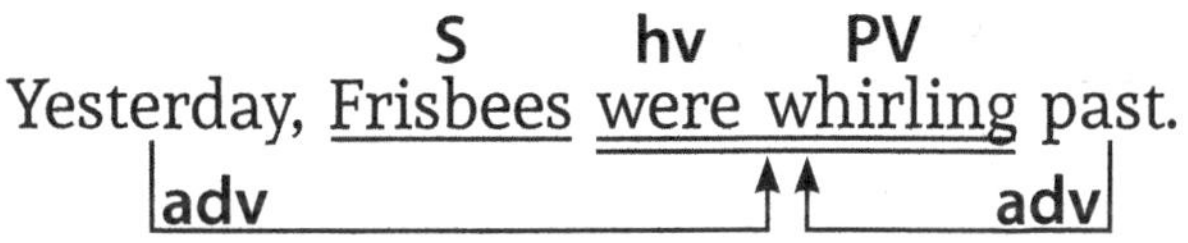

a. (First, read the sentence aloud.) "Yesterday, Frisbees were whirling past."

b. "This is a sentence because it is a group of words that expresses a complete thought."

c. "It is a declarative sentence because it makes a statement."

d. "This sentence is about *Frisbees*." (Underline the subject.) "So, *Frisbees* is the subject because it is what the sentence is about." (Place a capital letter *S* above the subject.)

e. "This sentence tells us that Frisbees *were whirling*." (Double underline the predicate.) "So, *were whirling* is the predicate because it is what the sentence tells us about *Frisbees*." (Place a capital letter *P* above the action verb.)

f. "It is a predicate verb because it shows action. There is no linking verb because predicate verbs do not need linking verbs." (Place a capital letter *V* to the right of the *P*.)

g. "*Were* is a helping verb because it helps the verb." (Place a lowercase *hv* above the helping verb.)

h. (Continue the analysis of the sentence, starting at the far right and moving toward the left.) "*Past* tells us *where* Frisbees were whirling." (Draw a straight line down from the adverb, then a horizontal line toward the word that it modifies, and then a straight line with an arrow pointing to the word it modifies.)

i. "So, *past* is an adverbial element because it modifies a verb. It is an adverb." (Write *adv* in lowercase letters in the elbow opposite the line with the arrow.)

j. "*Yesterday* tells us *when* Frisbees were whirling." (Draw a straight line down from the adverb, then a horizontal line toward the word that it modifies, and then a straight line with an arrow pointing to the word it modifies.)

k. "So, *yesterday* is an adverbial element because it modifies a verb. It is an adverb." (Write *adv* in lowercase letters in the elbow opposite the line with the arrow.)

Lesson to Learn

Adverbs

1. Analyze the following sentences.

   a. S hv PV
   Yesterday, Frisbees were whirling past.
   adv adv

   b. S hv PV
   Winston was dashing forward.
   adv

   c. S PV
   Rex followed behind too.
   adv adv

   d. S PV
   Unfortunately, Winston never catches.
   adv adv

2. An adverb answers the questions *how, when,* or *where* in a sentence. On the lines provided, list the adverbs from the sentences in exercise 1.

   a. yesterday
   b. past
   c. forward
   d. behind
   e. too
   f. unfortunately
   g. never

3. Rewrite sentence *b* from exercise 1 by adding an adverb that tells *how* Winston was dashing forward. **Awkwardly, Winston was dashing forward.**

4. Fill in each blank below with an adverb that answers *how* the action is being done. You may choose an adverb from the word bank or think of your own.

Word Bank: openly, carefully, tearfully, bravely, warmly, thoroughly

Answers may vary.

a. The nurse **warmly** welcomes.

b. Winston is explaining **tearfully**.

c. **Carefully**, the doctor examines.

d. The attendant is **thoroughly** bandaging.

e. Winston winces **openly**.

5. Imagine that a nurse is caring for a person's twisted ankle, and then write a declarative sentence about the nurse helping. Include an adverb in your sentence.

The nurse calmly helped.

Sentences for Practice—Fable

Adverbs

ANSWERS

Analyze the following sentences, which are based on "The Lion and the Mouse."

1. S PV
   Lion stretches out.
   adv

2. S hv PV
   Later, Lion was sleeping.
   adv

3. S PV
   Mouse quickly sprints past.
   adv adv

4. S PV
   Lion snatches furiously.
   adv

5. S PV
   Mouse woefully cries.
   adv

From the Sideline: These extra practice sentences are a synopsis of the fable "The Lion and the Mouse." The fable and the extended lesson notes are on the following pages.

Sentences for Practice—Fable

ANSWERS

Adverbs

6. Lightheartedly, Lion will release.
   (S: Lion; hv: will; PV: release; adv: Lightheartedly → release)

7. Lion howls continually.
   (S: Lion; PV: howls; adv: continually → howls)

8. Mouse eagerly comes.
   (S: Mouse; PV: comes; adv: eagerly → comes)

9. Quietly, Mouse kindly gnaws.
   (S: Mouse; PV: gnaws; adv: Quietly → gnaws; adv: kindly → gnaws)

10. Lion gratefully smiles.
    (S: Lion; PV: smiles; adv: gratefully → smiles)

Lessons to Enjoy—Fable
Adverbs

Sometimes we may think that big and strong people are the best at helping other people and solving problems. This fable, however, shows you that even those who are smaller and weaker can be just the kind of friend we need! You'll see that helpfulness and friendship come in all sizes.

The Lion and the Mouse

by Aesop

timid: lacking courage, fearful

roused: awakened from sleep

A Lion lay asleep in the shady forest, his great head resting on his paws. A timid little Mouse came upon him <u>unexpectedly</u>, and in her fright and haste to get <u>away</u>, she ran across the Lion's nose. Roused from his nap, the Lion laid his huge paw <u>angrily</u> on the tiny creature to kill her.

spare: decide not to harm or punish

"Spare me!" begged the poor Mouse. "<u>Please</u> let me go and <u>someday</u> I will <u>surely</u> repay you."

The Lion was <u>much</u> amused to think that a Mouse could <u>ever</u> help him. He laughed <u>so hard</u> that the whole ground shook. But as he was a generous Lion, he let the poor creature go.

stalking: quietly approaching

toils: the strings or ropes of a net

Some days <u>later</u>, while stalking his prey in the forest, the Lion was caught in the toils of a hunter's net. Unable to free himself, he filled the forest with his angry roaring. The Mouse knew the voice and <u>quickly</u> found the Lion struggling in the net. Running to one of the great ropes that bound him, she gnawed it until it parted, and <u>soon</u> the Lion was free.

"You laughed when I said I would repay you," said the Mouse. "<u>Now</u> you see that <u>even</u> a Mouse can help a Lion."

Moral: Little friends may prove great friends.[2]

2. Aesop, "The Lion and the Mouse," taken from *Writing & Rhetoric Book 1: Fable* by Paul Kortepeter (Camp Hill, PA: Classical Academic Press, 2013), 2–3.

Questions to Ponder

1. What happens that makes the Lion angry?
2. What does "caught in the toils of a hunter's net" mean?
3. Is there more than one meaning for the word "great" in the moral of this fable? What about in the first sentence of the story?

Well-Ordered Notes—Fable

Read

- Have students enjoy reading the fable aloud while eating your special homemade trail mix. (See recipe on next page.) Why trail mix? Well, what else would you take with you for a journey into the shady forest while reading a fable about lions?
- Have students sing the definition of a fable (1–14; see page 194 for lyrics).

Retell

- Use the Questions to Ponder as discussion starters:

  1. **What happens that makes the Lion angry?**
     The mouse accidentally runs across the lion's nose and wakes him up. This is a curious detail in the fable. How is it that the mouse ends up on the lion's nose? Ask your students to explain how they imagine it happening. Such a discussion tunes them in to the details of the story and allows for some variety in their interpretations. Ask them, "How are mistakes made when someone gets nervous or panicky? Do you blame the lion for being angry? Would you be angry in his place?"

  2. **What does "caught in the toils of a hunter's net" mean?**
     The lion is tangled up in the net. Help the students recognize that the struggle of this large beast would make the tangle worse. Also, point out that in his predicament, the *great* lion has been reduced.

  3. **Is there more than one meaning for the word "great" in the moral of this fable? What about in the first sentence of the story?**
     Great has at least two separate meanings: large and important. The whole story turns on the meaning of *great*. At the start, the lion is both large and important. He is the king of the forest, able to kill the mouse or choose to be amused and merciful. When he gets caught in the net, he may still be large, but his size is now a disadvantage. His importance is diminished, and he is at the mouse's mercy. The mouse is the opposite of great in size—as tiny as she can be. Seemingly, she has no importance, completely at the mercy of the lion. Her nervous, timid actions at the beginning show how *little* she is in both size and importance. But when the lion needs her, she is of utmost importance to him. She saves him. So, *great* also refers to moral character. The lion is great in his generous mercy toward the mouse. The mouse is great in her quick reaction to the problem and wholehearted assistance of the lion.

- Have the students identify the adverbs in the fable. On the board, make a list of the adverbs as the students say them. (Note that the helpful and polite word *please* is an adverb.) For your convenience, the adverbs have been underlined in the teacher's edition.

Record

- Have the students write their own version of the fable using other animals or even humans. Or have them write a story about what happens next for Lion and Mouse.
- Have students retell the fable using homemade sock puppets and a small net such as one that holds produce. You can make two puppets yourself and allow students to take turns being narrator, mouse, and lion. Or you could have the students make lion and mouse puppets at home. You can find simple instructions for sock puppets at: http://capress.link/wol1arev0401.

Lion and Mouse Trail Mix

from the kitchen of Tammy Peters

Ingredients:[1]

1 16-oz. jar of peanuts (salted or unsalted)

1 15-oz. box golden raisins

1 6-oz. bag of dried cranberries

2 3-oz. bags of dried bananas

1 10-oz. bag of chocolate chips

1 16-oz. bag pretzels

1 11-oz bag candy corn

2 cups of dry cereal, such as Cheerios or Chex

Directions:

In a large bowl, mix all of the ingredients together and serve.

1. Be mindful of children's allergies. If need be, eliminate or substitute ingredients with other options. Feel free to adjust the quantities of the listed ingredients to taste.

Review
Adverbs

ANSWERS

1. Analyze the following sentences.

   a. Clouds (S) are (hv) rolling (PV) gently (adv).

   b. Grandpa (S) hikes (PV) slowly (adv).

   c. Fritz (S) is (hv) munching (PV) noisily (adv).

   d. Rex (S) should (hv) follow (PV) obediently (adv).

> **From the Sideline:** The material in the following pages is not included in the student edition. You can find the Review lesson, the Quiz, the extra Sentences for Practice, and the second Lesson to Enjoy in reproducible form in the Extra Practice & Assessments PDF, available for purchase at ClassicalAcademicPress.com.

2. An adverb answers the questions *how, when,* or *where* in a sentence. On the lines provided, list the *adverbs* from the above sentences.

   a. gently   b. slowly

   c. noisily   d. obediently

3. Rewrite sentence *b* from exercise 1 by adding an adverb that tells ***when*** *Grandpa hikes.*

   Grandpa now hikes slowly.

4. Fill in each blank below with an adverb that answers how the action is being done. You can choose an adverb from the word bank or think of your own. **Answers may vary.**

Word Bank: around, not, well, suddenly, cautiously, willingly

a. **Cautiously**, the friends are following.

b. The guide is not leading **well**.

c. The kids are **not** cooperating.

d. **Suddenly**, the trails end.

e. The group turns **around**.

5. Imagine that a guide is getting lost in the woods with a group of people, and then write a declarative sentence about the guide leading them. Include an adverb in your sentence.

The guide foolishly leads.

Quiz
Adverbs

ANSWERS

1. Analyze the following sentences.

   a. Buses were stopping there.
   (S: Buses; hv: were; PV: stopping; adv: there → stopping)

   b. Theo did not wait patiently.
   (S: Theo; hv: did; PV: wait; adv: not → wait; adv: patiently → wait)

   c. Soon, doors were opening.
   (S: doors; hv: were; PV: opening; adv: Soon → opening)

   d. Suddenly, kids were rushing everywhere.
   (S: kids; hv: were; PV: rushing; adv: Suddenly → rushing; adv: everywhere → rushing)

2. An adverb answers the questions *how*, *when*, or *where* in a sentence. On the lines provided, list the adverbs from the sentences in exercise 1.

   a. **there**

   b. **not**

   c. **patiently**

   d. **soon**

   e. **suddenly**

   f. **everywhere**

3. Rewrite sentence *a* from exercise 1 above by adding an adverb that tells *how* buses were stopping there.

   Slowly, buses were stopping there.

4. Fill in each blank below with an adverb that answers *how* the action is being done. You can choose an adverb from the word bank or think of your own.

Word Bank: courageously, unexpectedly, fearfully, tightly, nervously, clearly

Answers may vary.

a. The zookeeper is ____**clearly**____ instructing.

b. Snakes can constrict ____**tightly**____.

c. ____**Courageously**____, a volunteer holds.

d. Friends were ____**nervously**____ watching.

e. ____**Unexpectedly**____, the snake slithered sideways.

5. Imagine that the zookeeper is telling about the snake, and then write a declarative sentence about what the zookeeper is doing. Include an adverb in your sentence.

The zookeeper skillfully instructs.

____

Sentences for Practice
Adverbs

ANSWERS

Analyze the following sentences.

1. Flags are waving high.
   (S: Flags; hv: are; PV: waving; adv: high → waving)

2. Trumpets should be sounding soon.
   (S: Trumpets; hv: should; hv: be; PV: sounding; adv: soon → sounding)

3. Veterans stand proudly.
   (S: Veterans; PV: stand; adv: proudly → stand)

4. Balloons are slowly floating up.
   (S: Balloons; hv: are; PV: floating; adv: slowly → floating; adv: up → floating)

5. Cornets blast again.
   (S: Cornets; PV: blast; adv: again → blast)

cornet: a type of horn or trumpet

Sentences for Practice

ANSWERS

Adverbs

S hv hv PV
6. Winston should be following closely.
adv

S hv PV
7. Urgently, Fritz is looking.
adv

S hv PV
8. Mom is searching too.
adv

S PV
9. Dad smiles reassuringly.
adv

S hv PV
10. Heidi is hiding nearby.
adv

Lessons to Enjoy—Poem

Adverbs

Sir Walter Scott was a writer and poet who wrote about the adventures of heroes and villains from Scotland. In the following short poem, Scott draws contrasting mental pictures, or images, for you of the men who are hunting and the animals who are being hunted. Now that you have analyzed how adverbs modify verbs, you will notice how Scott uses them to create those images vividly.

Hunter's Song

by Sir Walter Scott (1771–1832)

The toils are pitched, and the stakes are set,
Ever sing merrily, merrily;
The bows they bend, and the knives they whet,
Hunters live so cheerily.

toils: tightly woven nets used by hunters to hide behind; hunting blinds
pitched: set up
stakes: posts
whet: sharpen by grinding

It was a stag, a stag of ten,
Bearing its branches sturdily;
He came silently down the glen,
Ever sing hardily, hardily.

stag: an adult male deer
branches: antlers
sturdily: strongly
glen: small valley
hardily: boldly, courageously

It was there he met with a wounded doe,
She was bleeding deathfully;
She warned him of the toils below,
O so faithfully, faithfully!

doe: an adult female deer
bleeding deathfully: dying from her wound

He had an eye, and he could heed,
Ever sing so warily, warily;
He had a foot, and he could speed—
Hunters watch so narrowly.[2]

heed: give careful attention to
warily: cautiously
narrowly: closely, with great attention

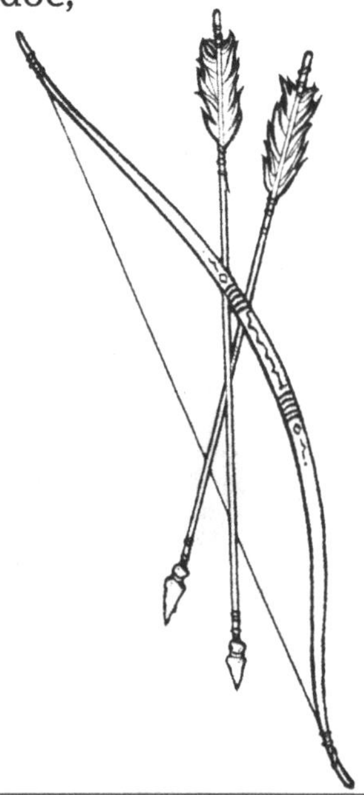

2. Sir Walter Scott, "Hunter's Song," in *Select Works of the British Poets*, ed. John Aikin (Philadelphia: Thomas Wardle, 1838), 702. Available at: https://books.google.com/books?id=PKgcAAAAMAAJ.

Questions to Ponder

1. In each stanza of the poem there are four lines. In each stanza, which lines rhyme with each other? How does this pattern make the poem like a song?
2. What does "The bows they bend, and the knives they whet" mean?
3. What happens in the last stanza? What do you think will happen next?

Well-Ordered Notes—Poem

Read

- Read the poem to the students while listening to a classical piece of music, such as "Royal Hunt and Storm" from Berlioz's *Les Troyens*. The poem is not a lighthearted one, but students can relish it for its drama and its unusual perspective from the animals' point of view.
- Bring in pictures of a hunter's blind and a majestic-looking stag with a large set of antlers to help the students understand the imagery of the poem.

Retell

- Use the Questions to Ponder as discussion starters:
  1. **In each stanza of the poem, there are four lines. In each stanza, which lines rhyme with each other? How does this pattern make the poem like a song?**
     In each stanza, lines 1 and 3 rhyme with each other, and lines 2 and 4 rhyme with each other, making for a rhyming pattern of *abab*. Such a rhyming pattern is typical of many songs the students may be familiar with, as varied as "Simple Simon" and "Amazing Grace." Point out that the rhymes and the title of "Hunter's Song" suggest that the poem is meant to be sung. Ask for a volunteer to try to sing the words with a made-up melody. Ask them when they think hunters would sing such a song? Hunters might sing it as they prepare for the hunt or as they gather to tell stories of hunting.
  2. **What does "The bows they bend, and the knives they whet" mean?**
     This question focuses the students' attention on the first stanza. The hunters are preparing for the hunt, sharpening their knives and testing their bows by bending them. The first line of this stanza describes the hunting blinds that the hunters have set up. During their preparations, they are cheerful and they sing. But there is another, darker side to the hunt—the rest of the poem lets us see it through the perspective of the deer.
  3. **What happens in the last stanza? What do you think will happen next?**
     In the last stanza, the bold song of the majestic stag turns wary. Witnessing the doe's trauma, the stag becomes cautious. He is controlled by instinct—he sees, he heeds, he runs. With the dash at the end of the third line of this stanza, the perspective shifts back to the hunters. They watch closely. The poem is open-ended. We don't know if they are watching closely enough to succeed in their hunt or if the stag escapes. Allow the students to imagine different endings. No matter how it ends, as a hunter's song, the poem celebrates the hunter's respect for the hunted and for the difficulty of the hunt.
- Have the students reread the poem looking for the adverbs. List the adverbs on the board as they say them. Help the students identify the common suffix *-ly* in most of the adverbs. For your convenience, the adverbs in the poem have been underlined in the teacher's edition only.

Record

- Have students write another stanza to the poem, addressing what they think will happen to the stag after being warned by the wounded doe. Will the stag escape the hunters?
- Have students draw a picture of what is happening in one of the stanzas in the poem. Or, have them draw a picture of the new stanza that they wrote for the poem.

Sentence Bank

These four additional sentences are for extra practice if needed. The scripts are provided for your reference as you model the marking on the board while the students analyze the sentences aloud.

S PV
Fritz laughs uncontrollably.
adv

a. (First, read the sentence aloud.) "Fritz laughs uncontrollably."

b. "This is a sentence because it is a group of words that expresses a complete thought. It is a declarative sentence because it makes a statement."

c. "This sentence is about *Fritz*." (Underline the subject.) "So, *Fritz* is the subject because it is what the sentence is about." (Place a capital letter *S* above the subject.)

d. "This sentence tells us that Fritz *laughs*." (Double underline the predicate.) "So, *laughs* is the predicate because it is what the sentence tells us about *Fritz*." (Place a capital letter *P* above the action verb.) "It is a predicate verb because it shows action." (Place a capital letter *V* to the right of the *P*.) "There is no linking verb because predicate verbs do not need linking verbs."

e. (Continue the analysis of the sentence, starting at the far right side and moving toward the left.) "*Uncontrollably* tells us how Fritz laughs." (Draw a straight line down from the adverb, then a horizontal line toward the word that it modifies, and then a straight line with an arrow pointing to the word it modifies.)

f. "So, *uncontrollably* is an adverbial element because it modifies a verb. It is an adverb." (Write *adv* in lowercase letters in the elbow opposite the line with the arrow.)

S PV
Softly Grandma whispered.
adv

a. (First, read the sentence aloud.) "Softly Grandma whispered."

b. "This is a sentence because it is a group of words that expresses a complete thought. It is a declarative sentence because it makes a statement."

c. "This sentence is about *Grandma*." (Underline the subject.) "So, *Grandma* is the subject because it is what the sentence is about." (Place a capital letter *S* above the subject.)

d. "This sentence tells us that Grandma *whispered*." (Double underline the predicate.) "So, *whispered* is the predicate because it is what the sentence tells us about *Grandma*." (Place a capital letter *P* above the action verb.) "It is a predicate verb because it shows action." (Place a capital letter *V* to the right of the *P*.) "There is no linking verb because predicate verbs do not need linking verbs."

e. (Continue the analysis of the sentence, starting at the far right side and moving toward the left.) "*Softly* tells us *how* Grandma whispered." (Draw a straight line down from the adverb, then a horizontal line toward the word that it modifies, and then a straight line with an arrow pointing to the word it modifies.)

f. "So, *softly* is an adverbial element because it modifies a verb. It is an adverb." (Write *adv* in lowercase letters in the elbow opposite the line with the arrow.)

S hv PV
Fritz is not swimming today.
adv adv

a. (First, read the sentence aloud.) "Fritz is not swimming today."

b. "This is a sentence because it is a group of words that expresses a complete thought. It is a declarative sentence because it makes a statement."

c. "This sentence is about *Fritz*." (Underline the subject.) "So, *Fritz* is the subject because it is what the sentence is about." (Place a capital letter *S* above the subject.)

d. "This sentence tells us that Fritz *is swimming*." (Double underline the predicate.) "So, *is swimming* is the predicate because it is what the sentence tells us about *Fritz*." (Place a capital letter *P* above the action verb.) "It is a predicate verb because it shows action." (Place a capital letter *V* to the right of the *P*.) "There is no linking verb because predicate verbs do not need linking verbs. *Is* is a helping verb because it helps the verb." (Place a lowercase *hv* above the helping verb.)

e. (Continue the analysis of the sentence, starting at the far right side and moving toward the left.) "*Today* tells us *when* Fritz is swimming." (Draw a straight line down from the adverb, then a horizontal line toward the word that it modifies, and then a straight line with an arrow pointing to the word it modifies.)

f. "So, *today* is an adverbial element because it modifies a verb. It is an adverb." (Write *adv* in lowercase letters in the elbow opposite the line with the arrow.)

g. "*Not* tells us *how* Fritz is swimming." (Draw a straight line down from the adverb, then a horizontal line toward the word that it modifies, and then a straight line with an arrow pointing to the word it modifies.)

h. "So, *not* is an adverbial element because it modifies a verb. It is an adverb." (Write *adv* in lowercase letters in the elbow opposite the line with the arrow.)

S hv PV
Lightning is suddenly flashing.
adv

a. (First, read the sentence aloud.) "Lightning is suddenly flashing."

b. "This is a sentence because it is a group of words that expresses a complete thought. It is a declarative sentence because it makes a statement."

c. "This sentence is about *lightning*." (Underline the subject.) "So, *lightning* is the subject because it is what the sentence is about." (Place a capital letter *S* above the subject.)

d. "This sentence tells us that lightning *is flashing*." (Double underline the predicate.) "So, *is flashing* is the predicate because it is what the sentence tells us about *lightning*." (Place a capital letter *P* above the action verb.) "It is a predicate verb because it shows action." (Place a capital letter *V* to the right of the *P*.) "There is no linking verb because predicate verbs do not need linking verbs. *Is* is a helping verb because it helps the verb." (Place a lowercase *hv* above the helping verb.)

e. "*Suddenly* tells us *how* lightning is flashing." (Draw a straight line down from the adverb, then a horizontal line toward the word that it modifies, and then a straight line with an arrow pointing to the word it modifies.)

f. "So, *suddenly* is an adverbial element because it modifies a verb. It is an adverb." (Write *adv* in lowercase letters in the elbow opposite the line with the arrow.)

From the Sideline: Expect 100 percent participation. Never let students sit back and watch when their participation is expected.

[A]Bring in cupcakes with icing for the students to eat after the lesson. Discuss how the frosting adds to the flavor of the cupcakes.

Chapter 5

Adjectives[A]

Most people do not consider a cupcake finished until it is frosted. If you give your friends cupcakes on your birthday, you probably choose the frosting carefully. Do you like rich, creamy homemade icing? Or do you prefer fancy, brightly colored bakery frosting covered in pink roses? The cake itself may be the same flavor, but your choice of frosting modifies it and makes it unique.

An **adjective**■ in a sentence works a bit like frosting on a cupcake—it adds flavor and interest. Like a cupcake before it is frosted, the core of a sentence—the subject and the predicate—is the most important part of the sentence. All the remaining parts modify or support those principal elements. You have learned how adverbs modify verbs; in this chapter you will learn about adjectives and what they do. While adverbs modify verbs, adjectives modify nouns. Using adjectives helps to clarify the meaning of nouns.

To the Source:
■ adjective
The word *adjective* comes from the Latin word *adjectivum,* meaning "that is added to (a noun)."

Adjectives are like icing on a cupcake—they bring flavor. As you know, frosting is not just for decoration: it changes the taste of the dessert. Similarly, a good adjective modifies the meaning of a noun.

Ideas to Understand

One of the eight parts of speech, adjectives describe or define nouns or pronouns. Adjectives answer the questions *how many, whose, which one,* or *what kind.* They are important because of the way they add to the meaning of a noun. For example, what if there were no adjectives to describe Tigger, a beloved character in A.A. Milne's book *The House at Pooh Corner*? He would be a rather ordinary creature and not at all bouncy. In chapter 7, "Tigger Is Unbounced," Milne tells the reader what kind of tigger Tigger is by using a number of descriptive adjectives:

> . . . Tigger was tearing around the Forest making loud yapping noises for Rabbit. And at last a very Small and Sorry Rabbit heard him. And the Small and Sorry Rabbit rushed through the mist at the noise, and it suddenly turned into Tigger; a Friendly Tigger, a Grand Tigger, a Large and Helpful Tigger, a Tigger who bounced, if he bounced at all, in just the beautiful way a Tigger ought to bounce.
>
> "Oh, Tigger, I *am* glad to see you," cried Rabbit.[1]

Milne seems to consider the adjectives describing Tigger so important that he capitalizes them even though we usually would not: Tigger is *Friendly*, *Grand*, *Large*, and *Helpful*. Those words are the icing on a Tigger cupcake. Notice that Rabbit is described with adjectives too, but he is *Small* and *Sorry*. If you read further in chapter 7 of *The House on Pooh Corner*, you will read how Rabbit feels guilty for having tried to take the bounce out of Tigger, and he is quite pleased that rambunctious, lovable Tigger is still very much himself.

Those adjectives all answer the question *what kind*. What kind of Tigger? What kind of Rabbit? Remember, adjectives may also tell *which one*, *whose*, or *how many*. For example, earlier in "Tigger Is Unbounced," Milne uses the adjective *twelve* to tell how many pots of honey there are in Pooh's cupboard: "But there are *twelve* pots of honey in my cupboard, and they've been calling to me for hours." Of course that silly old bear would know precisely how many pots of honey he has! With descriptive adjectives, Milne makes his characters from the Hundred Acre Wood jump out at you.

Milne also uses the words *the* and *a* as in "*the* pots" and "*a* shout."

> And just when he was getting so sure of himself that it didn't matter whether *the* pots went on calling or not, there was *a* shout from in front of them, and out of the mist came Christopher Robin.

These two words tell *which* or *how many* nouns; they are a subgroup of adjectives called articles. The English language has two articles: *a* (or *an*) and *the*.

Off the Shelf: You might be familiar with cartoon versions of Winnie the Pooh, but did you know that first there were two books? *Winnie the Pooh* and *The House at Pooh Corner* contain many more delightful stories about mishaps and adventures in the Hundred Acre Wood. Bounce on down to your local library to find the complete books.

From the Sideline: Read aloud the excerpt from *The House at Pooh Corner*, modulating your voice on the adjectives to exaggerate their effect. Milne capitalizes them in just this spirit of playful exaggeration, so "ham it up" a little. Then, reread the passage, this time omitting the capitalized adjectives. Call attention to how the meaning is changed without the modifiers; they are not just decorative.

1. A.A. Milne, *The House at Pooh Corner* (New York: Dell Publishing, Inc., Co., 1956), 124–127.

We count *a* and *an* as a single article because they mean the same thing. The word *a* stands before nouns (or adjectives) that begin with a **consonant** sound while *an* is used before words beginning with **vowel** sounds. We say "*a* shout," but we say "*an* alarming shout."

The article *a* (or *an*) is known as an **indefinite article**. It is placed before nonspecific nouns and identifies the nouns as being singular. When we read "there was *a* shout from in front of them," we know that Pooh and Piglet hear one nonspecific shout. It has not been mentioned before, so Pooh and Piglet cannot identify it definitely. It is indefinite.

On the other hand, the article *the* is known as a **definite article**. It identifies a particular noun and is placed before nouns or adjectives. When we read "it didn't matter whether *the* pots went on calling or not," we know Pooh is considering particular pots. He is thinking of the twelve honey pots in his own cupboard, not just any pots. They have already been mentioned in the story.

Most native speakers of English naturally hear the difference between the indefinite article *a* (or *an*) and the definite article *the*. When you say "*a* bear," you are referring to any old bear. When you say "*the* bear," you are talking about a specific, definite bear that we know something about. In this case, you could say "the bear" and mean that particular silly old Winnie the Pooh because he has already been mentioned in our explanation of adjectives.

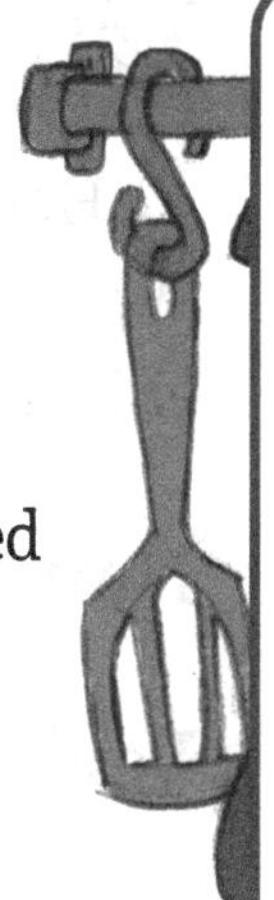

From the Sideline: Some classify articles as a separate part of speech, but we agree with grammarians who categorize articles and adjectives together, retaining the traditional eight parts of speech.

Note the exceptions to the *a*/*an* rule: *a* is used before words that begin with a *y* sound, such as *unique*, as well as before words that begin with a *w* sound, such as *one*. See this chapter's Moment for Mechanics for another exception.

Moment for Mechanics

Words starting with one of the five vowels—*a*, *e*, *i*, *o*, *u*—are not the only words that require the use of the indefinite article *an* before them. Sometimes the letter *h* is silent at the beginning of a word, so the word sounds like it starts with a vowel. Remember this rule: use *an* when you don't pronounce the *h*; use *a* when you do.

Examples:

Silent *h*	Consonant *h*
an honest mistake	*a* honey pot
an hour from now	*a* hungry bear

[B] For the lyrics to all of the songs, please see the Song Lyrics section on page 191. Play the appropriate audio tracks and have the students sing/chant along. Students should commit the songs to memory.

Terms to Remember[B]

Here are three definitions to review and one new one to memorize. What adjectives best describe your singing? Is it melodic, cheerful, and enjoyable? Make it memorable.

Noun *(1–5)*

Verb and Helping Verb *(1–6)*

Adverb *(1–7)*

NEW! **Adjective** *(1–8)*

Sentences to Analyze

By now, you have become familiar with and more skillful at analyzing sentences. As in the previous chapters, analyze the following sentence, saying the gray words in quotation marks with your teacher and your classmates. Use the unspoken black words in parentheses as hints to guide you. You know that the first step is to identify the words as a sentence, what kind of sentence it is, and then the principal elements. The next step is to identify adverbs and adjectives starting from the far right and moving backward toward the front of the sentence. Moving backward is a method of breaking a sentence apart that helps you focus your attention on each element in its turn, rather than on the whole sentence at once. That way, you don't miss any of the parts.

S (Tigger) PV (bounced)

A friendly Tigger bounced.

adj (A) adj (friendly) → Tigger

a. (First, read the sentence aloud.) "A friendly Tigger bounced."

b. "This is a sentence because it is a group of words that expresses a complete thought. It is a declarative sentence because it makes a statement."

c. "This sentence is about *Tigger*. So, *Tigger* is the subject because it is what the sentence is about." (Since *Tigger* is the subject, underline it and place a capital letter *S* above it.)

d. "This sentence tells us that Tigger *bounced*. So, *bounced* is the predicate because it is what the sentence tells us about *Tigger*." (Since *bounced* tells something about *Tigger*, double underline the predicate and place a capital letter *P* above it.) "It is a predicate verb because it shows action. There is no linking verb because predicate verbs do not need linking verbs." (Since *bounced* shows action, place a capital letter *V* to the right of the letter *P*.)

e. "*Friendly* tells us what kind of Tigger bounced." (To mark adjectives, carefully draw a straight line down from the adjective, then a horizontal line toward the word that it modifies, and then a straight line with an arrow pointing to the word it modifies.)

f. "So, *friendly* is an adjectival element because it modifies a noun. It is an adjective." (Write *adj* in lowercase letters in the elbow opposite the line with the arrow.)

g. "*A* tells us *which* Tigger." (Mark this adjective the same way by drawing a straight line down from the adjective, then a horizontal line toward the word that it modifies. However, connect this modifier line with the modifier line for *friendly* since both are **adjectival elements** modifying *Tigger*.)

h. "So, *a* is an adjectival element because it modifies a noun. It is an adjective." (Write *adj* in lowercase letters in the elbow opposite the line with the arrow.)

You are now ready to analyze longer sentences. Here is an example that includes not only multiple adjectives but also an adverb; plus, it has a helping verb. Notice how the modifier lines for the adjectives and the adverb do not cross each other. Also, the lines for the three adjectives join as one arrow pointing to the noun they modify.

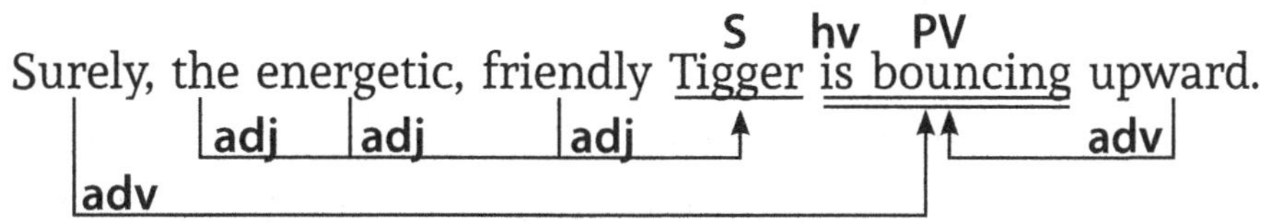

a. (First, read the sentence aloud.) "Surely, the energetic, friendly Tigger is bouncing upward."

From the Sideline: Remember, the marking of the sentence is done during the oral analysis. Note that an adjective (*adj*) is marked in lowercase letters underneath the adjective, and the modifying line is drawn neatly and connects to the noun that it modifies.

From the Sideline: When more than one adjective modifies the same noun, the modifier lines do not cross one another. In fact, the lines are connected, becoming one line with an arrow that points to the noun.

b. "This is a sentence because it is a group of words that expresses a complete thought. It is a declarative sentence because it makes a statement."

c. "This sentence is about *Tigger*. So, *Tigger* is the subject because it is what the sentence is about." (Since *Tigger* is the subject, underline it and place a capital letter *S* above the subject.)

d. "This sentence tells us that Tigger *is bouncing*. So, *is bouncing* is the predicate because it is what the sentence tells us about *Tigger*." (Since *is bouncing* tells us something about *Tigger*, double underline the predicate, including the helping verb, and place a capital letter *P* above the action verb.)

e. "It is a predicate verb because it shows action. There is no linking verb because predicate verbs do not need linking verbs." (Since *bouncing* shows action, place a capital letter *V* to the right of the letter *P*.)

f. "*Is* is the helping verb because it helps the verb." (Place the lowercase letters *hv* above the helping verb.)

g. "*Upward* tells us *where* Tigger is bouncing." (To mark an adverb, carefully draw a straight line down from the adverb, then a horizontal line toward the word that it modifies, and then a straight line with an arrow pointing to the word it modifies.)

h. "So, *upward* is an adverbial element because it modifies a verb. It is an adverb." (Write *adv* in lowercase letters in the elbow opposite the line with the arrow.)

i. "*Friendly* tells us *what kind* of Tigger." (To mark an adjective, carefully draw a straight line down from the adjective, then a horizontal line toward the word that it modifies, and then a straight line with an arrow pointing to the word it modifies.)

j. "So, *friendly* is an adjectival element because it modifies a noun. It is an adjective." (Write *adj* in lowercase letters in the elbow opposite the line with the arrow.)

k. "*Energetic* tells us *what kind* of Tigger." (To mark an adjective, carefully draw a straight line down from the adjective, then a horizontal line toward the word that it modifies. However, connect this modifier line with the modifier line for *friendly*, since both of the adjectival elements are modifying *Tigger*.)

l. "So, *energetic* is an adjectival element because it modifies a noun. It is an adjective." (Write *adj* in lowercase letters in the elbow opposite the line with the arrow.)

m. "*The* tells us *which* Tigger." (To mark an adjective, carefully draw a straight line down from the adjective, then a horizontal line toward the word that it modifies. Connect this modifier line with the modifier line for *energetic* and *friendly* since all three are adjectival elements modifying *Tigger*.)

n. "So, *the* is an adjectival element because it modifies a noun. It is an adjective." (Write *adj* in lowercase letters in the elbow opposite of the line with the arrow.)

o. "*Surely* tells us *how* Tigger is bouncing." (To mark an adverb, carefully draw a straight line down from the adverb, then a horizontal line toward the word that it modifies, and then a straight line with an arrow pointing to the word it modifies.)

p. "So, *surely* is an adverbial element because it modifies a verb. It is an adverb." (Write *adv* in lowercase letters in the elbow opposite the line with the arrow.)

Do you remember Stripes the cat in the last chapter? We used adverbs to describe the different ways she jumps. Those adverbs all modified the verb in the sentence and told how she jumps. For bouncy Tigger, we have focused on adjectives. Adjectives describe nouns or pronouns. Let's try some different adjectives in the simple sentence "Stripes jumps." *Little* Stripes jumps. *Lazy* Stripes jumps. *Hungry* Stripes jumps. *Sneaky* Stripes jumps. Adverbs and adjectives help you write with precise detail and power. You use them to help your reader imagine exactly what you mean.

Turn back to the cupcake illustration at the beginning of the chapter. Did you notice what Fritz is putting on his cupcake? Can you find the icing bag? What flavor frosting do you think it is? If you were decorating cupcakes, what would you put on yours?

Well-Ordered Notes A

Review It

Review the following:

What are the principal elements?
What are the twenty-three helping verbs?
What is an adverb?
What is an adjective?

Practice It

Lead the students in Lightning, an activity during which students quickly generate different nouns that can be modified by the same adjectives. Have the students stand. Say to the first student an adjective (e.g., *lazy*) and then "blank," which represents a noun. Once he answers (e.g., *lazy hound*), he may be seated. Use an adjective three times before changing to another adjective. If a student cannot think of an answer within five seconds, have her remain standing and give her a second chance at the end of the round.

Example: Teacher: "Lazy ____________."
Student 1: "*Lazy* hound."
Student 2: "*Lazy* cat."
Student 3: "*Lazy* day."

snarly	fuzzy	bumpy
honest	dark	sweet
creamy	rectangular	friendly
rough	crumbly	plaid
watery	humongous	tenth
scratchy	quiet	straight
lavender	spicy	

Analyze It

From the Sideline: Visit http://capress.link/wol1att for a video demonstration of analysis.

Now, as a class, analyze the four sentences in the lesson. Here is the script for the first one to help you lead the choral analysis and model the markings on the board. The words in parentheses are like stage directions to guide you and are not to be spoken. The words in gray and enclosed in quotation marks are for you and the students to speak in chorus.

S PV
White, fleecy clouds drift above.
adj adj adv

a. (First, read the sentence aloud.) "White, fleecy clouds drift above."

b. "This is a sentence because it is a group of words that expresses a complete thought."

c. "It is a declarative sentence because it makes a statement."

d. "This sentence is about *clouds*." (Underline the subject.) "So, *clouds* is the subject because it is what the sentence is about." (Place a capital letter *S* above the subject.)

e. "This sentence tells us that clouds *drift*." (Double underline the predicate.) "So, *drift* is the predicate because it is what the sentence tells us about *clouds*." (Place a capital letter *P* above the action verb.)

f. "It is a predicate verb because it shows action. There is no linking verb because predicate verbs do not need linking verbs." (Place a capital letter *V* to the right of the *P*.)

g. (Continue the analysis of the sentence, starting at the far right and moving toward the left.) "*Above* tells us *where* clouds drift." (Draw a straight line down from the adverb, then a horizontal line toward the word that it modifies, and then a straight line with an arrow pointing to the word it modifies.)

h. "So, *above* is an adverbial element because it modifies a verb. It is an adverb." (Write *adv* in lowercase letters in the elbow opposite the line with the arrow.)

i. "*Fleecy* tells us *what kind* of clouds." (Draw a straight line down from the adjective, then a horizontal line toward the word that it modifies, and then a straight line with an arrow pointing to the word it modifies.)

j. "So, *fleecy* is an adjectival element because it modifies a noun. It is an adjective." (Write *adj* in lowercase letters in the elbow opposite the line with the arrow.)

k. "*White* tells us *what kind* of clouds." (Draw a straight line down from the adjective, draw a horizontal line toward the word that it modifies, and connect this modifier line with the modifier line for *fleecy* since both the adjectival elements are modifying *clouds*.)

l. "So, *white* is an adjectival element because it modifies a noun. It is an adjective." (Write *adj* in lowercase letters in the elbow opposite the line with the arrow.)

From the Sideline: For extra guided practice, refer to the Sentence Bank at the end of this chapter.

Lesson to Learn
Adjectives

A

1. Analyze the following sentences.

   a. White, fleecy clouds drift above.
   (S: clouds; PV: drift; White — adj; fleecy — adj; above — adv)

   b. Ten ants are hunting together.
   (S: ants; hv: are; PV: hunting; Ten — adj; together — adv)

   c. Then, a curious black ant scurries away.
   (S: ant; PV: scurries; a — adj; curious — adj; black — adj; Then — adv; away — adv)

   d. The little ant wanders off alone.
   (S: ant; PV: wanders; The — adj; little — adj; off — adv; alone — adv)

From the Sideline: Remember that when you see the word *analyze* in instructions throughout this book, we mean both choral analysis and written notations. The two go hand in hand as a prediagramming system.

2. An adjective modifies a noun by answering the questions *how many*, *whose*, *which one*, or *what kind*. On the lines provided, list the adjectives from the sentences in exercise 1. (Do not include article adjectives.)

   a. white b. fleecy

   c. ten d. curious

   e. black f. little

3. Fill in each blank below with an adjective that modifies or describes the noun in the sentence. You may choose an adjective from the word bank or think of your own.

Word Bank: giggly, northern, wild, oak, small, autumn

Answers may vary.

a. A(n) autumn breeze blew gently.

b. The oak trees reached skyward.

c. Several ______wild______ geese honked together.

d. Two ______giggly______ girls skipped ahead.

e. A(n) ______small______ boy shuffled behind.

4. Imagine you are lying in the grass watching the clouds drift by in the sky. Rewrite sentence *a* from exercise 1 by adding an adjective that tells ***how many*** *white, fleecy clouds drift above.*

Four white, fleecy clouds drift above.

____

Well-Ordered Notes B

Review It

Review the following:

What are the eight parts of speech?
What is a verb?
What is an adjective?
What is a noun?
What is an adverb?

Practice It

Lead the students in Hot Potato, which encourages them to quickly think of appropriate adjectives for nouns. Have the students stand in a circle and pass a beanbag—the hot potato—from person to person while each student quickly thinks of an adjective. Start the activity by stating a noun (e.g., *seashells*) and hand the beanbag to the first student. She must quickly provide an appropriate adjective (e.g., *cockle seashells*) while she passes the beanbag to the next student. If she cannot think of an adjective within five seconds, she stands in the middle of the circle. Begin a new round with a new noun (e.g., *snail*). Once there are five students inside the circle, pause the activity and let the students return to the circle. Use the provided list of nouns or create a list of your own.

Fewer than Five: If there are too few students to create a circle, have each student stand and pass the Hot Potato back and forth from you to the first student, then back to you, and then to the next student. The goal is the same: the students are to quickly think of an adjective that would complement the stated noun.

Example:
Teacher: "Seashells"
Student 1: "Cockle seashells"
Student 2: "Tiny seashells"

- snail
- driftwood
- sunscreen
- seaweed
- towel
- pail
- sunglasses
- sandcastle
- fish
- goggles

Analyze It

From the Sideline: Visit http://capress.link/wol1att for a video demonstration of analysis.

Now, as a class, analyze the four sentences in the lesson. Here is the script for the first one to help you lead the choral analysis and model the markings on the board. The words in parentheses are like stage directions to guide you and are not to be spoken. The words in gray and enclosed in quotation marks are for you and the students to speak in chorus.

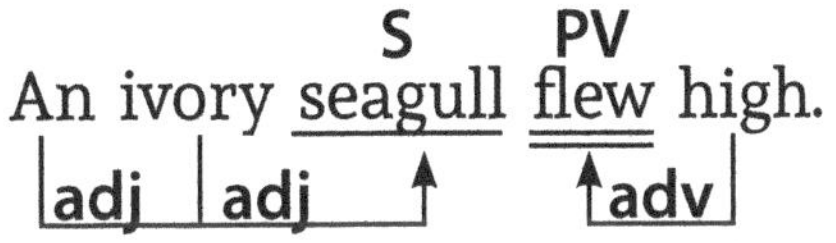

a. (First, read the sentence aloud.) "An ivory seagull flew high."

b. "This is a sentence because it is a group of words that expresses a complete thought."

c. "It is a declarative sentence because it makes a statement."

d. "This sentence is about *seagull*." (Underline the subject.) "So, *seagull* is the subject because it is what the sentence is about." (Place a capital letter *S* above the subject.)

e. "This sentence tells us that seagull *flew*." (Double underline the predicate.) "So, *flew* is the predicate because it is what the sentence tells us about *seagull*." (Place a capital letter *P* above the action verb.)

f. "It is a predicate verb because it shows action. There is no linking verb because predicate verbs do not need linking verbs." (Place a capital letter *V* to the right of the *P*.)

g. (Continue the analysis of the sentence, starting at the far right and moving toward the left.) "*High* tells us *where* seagull flew." (Draw a straight line down from the adverb, then a horizontal line toward the word that it modifies, and then a straight line with an arrow pointing to the word it modifies.)

h. "So, *high* is an adverbial element because it modifies a verb. It is an adverb." (Write *adv* in lowercase letters in the elbow opposite the line with the arrow.)

i. "*Ivory* tells us *what kind* of seagull." (Draw a straight line down from the adjective, then a horizontal line toward the word that it modifies, and then a straight line with an arrow pointing to the word it modifies.)

j. "So, *ivory* is an adjectival element because it modifies a noun. It is an adjective." (Write *adj* in lowercase letters in the elbow opposite the line with the arrow.)

k. "*An* tells us *how many* seagulls." (Draw a straight line down from the adjective, then a horizontal line toward the word that it modifies, and then connect this modifier line with the modifier line for *ivory* since both adjectival elements are modifying *seagull*.)

l. "So, *an* is an adjectival element because it modifies a noun. It is an adjective." (Write *adj* in lowercase letters in the elbow opposite the line with the arrow.)

Lesson to Learn
Adjectives

B

1. Analyze the following sentences.

    a. An ivory seagull flew high.
    S: seagull; PV: flew; adj: An, ivory; adv: high

    b. Three children eagerly splashed about.
    S: children; PV: splashed; adj: Three; adv: eagerly, about

    c. Suddenly, a long, slender snake appeared.
    S: snake; PV: appeared; adj: a, long, slender; adv: Suddenly

    d. The fretful children screamed uncontrollably.
    S: children; PV: screamed; adj: The, fretful; adv: uncontrollably

2. An adjective modifies a noun by answering the questions *how many, whose, which one,* or *what kind*. On the lines provided, list the *adjectives* from the above sentences. (Do not include article adjectives.)

    a. ivory

    b. three

    c. long

    d. slender

    e. fretful

3. Circle the correct indefinite article. Remember, *a* comes before words that begin with a consonant sound, while *an* comes before words that begin with a vowel or silent h.
   a. A / An hourly battle begins there.
   b. A / An pesky seagull squawked wildly.
   c. A / An angry crab snapped defensively.
   d. A / An curious sandpiper watched calmly.
   e. A / An hungry seagull flew away.

4. Imagine you are sitting on a beach watching the waves roll in. Then rewrite sentence *b* from exercise 1 by adding an adjective that tells *what kind* of children eagerly splashed about.

   Three young children eagerly splashed about.

Well-Ordered Notes C

Review It

Review the following:

What is a sentence?
What is a verb?
What are helping verbs?
What is an adverb?

Practice It

Lead the students in Guess the Adjective, using index cards and a whiteboard. Write the following adjective-noun pairs on four index cards. Have one student choose a card, silently read the phrase on the card, and then draw a picture that describes the card. Have a fellow student guess what was drawn and explain which word is the adjective and why it is an adjective.

Example: Large spider
Student 1: Student draws a large spider.
Teacher: "Can anyone guess what this is a picture of?"
Student 2: "It is a picture of a large spider."
Teacher: "What kind of spider did she draw? What is the adjective and why?"
Student 2: "She drew a *large* spider. *Large* tells us *what kind* of spider, so *large* is an adjectival element because it modifies a noun. It is an adjective."

1. Two boats: *Two* tells us *how many* boats, so *two* is an adjectival element because it modifies a noun. It is an adjective.
2. Black flies: *Black* tells us *what kind* of flies, so *black* is an adjectival element because it modifies a noun. It is an adjective.
3. Furry caterpillars: *Furry* tells us *what kind* of caterpillars, so *furry* is an adjectival element because it modifies a noun. It is an adjective.
4. Bug repellent: *Bug* tells us *what kind* of repellent, so *bug* is an adjectival element because it modifies a noun. It is an adjective.

Analyze It

Now, as a class, analyze the four sentences in the lesson. Here is the script for the first one to help you lead the choral analysis and model the markings on the board. The words in parentheses are like stage directions to guide you and are not to be spoken. The words in gray and enclosed in quotation marks are for you and the students to speak in chorus.

S hv PV
Colorful maple leaves are slowly swirling down.
adj adj adv adv

e. (First, read the sentence aloud.) "Colorful maple leaves are slowly swirling down."

f. "This is a sentence because it is a group of words that expresses a complete thought."

g. "It is a declarative sentence because it makes a statement."

h. "This sentence is about *leaves*." (Underline the subject.) "So, *leaves* is the subject because it is what the sentence is about." (Place a capital letter *S* above the subject.)

i. "This sentence tells us that leaves *are swirling*." (Double underline the predicate.) "So, *are swirling* is the predicate because it is what the sentence tells us about *leaves*." (Place a capital letter *P* above the action verb.)

j. "It is a predicate verb because it shows action. There is no linking verb because predicate verbs do not need linking verbs." (Place a capital letter *V* to the right of the *P*.)

k. "*Are* is a helping verb because it helps the verb." (Place a lowercase *hv* above the helping verb.)

l. (Continue the analysis of the sentence, starting at the far right and moving toward the left.) "*Down* tells us *where* leaves are swirling." (Draw a straight line down from the adverb, then a horizontal line toward the word that it modifies, and then a straight line with an arrow pointing to the word it modifies.)

m. "So, *down* is an adverbial element because it modifies a verb. It is an adverb." (Write *adv* in lowercase letters in the elbow opposite the line with the arrow.)

n. "*Slowly* tells us *how* leaves are swirling." (Draw a straight line down from the adverb, then a horizontal line toward the word that it modifies, and then a straight line with an arrow pointing to the word it modifies.)

o. "So, *slowly* is an adverbial element because it modifies a verb. It is an adverb." (Write *adv* in lowercase letters in the elbow opposite the line with the arrow.)

p. "*Maple* tells us *what kind* of leaves." (Draw a straight line down from the adjective, then a horizontal line toward the word that it modifies, and then a straight line with an arrow pointing to the word it modifies.)

q. "So, *maple* is an adjectival element because it modifies a noun. It is an adjective." (Write *adj* in lowercase letters in the elbow opposite the line with the arrow.)

r. "*Colorful* tells us *what kind* of leaves." (Draw a straight line down from the adjective, then a horizontal line toward the word that it modifies, and connect this modifier line with the modifier line for *maple* since both the adjectival elements are modifying *leaves*.)

s. "So, *colorful* is an adjectival element because it modifies a noun. It is an adjective." (Write *adj* in lowercase letters in the elbow opposite the line with the arrow.)

Lesson to Learn
Adjectives

1. Analyze the following sentences.

   a. Colorful maple leaves are slowly swirling down.
   S hv PV
   adj adj adv adv

   b. Two yellow canoes glide smoothly.
   S PV
   adj adj adv

   c. One clever hawk is circling overhead.
   S hv PV
   adj adj adv

   d. Frantically, the small, gray mice scurry away.
   S PV
   adj adj adj adv
   adv

2. An adjective modifies a noun by answering the questions *how many*, *whose*, *which one*, or *what kind*. On the lines provided, list the adjectives from the sentences in exercise 1. (Do not include article adjectives.)

   a. colorful
   b. maple
   c. two
   d. yellow
   e. one
   f. clever
   g. small
   h. gray

3. Fill in each blank below with an adjective that modifies or describes the noun in the sentence. You may choose an adjective from the word bank or think of your own.

Word Bank: hungry, curious, icy, unfortunate, brown, silvery

Answers may vary.

a. The **brown** bears fish.

b. The **icy** rivers rapidly flow.

c. Later, **silvery** salmon swam upstream.

d. Several **curious** bears watched together.

e. One **unfortunate** fish jumped high.

f. A **hungry** bear grabbed eagerly.

4. Imagine you are taking a canoe trip down a river when you spot mice scurrying away because of a hawk. Rewrite sentence *d* from exercise 1 by adding an adjective that tells *how many* gray field mice scurry away.

Frantically, five small, gray mice scurry away.

Well-Ordered Notes D

Review It

Review the following:

What is a sentence?
What is a adverb?
What are the four kinds of sentences?
What is an adjective?

Practice It

Lead the students in Add an Adjective, which is an oral exercise. Use nouns that can be described, such as the words in the following list, or generate your own. Ask the first student to give an adjective to modify the noun. Ask the next student to add an adjective to that adjective-noun pair. Ask the third student to add one more adjective. Switch to a new noun to describe and continue around the room. Let all your students have a chance to provide an adjective.

Example: Teacher: "Ladybugs"
Student 1: "*Red* ladybugs"
Student 2: "*Small red* ladybugs"
Student 3: "*Three small red* ladybugs"

ladybugs	moths	ferns
dragonflies	moss	earthworms
vines	beetles	leaves
gnats	centipedes	webs

Analyze It

Now, as a class, analyze the four sentences in the lesson. Here is the script for the first one to help you lead the choral analysis and model the markings on the board. The words in parentheses are like stage directions to guide you and are not to be spoken. The words in gray and enclosed in quotation marks are for you and the students to speak in chorus.

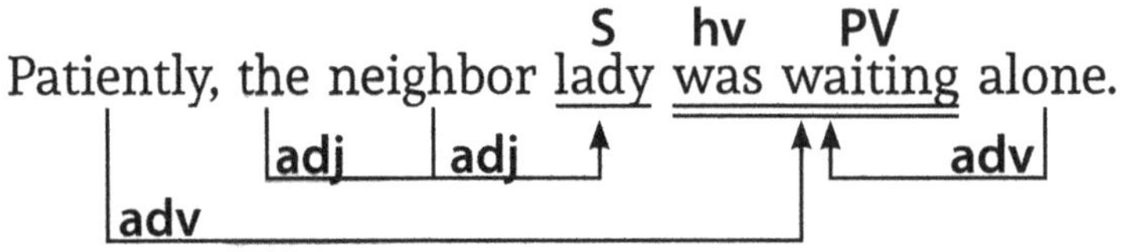

a. (First, read the sentence aloud.) "Patiently, the neighbor lady was waiting alone."

b. "This is a sentence because it is a group of words that expresses a complete thought."

c. "It is a declarative sentence because it makes a statement."

d. "This sentence is about *lady*." (Underline the subject.) "So, *lady* is the subject because it is what the sentence is about." (Place a capital letter *S* above the subject.)

e. "This sentence tells us that lady *was waiting*." (Double underline the predicate.) "So, *was waiting* is the predicate because it is what the sentence tells us about *lady*." (Place a capital letter *P* above the action verb.)

f. "It is a predicate verb because it shows action. There is no linking verb because predicate verbs do not need linking verbs." (Place a capital letter *V* to the right of the *P*.)

g. "*Was* is a helping verb because it helps the verb." (Place a lowercase *hv* above the helping verb.)

h. (Continue the analysis of the sentence, starting at the far right and moving toward the left.) "*Alone* tells us *how* lady was waiting." (Draw a straight line down from the adverb, then a horizontal line toward the word that it modifies, and then a straight line with an arrow pointing to the word it modifies.)

i. "So, *alone* is an adverbial element because it modifies a verb. It is an adverb." (Write ***adv*** in lowercase letters in the elbow opposite the line with the arrow.)

j. "*Neighbor* tells us *what kind* of lady." (Draw a straight line down from the adjective, then a horizontal line toward the word that it modifies, and then a straight line with an arrow pointing to the word it modifies.)

k. "So, *neighbor* is an adjectival element because it modifies a noun. It is an adjective." (Write ***adj*** in lowercase letters in the elbow opposite the line with the arrow.)

l. "*The* tells us *which* lady." (Draw a straight line down from the adjective, draw a horizontal line toward the word that it modifies, and connect this modifier line with the modifier line for ***neighbor*** since both adjectival elements are modifying *lady*.)

m. "So, *the* is an adjectival element because it modifies a noun. It is an adjective." (Write ***adj*** in lowercase letters in the elbow opposite the line with the arrow.)

n. "*Patiently* tells us *how* lady was waiting." (Draw a straight line down from the adverb, then a horizontal line toward the word that it modifies, and then a straight line with an arrow pointing to the word it modifies.)

o. "So, *patiently* is an adverbial element because it modifies a verb. It is an adverb." (Write ***adv*** in lowercase letters in the elbow opposite the line with the arrow.)

Lesson to Learn D
Adjectives

1. Analyze the following sentences.

   S hv PV
   a. Patiently, the neighbor lady was waiting alone.
   adj adj adv
   adv

   S hv hv PV
   b. Eight kids should be raking now.
   adj adv

   S PV
   c. Suddenly, sheepish youngsters snuck outside.
   adj adv
   adv

   S PV
   d. The thoughtless children forgot again.
   adj adj adv

2. On the lines provided, list the *adjectives* from the above sentences. (Do not include article adjectives.)

   a. **neighbor**

   b. **eight**

   c. **sheepish**

   d. **thoughtless**

3. Add a few creative adjectives to spice up the following old nursery rhyme.

   a. The ______nippy______ south wind brings wet weather.

   b. The ______gnawing______ north wind blows wet and cold together.

   c. The ______wheezy______ west wind brings us rain.

   d. The ______freezing______ east wind blows it back again.

4. Imagine you are watching some children playing games and not doing the raking they should be doing. Rewrite sentence *b* from exercise 1 by adding an adjective that tells *what kind* of kids should be raking.

   Eight forgetful kids should be raking now.

   ____

Sentences for Practice

Adjectives

Analyze the following sentences.

S PV
1. Loudly, the big gray clouds rumbled.
adj adj adj adv

S hv PV
2. Two parents were watching cautiously.
adj adv

S PV
3. Four children waited patiently.
adj adv

S hv PV
4. Passengers were scattering everywhere.
adv

S PV
5. An old, smiley man waved kindly.
adj adj adj adv

From the Sideline: In each chapter, an extra practice sheet provides more sentences for analysis to use as needed—perhaps for review as a class, for individual students requiring more practice, or even as a refresher for students later in the year.

6. One giant airplane flew overhead.
(S: airplane; PV: flew; adj: One, giant; adv: overhead)

7. The four eager children were hurrying aboard.
(S: children; hv: were; PV: hurrying; adj: The, four, eager; adv: aboard)

8. Again, the weary parents watched.
(S: parents; PV: watched; adj: the, weary; adv: Again)

9. Then, a cheerful stewardess warmly greeted.
(S: stewardess; PV: greeted; adj: a, cheerful; adv: Then, warmly)

10. Suddenly, a brilliant rainbow appeared.
(S: rainbow; PV: appeared; adj: a, brilliant; adv: Suddenly)

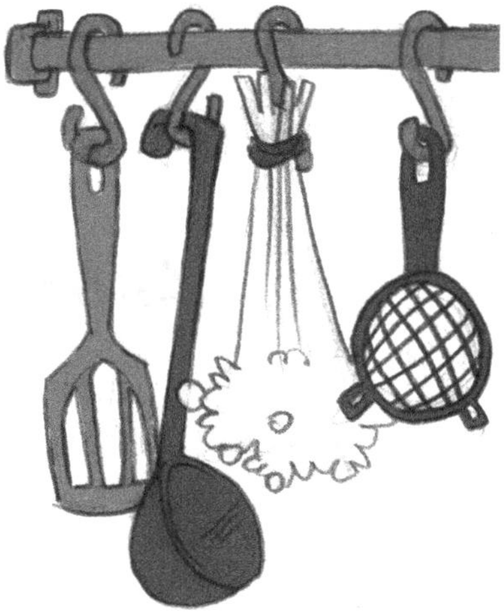

Irene Rutherford McLeod was an Australian-born poet who loved words. In her most famous poem, "Lone Dog," she uses adjectives to describe a courageous, mischievous dog that would rather be a wild dog than a sleek one. Where would you find a dog like this?

Lone Dog

Irene Rutherford McLeod (1891–1968)

keen: sharply eager
lone: alone
bay: howl at

I'm a lean dog, a keen dog, a wild dog, and lone;
I'm a rough dog, a tough dog, hunting on my own;
I'm a bad dog, a mad dog, teasing silly sheep;
I love to sit and bay the moon, to keep fat souls from sleep.

sleek: carefully groomed, with smooth, glossy fur
meek: humble
cringing: shrinking in fright
cuff: a punch with a hand
bide: last a long time or endure
quest: an adventurous search

I'll never be a lap dog, licking dirty feet,
A sleek dog, a meek dog, cringing for my meat,
Not for me the fireside, the well-filled plate,
But shut door, and sharp stone, and cuff and kick, and hate.

Not for me the other dogs, running by my side,
Some have run a short while, but none of them would bide.
O mine is still the lone trail, the hard trail, the best!
Wide wind, and wild stars, and hunger of the quest![2]

Questions to Ponder

1. What does "bay the moon" mean? What else does the dog in the poem do?
2. What happens to the dogs that run with the lone dog?
3. The voice we hear speaking in this poem is the dog's. How does that help you to imagine the life of this dog?

2. Irene Rutherford McLeod, "Lone Dog," in *Favorite Poems Old and New*, ed. Helen Ferris (New York: Doubleday & Company, Inc., 1957), 155–156.

Lesson to Enjoy—Poem
Adjectives

Here is an extra poem for you to enjoy. This poem is like a game or puzzle. It depends on sequential (placed in order) numbers, such as *first*, *second*, and *third*, which are adjectives that help define nouns. Numbers that are used as adjectives and that show place order are called **ordinal**■ **numbers**. Most of them end in *-th*. In the following puzzle poem, see if you can use the adjective clues to figure out the name of a famous person. Best wishes with the riddle. It may be challenging, but without this special kind of adjective—the ordinal number—it would be impossible.

To the Source:
■ **ordinal**
Ordinal comes from the Latin word *ordinalis*, meaning "in order of succession, of an order."

What's My Name?

by Tammy Peters

My first letter is in *woe*, but not in *grief*.
My second letter is in *cattle*, but not in *beef*.
My third letter is in *icicles*, but not in *cold*.
My fourth letter is in *youthful*, but not in *old*.
My fifth letter is in *Jim*, but not in *Kate*.
My sixth letter is in *present*, but not in *late*.
My seventh letter is in *burgeon*, but not in *poor*.
My eighth letter is in *tiling*, but not in *floor*.
My ninth letter is in *opaque*, but not in *black*.
My tenth letter is in *front*, but not in *back*.
What's my name? 'Tis hidden in the letters.
I was once known for my statesman's endeavors.

burgeon: grow quickly, flourish

opaque: not transparent or see-through

endeavors: attempts at difficult things

Answer: Washington

From the Sideline: See Well-Ordered Notes—Poem for some hints for the puzzle poem.

Well-Ordered Notes—Poem

Read

- Read the poem aloud to the students. Show pictures of sleek, meek dogs (e.g., Labrador Retrievers) and lone, wild dogs (e.g., Australian dingoes) while playing a recording of a howling dog (such as the one found here: http://capress.link/wol1arev0501).
- Encourage the students to focus on the poem's intriguing rhythms and sound effects. First, have them clap in time as you read the poem with exaggerated stresses. Next, read the poem aloud again, having the class say "dog" every time the word appears. Point out that the sound effect is similar to barking. Have them identify rhymes and repeated consonant sounds (alliteration).

Retell

- Use the Questions to Ponder as discussion starters:

  1. **What does "bay the moon" mean? What else does the dog in the poem do?**
     "Bay the moon" means "howl at the moon." The dog is like a wolf (or a dingo in Australia), one of the most untamable creatures on earth. In addition to howling, the dog hunts, torments the sheep, welcomes punches/kicks/hate, and runs wildly in an endless adventure. These characteristics are more wolflike than domesticated.

  2. **What happens to the dogs that run with the lone dog?**
     According to the lone dog, even wilder dogs than the domesticated ones he disdains can't keep up with him or long endure his chosen life. They only can run with him for a while. He is the toughest, the wildest.

  3. **The voice we hear speaking in this poem is the dog's. How does that help you to imagine the life of this dog?**
     Answers to this question will vary. The point is for the students to notice that they are seeing through a dog's perspective. Challenge them with these related questions, for which there are no right or wrong answers: Is the dog really everything it describes itself to be? Or is the dog putting on airs, pretending to be tougher and wilder than it is? Are there any people who would describe themselves as "lone people"—tough and not needing anyone else?

- Have students make a list of the adjectives in the poem that describe *dog* (*lean, keen, wild, lone, rough, tough, bad, mad, lap, sleek, meek, other*).

Record

- Have students copy their favorite of the three stanzas from the poem into their copybook or on lined paper. Ask them to decorate it with a border, such as paw prints.

Puzzle Hint for "What's My Name?"

The clues are in the given words. The first letter is in the woe (w-o-e), but not in grief (g-r-i-e-f). One of those letters will be the first letter. The second letter is in the cattle (c-a-t-t-l-e), but not in beef (b-e-e-f). List on the board the options using the following chart. The answer is in bold in each word.

first	**w**-o-e	g-r-i-e-f
second	c-**a**-t-t-l-e	b-e-e-f
third	i-c-i-c-l-e-**s**	c-o-l-d
forth	y-o-u-t-**h**-f-u-l	o-l-d
fifth	J-**i**-m	K-a-t-e
sixth	p-r-e-s-e-**n**-t	l-a-t-e
seventh	b-u-r-**g**-e-o-n	p-o-o-r
eighth	**t**-i-l-i-n-g	f-l-o-o-r
ninth	**o**-p-a-q-u-e	b-l-a-c-k
tenth	f-r-o-**n**-t	b-a-c-k

Review
Adjectives

ANSWERS

1. Analyze the following sentences.

From the Sideline: The material in the following pages is not included in the student edition. You can find the Review lesson, the Quiz, the extra Sentences for Practice, and the second Lesson to Enjoy in reproducible form in the Extra Practice & Assessments PDF, available for purchase at ClassicalAcademicPress.com.

a. The eager parents watched patiently.
(S: parents; PV: watched; The — adj; eager — adj; patiently — adv)

b. Little dancers twirled merrily around.
(S: dancers; PV: twirled; Little — adj; merrily — adv; around — adv)

c. Nine additional dancers joined in.
(S: dancers; PV: joined; Nine — adj; additional — adj; in — adv)

d. Afterward, the attentive parents clapped loudly.
(S: parents; PV: clapped; Afterward — adv; the — adj; attentive — adj; loudly — adv)

2. On the lines provided, list the *adjectives* from the above sentences. (Do not include article adjectives.)

a. eager

b. little

c. nine

d. additional

e. attentive

3. Fill in each blank below with an adjective that modifies or describes the noun in the sentence. You may choose an adjective from the word bank or think of your own.

Word Bank: speechless, awkward, kind, brave, unsteady, young

Answers may vary.

a. An **unsteady** dancer stumbled awkwardly.

b. The **speechless** audience gasped.

c. Unfortunately, the **young** girl fell.

d. Fortunately, a **kind** gentleman stepped forward.

e. The **brave** dancer landed well.

4. Imagine some of your friends are part of a dance performance and then rewrite sentence *a* from exercise 1 by adding an adjective that tells *how many* eager parents watched patiently.

Eight eager parents watched patiently.

Quiz
Adjectives

ANSWERS

1. Analyze the following sentences.

   S hv PV
   a. The full moon was shining brightly.
   adj adj adv

   S PV
   b. Autumn leaves rustled overhead.
   adj adv

   S PV
   c. Noisily, the forest birds chirped.
   adj adj
   adv

   S PV
   d. Three weary campers listened intently.
   adj adj adv

2. An adjective modifies a noun by answering the questions *how many*, *whose*, *which one*, or *what kind*. On the lines provided, list the *adjectives* from the above sentences. (Do not include article adjectives.)

   a. full
   b. autumn
   c. forest
   d. three
   e. weary

3. Fill in each blank below with an adjective that modifies or describes the noun in the sentence. You may choose an adjective from the word bank or think of your own.

Word Bank: adventurous, nervous, brave, angry, fearful, wobbly

Answers may vary.

a. An ___**angry**___ owl hooted loudly.

b. The ___**nervous**___ boys stirred restlessly.

c. Suddenly, the ___**wobbly**___ tent collapsed.

d. Two ___**fearful**___ campers yelled helplessly.

e. One ___**brave**___ boy crawled out quickly.

4. Imagine you are camping outside on a cool autumn night and then rewrite sentence *c* from exercise 1 by adding an adjective that tells *how many* forest birds chirped noisily.

Noisily, ten forest birds chirped.

Sentences for Practice—Fable
Adjectives

Analyze the following sentences.

1. The pleasant sun shone brightly.
   (S: sun; PV: shone; adj: The, pleasant → sun; adv: brightly → shone)

2. Three young Bulls were feeding merrily together.
   (S: Bulls; hv: were; PV: feeding; adj: Three, young → Bulls; adv: merrily, together → feeding)

3. Hungry Lion watched patiently.
   (S: Lion; PV: watched; adj: Hungry → Lion; adv: patiently → watched)

4. One Bull argued selfishly.
   (S: Bull; PV: argued; adj: One → Bull; adv: selfishly → argued)

5. Another Bull strode away sorrowfully.
   (S: Bull; PV: strode; adj: Another → Bull; adv: away, sorrowfully → strode)

strode: walked with long steps

From the Sideline: These extra practice sentences are a synopsis of the fable "The Young Bulls and a Lion." The fable and the extended lesson notes are on the following pages.

6. The third Bull retreated bitterly.
   - S: Bull; PV: retreated
   - adj: The, third → Bull; adv: bitterly → retreated

7. Three quarrelsome Bulls separated.
   - S: Bulls; PV: separated
   - adj: Three, quarrelsome → Bulls

quarrelsome: likely to argue a lot

8. Slowly, the sly Lion attacked.
   - S: Lion; PV: attacked
   - adj: the, sly → Lion; adv: Slowly → attacked

9. The clever Lion pounced twice.
   - S: Lion; PV: pounced
   - adj: The, clever → Lion; adv: twice → pounced

pounced: jumped and grabbed prey

10. The greedy Lion finally struck thrice.
    - S: Lion; PV: struck
    - adj: The, greedy → Lion; adv: finally → struck; adv: thrice → struck

thrice: three times

Lesson to Enjoy—Fable
Adjectives

Friendship is like glue. When friends are getting along and caring for one another, the "stickiness" of the glue keeps them together. Yet when everyone is at odds with one another, the "stickiness" loses its ability to stick. In other words, the friends don't act like friends, and they could hurt others. Being divided is the opposite of being united. In this next fable, Aesop warns that a lion can best devour his prey when they are divided among themselves.

Three Young Bulls and a Lion

by Aesop

A Lion was watching three young Bulls feeding in an open field. He tried to attack them several times, but they kept together and helped each other to drive him off. The Lion had little hope of eating them because he was no match for three strong Bulls with their sharp horns and hoofs. But he could not keep away from that field, for it is hard to resist watching a good meal, even when there is little chance of getting it.

Then one day the young Bulls quarreled over which one of them should eat a patch of sweet clover. They pawed the ground angrily, butted each other, and scratched each other with their horns. When the hungry Lion came to look at them and lick his chops, he found them in separate corners of the field, as far away from one another as they could get.

It was now an easy matter for the Lion to attack them one at a time. He ate all three young Bulls with the greatest satisfaction and relish.

Moral: In unity is strength.[1]

1. Aesop, "Three Young Bulls and a Lion," taken from *Writing & Rhetoric Book 1: Fable* by Paul Kortepeter (Camp Hill, PA: Classical Academic Press, 2013), 15.

Questions to Ponder

1. What does the Lion in the story want? Why can't he get it at first?
2. What are the young Bulls quarreling over?
3. How does the Lion get what he wants?

Well-Ordered Notes—Fable

Read

- Read the fable to the students and show them pictures of young bulls and a lion to help them enjoy this as story time.
- Have the students act out the fable. Choose volunteers to play the parts of the bulls, the lion, and narrator. Have the rest of the students be the fence. Have the students act out the fable several times, changing the characters each time, so everyone will get a turn to have a part.

Retell

- Use the Questions to Ponder as discussion starters:
  1. **What does the Lion in the story want? Why can't he get it at first?**
     The Lion wants to eat the Bulls. As long as the Bulls stay in a group, he does not attack them because he knows together they could fight him off. They are safe as long as they get along with each other and cooperate.
  2. **What are the young Bulls quarreling over?**
     They quarrel over which of them should have the best clover to eat. Encourage the students to think of adjectives that describe them: angry, greedy, selfish, foolish.
  3. **How does the Lion get what he wants?**
     Once the angry Bulls desert each other, they are easy prey for the Lion. In disunity, they are weak. Challenge the students to think about specific ways they can be united with each other. What are possible consequences when they are not unified?
- Have the students reread the fable, looking for adjectives. Focus on the adjectives that answer the questions *how many* or *what kind* as they modify nouns: e.g., *three* bulls, *young* bulls, *open* field, *several* times, *little* hope, *strong* bulls, *sharp* horns and hoofs, *good* meal, *little* chance, *one* day, *sweet* clover, *hungry* Lion, *greatest* satisfaction.

Record

- Have the students think of another moral to conclude the fable (e.g., United we stand, divided we fall; A kingdom divided against itself cannot stand; A scattered army claims no victory). Have the students share their morals with the other students. Write the different options on the board and have the students choose one to use for their copybook.

Notes

Sentence Bank

These four additional sentences are for extra practice if needed. The scripts are provided for your reference as you model the marking on the board while the students analyze the sentences aloud.

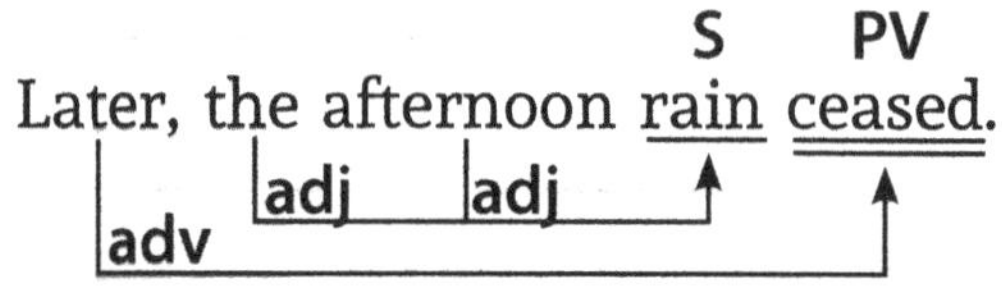

a. (First, read the sentence aloud.) "Later, the afternoon rain ceased."

b. "This is a sentence because it is a group of words that expresses a complete thought. It is a declarative sentence because it makes a statement."

c. "This sentence is about *rain.*" (Underline the subject.) "So, *rain* is the subject because it is what the sentence is about." (Place a capital letter *S* above the subject.)

d. "This sentence tells us that rain *ceased.*" (Double underline the predicate.) "So, *ceased* is the predicate because it is what the sentence tells us about *rain.*" (Place a capital letter *P* above the action verb.) "It is a predicate verb because it shows action." (Place a capital letter *V* to the right of the *P*.) "There is no linking verb because predicate verbs do not need linking verbs."

e. (Continue the analysis of the sentence, starting at the far right side and moving toward the left.) "*Afternoon* tells us *what kind* of rain." (Draw a straight line down from the adjective, then a horizontal line toward the word that it modifies, and then a straight line with an arrow pointing to the word it modifies.)

f. "So, *afternoon* is an adjectival element because it modifies a noun. It is an adjective." (Write *adj* in lowercase letters in the elbow opposite the line with the arrow.)

g. "*The* tells us *which* rain." (Draw a straight line down from the adjective, then a horizontal line toward the word that it modifies and connect the line to the modifying line of the word *afternoon.* The two modifying lines are joined and point, with a straight line, toward the word they modify.)

h. "So, *the* is an adjectival element because it modifies a noun. It is an adjective." (Write *adj* in lowercase letters in the elbow opposite the line with the arrow.)

i. "*Later* tells us *when* the rain ceased." (Draw a straight line down from the adverb, then a horizontal line toward the word that it modifies, and then a straight line with an arrow pointing to the word it modifies. ***Do not connect this adverbial modifying line with the adjectival modifying line.***)

j. "So, *later* is an adverbial element because it modifies a verb. It is an adverb." (Write *adv* in lowercase letters in the elbow opposite the line with the arrow.)

S hv PV
Together tiny crickets were chirping joyfully.
adj adv
adv

a. (First, read the sentence aloud.) "Together tiny crickets were chirping joyfully."

b. "This is a sentence because it is a group of words that expresses a complete thought. It is a declarative sentence because it makes a statement."

c. "This sentence is about *crickets*." (Underline the subject.) "So, *crickets* is the subject because it is what the sentence is about." (Place a capital letter *S* above the subject.)

d. "This sentence tells us that crickets *were chirping*." (Double underline the predicate.) "So, *were chirping* is the predicate because it is what the sentence tells us about *crickets*." (Place a capital letter *P* above the action verb.) "It is a predicate verb because it shows action." (Place a capital letter *V* to the right of the *P*.) "There is no linking verb because predicate verbs do not need linking verbs. *Were* is the helping verb because it helps the verb." (Place a lowercase *hv* above the helping verb.)

e. (Continue the analysis of the sentence, starting at the far right side and moving toward the left.) "*Joyfully* tells us *how* crickets were chirping." (Draw a straight line down from the adverb, then a horizontal line toward the word that it modifies, and then a straight line with an arrow pointing to the word it modifies.)

f. "So, *joyfully* is an adverbial element because it modifies a verb. It is an adverb." (Write *adv* in lowercase letters in the elbow opposite the line with the arrow.)

g. "*Tiny* tells us *what kind* of crickets." (Draw a straight line down from the adjective, then a horizontal line toward the word that it modifies, and then a straight line with an arrow pointing to the word it modifies.)

h. "So, *tiny* is an adjectival element because it modifies a noun. It is an adjective." (Write *adj* in lowercase letters in the elbow opposite the line with the arrow.)

i. "*Together* tells us *how* crickets were chirping." (Draw a straight line down from the adverb, then a horizontal line toward the word that it modifies, and then a straight line with an arrow pointing to the word it modifies.)

j. "So, *together* is an adverbial element because it modifies a verb. It is an adverb." (Write *adv* in lowercase letters in the elbow opposite the line with the arrow.)

S hv PV
Five frisky otters were swimming about.
adj adj adv

a. (First, read the sentence aloud.) "Five frisky otters were swimming about."

b. "This is a sentence because it is a group of words that expresses a complete thought. It is a declarative sentence because it makes a statement."

c. "This sentence is about *otters*." (Underline the subject.) "So, *otters* is the subject because it is what the sentence is about." (Place a capital letter *S* above the subject.)

d. "This sentence tells us that otters *were swimming*." (Double underline the predicate.) "So, *were swimming* is the predicate because it is what the sentence tells us about *otters*." (Place a capital letter *P* above the action verb.) "It is a predicate verb because it shows action." (Place a capital letter *V* to the right of the *P*.) "There is no linking verb because predicate verbs do not need linking verbs. *Were* is the helping verb because it helps the verb." (Place a lowercase *hv* above the helping verb.)

e. (Continue the analysis of the sentence, starting at the far right side and moving toward the left.) "*About* tells us *where* otters were swimming." (Draw a straight line down from the adverb, then a horizontal line toward the word that it modifies, and then a straight line with an arrow pointing to the word it modifies.)

f. "So, *about* is an adverbial element because it modifies a verb. It is an adverb." (Write *adv* in lowercase letters in the elbow opposite the line with the arrow.)

g. "*Frisky* tells us *what kind* of otters." (Draw a straight line down from the adjective, then a horizontal line toward the word that it modifies, and then a straight line with an arrow pointing to the word it modifies.)

h. "So, *frisky* is an adjectival element because it modifies a noun. It is an adjective." (Write *adj* in lowercase letters in the elbow opposite the line with the arrow.)

i. "*Five* tells us *how many* otters." (Draw a straight line down from the adjective, then a horizontal line toward the word that it modifies and connect the line to the modifying line of the word *frisky*. The two modifying lines are joined and point, with a straight line, toward the word they modify.)

j. "So, *five* is an adjectival element because it modifies a noun. It is an adjective." (Write *adj* in lowercase letters in the elbow opposite the line with the arrow.)

S PV
The cold autumn rain falls endlessly.
adj adj adj adv

a. (First, read the sentence aloud.) "The cold autumn rain falls endlessly."

b. "This is a sentence because it is a group of words that expresses a complete thought. It is a declarative sentence because it makes a statement."

c. "This sentence is about *rain*." (Underline the subject.) "So, *rain* is the subject because it is what the sentence is about." (Place a capital letter *S* above the subject.)

d. "This sentence tells us that rain *falls*." (Double underline the predicate.) "So, *falls* is the predicate because it is what the sentence tells us about *rain*." (Place a capital letter *P* above the action verb.) "It is a predicate verb because it shows action." (Place a capital letter *V* to the right of the *P*.) "There is no linking verb because predicate verbs do not need linking verbs."

e. (Continue the analysis of the sentence, starting at the far right side and moving toward the left.) "*Endlessly* tells us *how* rain falls." (Draw a straight line down from the adverb, then a horizontal line toward the word that it modifies, and then a straight line with an arrow pointing to the word it modifies.)

f. "So, *endlessly* is an adverbial element because it modifies a verb. It is an adverb." (Write *adv* in lowercase letters in the elbow opposite the line with the arrow.)

g. "*Autumn* tells us *what kind* of rain." (Draw a straight line down from the adjective, then a horizontal line toward the word that it modifies, and then a straight line with an arrow pointing to the word it modifies.)

h. "So, *autumn* is an adjectival element because it modifies a noun. It is an adjective." (Write *adj* in lowercase letters in the elbow opposite the line with the arrow.)

i. "*Cold* tells us *what kind* of rain." (Draw a straight line down from the adjective, then a horizontal line toward the word that it modifies and connect the line to the modifying line of the word *autumn*. The two modifying lines are joined and point, with a straight line, toward the word they modify.)

j. "So, *cold* is an adjectival element because it modifies a noun. It is an adjective." (Write *adj* in lowercase letters in the elbow opposite the line with the arrow.)

k. "*The* tells us *which* rain." (Draw a straight line down from the adjective, then a horizontal line toward the word that it modifies and connect the line to the modifying line of the words *cold* and *autumn*. The three modifying lines are joined and point, with a straight line, toward the word they modify.)

l. "So, *the* is an adjectival element because it modifies a noun. It is an adjective." (Write *adj* in lowercase letters in the elbow opposite the line with the arrow.)

REX

From the Sideline: Expect the best work. Teach your students to do their work neatly and carefully. We use the phrase, "Please be neat and petite."

[A]Bring in a clock or a picture of the inner workings of a clock. You can use it to explain the interconnectedness of the parts of a sentence.

Chapter 6

Direct Objects[A]

Have you ever wondered how an old grandfather clock, with its wheels and dials, works? If you look at a clock's manual, you will see many parts listed and labeled: suspension spring, pendulum bob, fork, pallet, escape wheel, ratchet wheel, spindle, pinion, and drum. Each part works exactly and correctly with the other parts to tell time. If just one cog is out of position, the rhythm of the clock is thrown off and it will not work properly. The parts of a sentence are similar to the parts of a clock: just as the clock's parts work together to tell time, the principal elements and modifiers of a sentence work together to convey meaning.

While the logic that makes our language tick is fairly simple, there is still more for us to learn about it. Let's take another look at the predicate verb and see what else we can discover. Some predicate verbs are complete in their action, such as "Winston sits." This sentence needs nothing else. Winston is doing the sitting, but no person or thing receives that action. The questions *Winston sits what?* or *Winston sits whom?* are nonsense. Other verbs are incomplete without an additional word—an **object**. The object names the person or thing that directly receives the action of the verb. In other words, the verb has a partial, or incomplete, meaning without something or someone completing its action, such as "Winston fixes clocks." The word *clocks* is *what* Winston fixes. It is the object of Winston's fixing. This type of object, which directly receives the action of the verb, is called a **direct object**■ and it is an important part of what makes a sentence work.

Let's take apart the clock of language and see how a predicate verb operates with a direct object.

To the Source:
■ object
The word *object* comes from the Latin word *obicio*, meaning "I throw toward," from *ob-*, "toward, to," and *iacio*, "I throw."

From the Sideline: If your students are studying Latin, point out to them that the accusative case of a noun is used for the direct object of a transitive verb in a sentence.

From the Sideline: Write on the board the excerpt from the poem "Of a Spider" by Wilfrid Thorley. The entire poem is available in The Curious Child's Literary Appendix. Note that it's a short poem, so you could read it with your students before discussing the passage and discuss briefly with them what the spider is doing.

Ideas to Understand

Look closely at the first four lines of the poem "Of a Spider" by Wilfrid Thorley. If you take apart what makes them tick, you will find a direct object in the first line.

> The spider weaves his silver wire
> Between the cherry and the brier.
>
> He runs along and sees the thread
> Well-fastened on each hawser-head.[1]

brier: prickly bush

hawser-head: the top of a small cable

Do you see the direct object in the first stanza? *Wire* tells *what* the spider weaves, and thus *wire* completes the meaning of the verb *weaves*, making it the direct object. A direct object tells what the subject is acting on. It is a noun or pronoun that comes after a verb. It answers the question *what* or *whom* in a sentence.

Can you find another direct object in these opening lines from "Of a Spider"? *Thread* is the direct object of the verb *sees. He sees* what? *He sees the thread.*

While you were examining the lines of the poem, did you also find another verb? That's right: The verb *runs* is in the third line. But where is its direct object? What noun is receiving its action? *He runs* what? or *He runs* whom? In this instance, this verb has no direct object because it is complete without one. The adverb *along* tells where the spider runs, but it does not receive the action as the noun *wire* receives the action of *weaves*. The adverb *along* does not answer the question *what* or *whom*.

Weaves and *runs* in "Of a Spider" are two different kinds of verbs. One needs a direct object, and the other does not. In order to understand direct objects better, you need to know the four verb classes, which are **transitive▪ verbs**, **intransitive▪ verbs**, helping verbs, and linking verbs. Verbs are divided into these four classes based on their meaning and their use.

To the Source: ▪ transitive
The word *transitive* comes from the Latin *transire*, meaning "to cross." A transitive verb makes a transition from the subject to the direct object.

To the Source: ▪ intransitive
The Latin stem *in*, meaning "not," is added to *transire* (remember, that means "to cross"), so intransitive verbs do not cross—they do not make a transition to something else. They are complete on their own.

A *transitive verb* takes an **objective element**, which is a word (or a group of words) that tells us what or whom the subject is acting on in a sentence. For example, in the following sentence, *what* did the spider weave?

1. Wilfrid Thorley, "Of a Spider," in *Favorite Poems Old and New*, ed. Helen Ferris (New York: Doubleday & Company, Inc., 1957), 141–142.

The spider *weaves* a wire.

The spider weaves a *wire*, which means that *wire* is the direct object. Transitive verbs, such as *weaves* in this sentence, always have direct objects.

An *intransitive verb* is a predicate verb, but it does not have an objective element. If you ask *what* or *whom* after an intransitive verb, you find no answer in the sentence. The action is complete without an object. Take a look at the following sentence:

The spider *runs*.

The sentence is complete in itself. Intransitive verbs, such as *runs* in this sentence, do not have direct objects.

A *helping verb* (or auxiliary verb) helps another verb express its meaning. It is placed alongside a transitive, linking, or intransitive verb to form a verb phrase. Both words work together as one action. Which of the two verbs in the following sentence is the helping verb?

The spider is weaving the thread.

The verb *is* is the helping verb. It works together with *weaving* as one unit. Together they represent a simple predicate because they explain what the sentence tells about the spider. A sentence that includes a helping verb may or may not have a direct object, depending on whether or not it is placed alongside a transitive verb.

A *linking verb* joins the subject to the predicate. In other words, it is the glue that joins the subject either to a noun that renames the subject or to an adjective that describes the subject. Linking verbs express a state of being. Can you find the linking verbs in the following sentences?

The spider was an orb-weaver.

The spider was black.

The verb *was* is the linking verb in both sentences. You could almost replace *was* with an equals sign: *spider = orb-weaver* and *spider = black*. We will discuss linking verbs in detail in *Well-Ordered Language Level 2*. For now, let us point out that linking verbs do not have direct objects. *Orb-weaver* and *black* are not direct objects because they do not receive the action of a transitive verb; instead, they rename or describe the subject.

From the Sideline: Some words in the list of helping verbs can function as transitive verbs (*have, has, had, do, did, does*) as in *The spider **has** a web*. Others can function as linking verbs (*am, is, are, was, were, be, being, been*) as in *The spider **was** black*. Identifying a particular verb's class depends on understanding its meaning and use. Such distinctions will be explored further in *WOL Level 2*.

Moment for Mechanics

Some verbs can be either transitive or intransitive depending on how they are used in a sentence. If the verb is behaving as a *transitive* verb, the sentence will have a direct object that answers the question *what* or *whom*. If the verb is behaving as an *intransitive* verb, the sentence will not include a word that answers either of those questions.

- Winston *reads* the clock manual quietly. [Winston reads *what*? Manual.]
- Winston *reads* quietly. [The adverb *quietly* tells *how* Winston reads, not *what*.]

Some verbs are usually transitive and require a direct object.

- Winston *bought* a new book. [Winston bought *what*? Book.]
- Winston *bought*. [The verb doesn't make sense without an object.]

On the other hand, some verbs are usually intransitive and never take a direct object.

- Winston *sits*. [The verb completes the thought. An object would make no sense.]

[B] For the lyrics to all of the songs, please see the Song Lyrics section on page 191. Play the appropriate audio tracks and have students sing/chant along. Students should commit the songs to memory.

Terms to Remember[B]

Knowing about the different classes of verbs helps you understand direct objects better. Notice that the following definition of a direct object includes the terms *objective element* and *transitive verb*.

NEW! **Direct Object** *(1–9)*

NEW! **Four Classes of Verbs** *(1–10)*

Sentences to Analyze

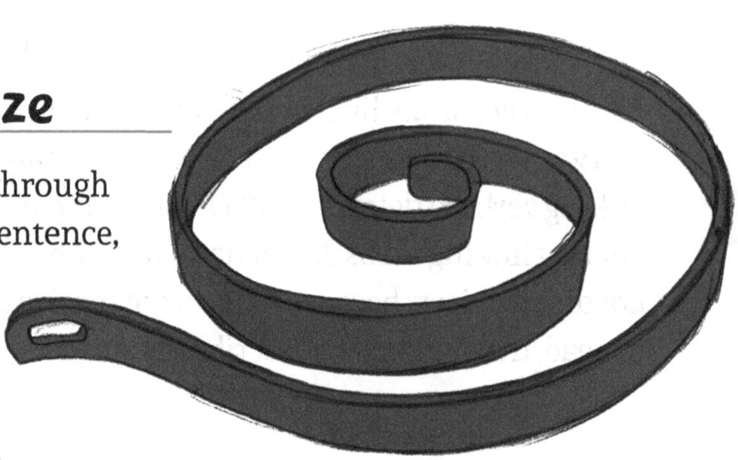

As your teacher leads you through the analysis of the following sentence, you will notice a slight change because a transitive verb is present. You will still need to identify the subject and then the predicate first. Then you are to identify the direct object. The sentence is already marked in your book, so you can watch your teacher closely as you speak the words expressively.

S PV
Spiders weave webs.
do

a. (First, read the sentence aloud.) "Spiders weave webs."

b. "This is a sentence, and it is declarative."

c. "This sentence is about *spiders*. So, *spiders* is the subject because it is what the sentence is about." (Since *spiders* is the subject, underline it and place a capital letter *S* above it.)

d. "This sentence tells us that spiders *weave*. So, *weave* is the predicate because it is what the sentence tells us about *spiders*." (Since *weave* tells something about *spiders*, double underline the predicate and a capital letter *P* above it.)

e. "It is a predicate verb because it shows action. There is no linking verb because predicate verbs do not need linking verbs." (Since *weave* shows action, place a capital letter *V* to the right of the letter *P*.)

f. (Pause and think about *what* or *whom* would complete the verb before identifying the objective element.) "*Webs* tells us *what* spiders weave." (Since *webs* tells us *what* spiders weave, draw a circle around it.)

g. "So, *webs* is an objective element because it completes the meaning of an action verb. It is a direct object because it tells *what* spiders weave." (Write *do* in lowercase letters beneath the direct object.)

Order is key when analyzing sentences. For a sentence like the following, which includes a helping verb and modifiers, you first identify the principal elements and then the direct object, if present. After that, you identify each adverb and adjective starting at the end of the sentence and working toward the front. Follow these steps to analyze the sentence with your teacher's guidance.

From the Sideline: Model the steps of the analysis on the board for the students. The repetition is important for learning the relationships among the words in the sentences. Use the parenthetical directions for guidance, and speak the words in quotation marks in chorus with the students. As each chapter adds a grammatical element to analyze, you will notice that the students have an increasingly sophisticated grasp of the process. Therefore, the script is condensed or streamlined in places.

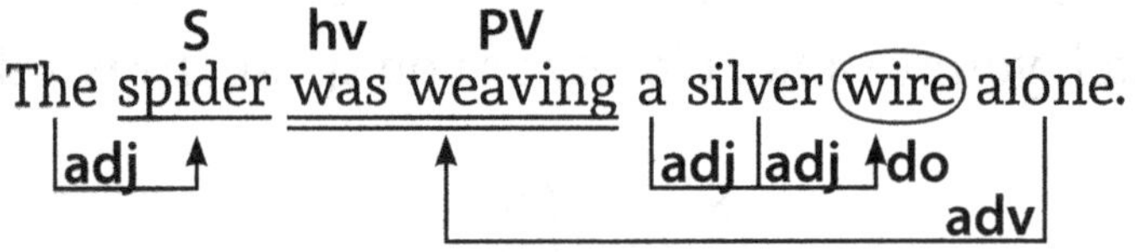

a. (Read the sentence first aloud.) "The spider was weaving a silver wire alone."

b. "This is a sentence and it is declarative."

c. "This sentence is about *spider*. So, *spider* is the subject because it is what the sentence is about." (Since *spider* is the subject, underline it and place a capital letter *S* above the subject.)

d. "This sentence tells us that spider *was weaving*. So, *was weaving* is the predicate because it is what the sentence tells us about *spider*." (Since *weaving* tells us something about *spider*, double underline the predicate, including the helping verb, and place a capital letter *P* above the action verb.)

e. "It is a predicate verb because it shows action. There is no linking verb because predicate verbs do not need linking verbs." (Since *weaving* shows action, place a capital letter *V* to the right of the *P*.)

f. "*Was* is the helping verb because it helps the verb." (Place the lowercase letters *hv* above the helping verb.)

g. (Before identifying the objective element, pause and think about *what* or *whom* would complete the verb.) "*Wire* tells us *what* spider was weaving." (Since *wire* tells us *what* spider was weaving, draw a circle around it.)

h. "So, *wire* is an objective element because it completes the meaning of an action verb. It is a direct object because it tells us *what* spider was weaving." (Write *do* in lowercase letters underneath the direct object.)

i. "*Alone* tells us *how* spider was weaving." (Draw a straight line down from the adverb, then a horizontal line toward the word that it modifies, and then a straight line with an arrow pointing to the word it modifies.)

j. "So, *alone* is an adverbial element because it modifies a verb. It is an adverb." (Write *adv* in lowercase letters in the elbow opposite the line with the arrow.)

k. "*Silver* tells us *what kind* of wire." (Draw a straight line down from the adjective, then a horizontal line toward the word that it modifies, and then a straight line with an arrow pointing to the word it modifies.)

l. "So, *silver* is an adjectival element because it modifies a noun. It is an adjective." (Write *adj* in lowercase letters in the elbow opposite the line with the arrow.)

m. "*A* tells us *how many* wires." (Draw a straight line down from the adjective, then a horizontal line toward the word that it modifies. Connect this modifier line with the modifier line for *silver* since both adjectival elements are modifying *wire.*)

n. "So, *a* is an adjectival element because it modifies a noun. It is an adjective." (Write *adj* in lowercase letters in the elbow opposite the line with the arrow.)

o. "*The* tells us *which* spider." (Draw a straight line down from the adjective, then a horizontal line toward the word that it modifies, and then a straight line with an arrow pointing to the word it modifies.)

p. "So, *the* is an adjectival element because it modifies a noun. It is an adjective." (Write *adj* in lowercase letters in the elbow opposite the line with the arrow.)

An old grandfather clock counts away the hours with efficiency and stands in the corner of a room looking majestic. It does its job, and it does it beautifully. We hardly ever think about how it works. It is the same with sentences. You use subjects, verbs of all sorts, and modifiers nearly every time you speak. You use them efficiently and beautifully to communicate meaning. Just as it is captivating to look behind the clock's face and see the mechanism that makes it work, it can be fascinating to examine the grammar that makes your sentences tick.

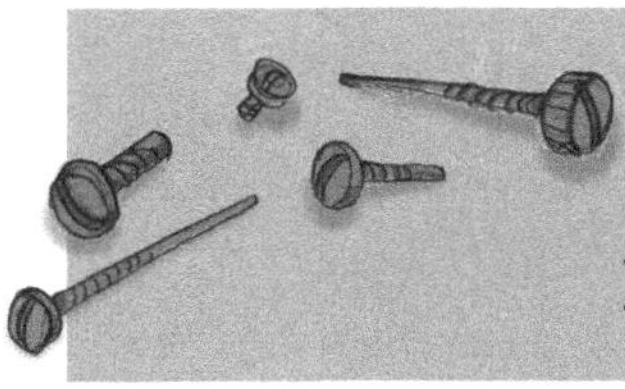

Take a look at the illustration at the beginning of this chapter. Which piece is considered the face of the clock? Can you find the two hands? How many screws do you see?

Well-Ordered Notes A

Review It

Review the following:

What are the four kinds of sentences?
What are the eight parts of speech?
What is a noun?
What is a direct object?

Practice It

Lead the students in Stage a Sentence, an interactive activity that reinforces their understanding of transitive verbs. For each of the following sentences, select enough students to represent each word. For example, in the sentence "Winston studies autumn birds," four students are needed: one student to hold the card for the word *Winston*, one to hold the word *studies*, one to hold the word *autumn*, and one to hold the word *birds*. Discuss whether the verb in the sentence is transitive or intransitive. Help the students to see the placement of the direct object (e.g., *birds*) completes the meaning of the action verb by answering *what* or *whom*, making the verb a transitive verb (e.g., *studies* is transitive). If the sentence has an intransitive verb, emphasize that there is no word that answers *what* or *whom*, so there is no direct object. For example, in the sentence "Winston studies carefully," three students would stand, each holding a word card: one to hold the word *Winston*, one to hold the word *studies*, and one to hold the word *carefully*. Help the students to see that *carefully* is an adverb and there is no direct object, so the verb is an intransitive verb in this sentence.

Fewer than Five: Adapt the activity by creating color-coded cards. Write each word of each sentence in the same color (e.g., sentence 1 is red; sentence 2 is blue, etc.). Mix the cards up. Have the student(s) sort the cards into piles according to color and then unscramble them to make complete sentences. Discuss which sentences have transitive verbs and which have intransitive verbs.

Example:
Winston studies autumn birds. (transitive verb)
Winston studies carefully. (intransitive verb)

1. Some autumn birds migrate south. (intransitive verb)
2. Winston carefully watched the barn swallows. (transitive verb)
3. Swallows often swoop low. (intransitive verb)
4. These lively birds are eating pesky insects. (transitive verb)
5. Many birds restlessly gather together. (intransitive verb)
6. Winston spotted a wayward flock. (transitive verb)

Analyze It

From the Sideline: Visit http://capress.link/wol1att for a video demonstration of analysis.

Now, as a class, analyze the four sentences in the lesson. Here is the script for the first one to help you lead the choral analysis and model the markings on the board. The words in parentheses are like stage directions to guide you and are not to be spoken. The words in gray and enclosed in quotation marks are for you and the students to speak in chorus.

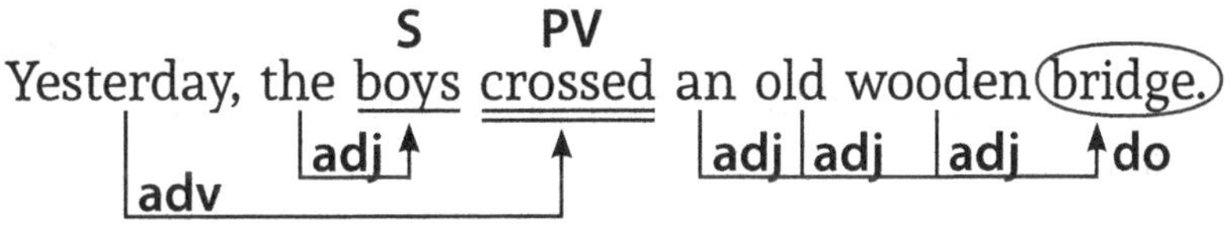

a. (First, read the sentence aloud.) "Yesterday, the boys crossed an old wooden bridge."

b. "This is a sentence and it is declarative."

c. "This sentence is about *boys*." (Underline the subject.) "So, *boys* is the subject because it is what the sentence is about." (Place a capital letter *S* above the subject.)

d. "This sentence tells us that boys *crossed*." (Double underline the predicate.) "So, *crossed* is the predicate because it is what the sentence tells us about *boys*." (Place a capital letter *P* above the action verb.)

e. "It is a predicate verb because it shows action. There is no linking verb because predicate verbs do not need linking verbs." (Place a capital letter *V* to the right of the *P*.)

f. (Before identifying the objective element, pause and think about *what* or *whom* would complete the verb.) "*Bridge* tells us *what* the boys crossed." (Draw a circle around the word.)

g. "So, *bridge* is an objective element that completes the meaning of the action verb. It is a direct object because it tells us *what* the boys crossed." (Write *do* in lowercase letters underneath the direct object.)

h. "*Wooden* tells us *what kind* of bridge." (Draw a straight line down from the adjective, then a horizontal line toward the word that it modifies, and then a straight line with an arrow pointing to the word it modifies.)

i. "So, *wooden* is an adjectival element because it modifies a noun. It is an adjective." (Write *adj* in lowercase letters in the elbow opposite the line with the arrow.)

j. "*Old* tells us *what kind* of bridge." (Draw a straight line down from the adjective, then a horizontal line toward the word that it modifies, and connect this modifier line with the modifier line for *wooden* since both adjectival elements are modifying *bridge*.)

k. "So, *old* is an adjectival element because it modifies a noun. It is an adjective." (Write *adj* in lowercase letters in the elbow opposite the line with the arrow.)

l. "*An* tells us *how many* bridges." (Draw a straight line down from the adjective, then a horizontal line toward the word that it modifies, and connect this modifier line with the modifier line for *old* and *wooden* since they are adjectival elements modifying *bridge*.)

m. "So, *an* is an adjectival element because it modifies a noun. It is an adjective." (Write *adj* in lowercase letters in the elbow opposite the line with the arrow.)

n. "*The* tells us *which* boys." (Draw a straight line down from the adjective, then draw a horizontal line toward the word that it modifies, and then a straight line with an arrow pointing to the word it modifies.)

o. "So, *the* is an adjectival element because it modifies a noun. It is an adjective." (Write *adj* in lowercase letters in the elbow opposite the line with the arrow.)

p. "*Yesterday* tells us *when* the boys crossed." (Draw a straight line down from the adverb, then a horizontal line toward the word that it modifies, and then a straight line with an arrow pointing to the word it modifies.)

q. "So, *yesterday* is an adverbial element because it modifies a verb. It is an adverb." (Write *adv* in lowercase letters in the elbow opposite the line with the arrow.)

From the Sideline: For extra guided practice, refer to the Sentence Bank at the end of this chapter.

Notes

Lesson to Learn
Direct Objects

1. Analyze the following sentences.

   a. S: boys, PV: crossed
   Yesterday, the boys crossed an old wooden (bridge).
   adv, adj, adj, adj, adj, do

   b. S: Winston, PV: helped
   Winston helped the (guys) along.
   adj, do, adv

   c. S: Fritz, PV: found
   Suddenly, Fritz found a small (nest).
   adv, adj, adj, do

   d. S: boys, hv: did, PV: disturb
   The three boys did not disturb the tiny (home).
   adj, adj, adv, adj, adj, do

2. On the lines provided, list all the *nouns* from the above sentences.

a. boys	b. bridge
c. Winston	d. guys
e. Fritz	f. nest
g. boys	h. home

From the Sideline:
Remember that when you see the word *analyze* in instructions throughout this book, we mean both choral analysis and written notations. The two go hand in hand as a prediagramming system.

3. The order of words is important for understanding the meaning of a sentence. Unscramble the following sentences. Remember that adverbs can show up in different places and still make sense. **Answers may vary.**

Example:
tuna not the want Fritz sandwich did **Fritz did not want the tuna sandwich.**

a. along brought few Winston sandwiches a **Winston brought a few sandwiches along. OR: Winston brought along a few sandwiches.**

b. butter away Winston the gave sandwich peanut **Winston gave the peanut butter sandwich away. OR: Winston gave away the peanut butter sandwich.**

c. alone two sandwiches boy ham ate one **One boy ate two ham sandwiches alone. OR: Alone, one boy ate two ham sandwiches. OR One boy alone ate two ham sandwiches.**

d. three eagerly oatmeal friends cookies the shared **The three friends eagerly shared oatmeal cookies. OR: Eagerly, the three friends shared oatmeal cookies.**

4. What questions does a *direct object* answer? (Answer using a complete sentence.)

Direct objects answer the questions *what* or *whom*.

5. Imagine some boys exploring the woods, and then write a sentence about it, being sure to include a *direct object* in it.

The boys found a nest.

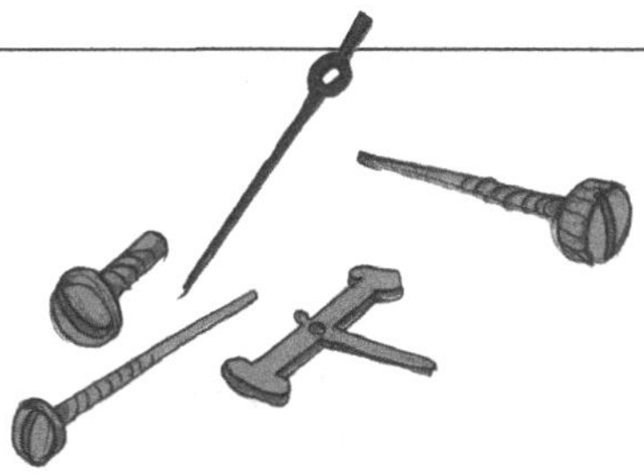

Well-Ordered Notes B

Review It

Review the following:

What is a verb?
What are the twenty-three helping verbs?
What are the four classes of verbs?
What s an adverb?

Practice It

Lead the students in What Makes Sense, an activity in which they construct sentences that include direct objects. Write the following transitive verbs on Popsicle sticks and place them in a container. Have a volunteer draw the first stick and read the verb aloud (e.g., *crack*). Have each student construct a sentence on scrap paper by adding a subject and direct object to the chosen verb (e.g., "Isaac cracks eggs."). They should feel free to change the form or the tense of the verb. Have three students share their sentence (e.g., "Isaac cracks eggs."). Continue with the other popsicle sticks. This activity can be either oral or written.

Example: "Crack" (a chosen popsicle stick word)
Student 1: "Isaac *cracks* eggs."
Student 2: "The boys *are cracking* jokes outside."
Student 3: "Elise *cracked* the glass bowl."

Suggested transitive verbs: crack, spin, shake, break, mix, blend, turn, toss, stop, chop, bump, cook

Analyze It

Now, as a class, analyze the four sentences in the lesson. Here is the script for the first one to help you lead the choral analysis and model the markings on the board. The words in parentheses are like stage directions to guide you and are not to be spoken. The words in gray and enclosed in quotation marks are for you and the students to speak in chorus.

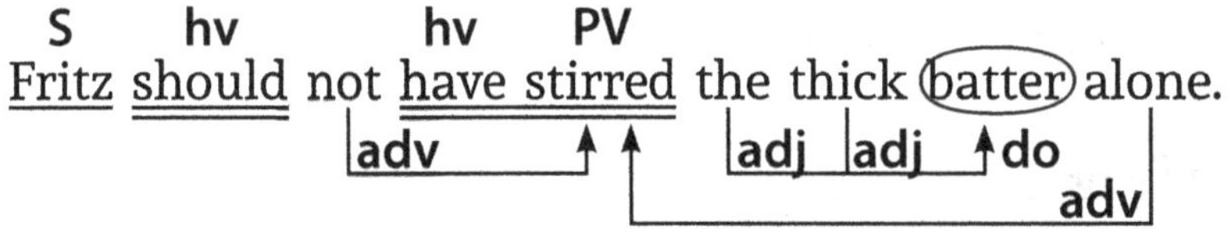

a. (First, read the sentence aloud.) "Fritz should not have stirred the thick batter alone."

b. "This is a sentence and it is declarative."

c. "This sentence is about *Fritz*." (Underline the subject.) "So, *Fritz* is the subject because it is what the sentence is about." (Place a capital letter *S* above the subject.)

d. "This sentence tells us that Fritz *should have stirred*." (Double underline the predicate.) "So, *should have stirred* is the predicate because it is what the sentence tells us about *Fritz*." (Place a capital letter *P* above the action verb.)

e. "It is a predicate verb because it shows action. There is no linking verb because predicate verbs do not need linking verbs." (Place a capital letter *V* to the right of the *P*.)

f. "*Should have* are helping verbs because they help the verb." (Place a lowercase *hv* above both helping verbs.)

g. (Before identifying the objective element, pause and think about *what* or *whom* would complete the verb.) "*Batter* tells us *what* Fritz should have stirred." (Draw a circle around the word.)

h. "So, *batter* is an objective element because it completes the meaning of the action verb. It is a direct object because it tells us *what* Fritz should have stirred." (Write *do* in lowercase letters beneath the direct object.)

i. "*Alone* tells us *how* Fritz should have stirred." (Draw a straight line down from the adverb, then a horizontal line toward the word that it modifies, and then a straight line with an arrow pointing to the word it modifies.)

j. "So, *alone* is an adverbial element because it modifies a verb. It is an adverb." (Write *adv* in lowercase letters in the elbow opposite the line with the arrow.)

k. "*Thick* tells us *what kind* of batter." (Draw a straight line down from the adjective, then a horizontal line toward the word that it modifies, and then a straight line with an arrow pointing to the word it modifies.)

l. "So, *thick* is an adjectival element because it modifies a noun. It is an adjective." (Write *adj* in lowercase letters in the elbow opposite the line with the arrow.)

m. "*The* tells us *which* batter." (Draw a straight line down from the adjective, then a horizontal line toward the word that it modifies, and connect this modifier line with the modifier line for *thick* since both adjectival elements are modifying *batter*.)

n. "So, *the* is an adjectival element because it modifies a noun. It is an adjective." (Write *adj* in lowercase letters in the elbow opposite the line with the arrow.)

o. "*Not* tells us *how* Fritz should have stirred." (Draw a straight line down from the adverb, then a horizontal line toward the word that it modifies, and then a straight line with an arrow pointing to the word it modifies.)

p. "So, *not* is an adverbial element because it modifies a verb. It is an adverb." (Write *adv* in lowercase letters in the elbow opposite the line with the arrow.)

Lesson to Learn
Direct Objects

B

1. Analyze the following sentences.

    a. Fritz should not have stirred the thick batter alone.
    (S: Fritz; hv: should; hv: have; PV: stirred; adv: not; adj: the; adj: thick; do: batter; adv: alone)

    b. The youngster wanted blueberry pancakes.
    (S: youngster; PV: wanted; adj: The; adj: blueberry; do: pancakes)

    c. Fritz will now use the electric mixer.
    (S: Fritz; hv: will; PV: use; adv: now; adj: the; adj: electric; do: mixer)

    d. Afterward, Rex licked the sticky floor.
    (S: Rex; PV: licked; adv: Afterward; adj: the; adj: sticky; do: floor)

2. On the lines provided, list all the *nouns* from the above sentences.

a. Fritz	b. batter
c. youngster	d. pancakes
e. Fritz	f. mixer
g. Rex	h. floor

3. Read each sentence carefully and decide whether the verb is transitive or intransitive. Circle the correct response. Keep in mind that some verbs can be either transitive or intransitive depending on whether or not there is a direct object in the sentence.

a. An inventor once watched a baker.	(transitive)	intransitive
b. The clever man watched closely.	transitive	(intransitive)
c. The baker was stirring quickly.	transitive	(intransitive)
d. Next, the inventor was stirring an idea.	(transitive)	intransitive
e. Later, this man designed the first mixer.	(transitive)	intransitive

4. What questions does a *direct object* answer? (Answer using a complete sentence.)

Direct objects answer the questions *what* or *whom*.

5. Imagine Fritz is preparing breakfast for the family, and then write a sentence about it, being sure to include a *direct object* in it.

Fritz sets the table.

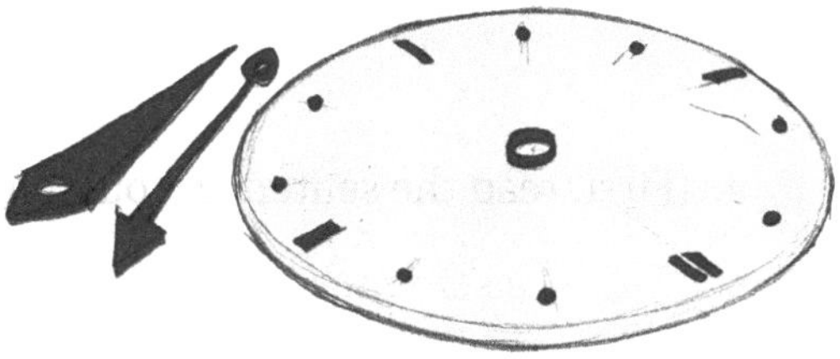

Well-Ordered Notes C

Review It

Review the following:

What are the principal elements?
What is an adverb?
What are the three parts of speech an adverb modifies?
What is an adjective?
What are the two parts of speech an adjective modifies?

Practice It

Lead the students in Lightning to reinforce constructing sentences that have transitive verbs. Have the students stand by their desks. Using the list of verbs below or supplying your own list, give the first student a verb. He then has five seconds to create a sentence by providing a subject and a direct object that go with the verb. Continue with the exercise until all students have had the opportunity to create a sentence.

Example: Teacher: "Crossed"
Student: *"The neighbor kids crossed the street."*

bakes	plants	rakes
expands	makes	shapes
jabs	sketches	rides
eats	discovers	invents

Analyze It

Now, as a class, analyze the four sentences in the lesson. Here is the script for the first one to help you lead the choral analysis and model the markings on the board. The words in parentheses are like stage directions to guide you and are not to be spoken. The words in gray and enclosed in quotation marks are for you and the students to speak in chorus.

S (children) PV (climbed)
The neighbor children climbed the stone wall
adj adj (→ children) adj adj (→ wall) do

a. (First, read the sentence aloud.) "The neighbor children climbed the stone wall."

b. "This is a sentence and it is declarative."

c. "This sentence is about *children.*" (Underline the subject.) "So, *children* is the subject because it is what the sentence is about." (Place a capital letter *S* above the subject.)

d. "This sentence tells us that children *climbed.*" (Double underline the predicate.) "So, *climbed* is the predicate because it is what the sentence tells us about *children.*" (Place a capital letter *P* above the action verb.)

e. "It is a predicate verb because it shows action. There is no linking verb because predicate verbs do not need linking verbs." (Place a capital letter *V* to the right of the *P*.)

f. (Before identifying the objective element, pause and think about what or whom would complete the verb.) "*Wall* tells us *what* children climbed." (Draw a circle around the word.)

g. "So, *wall* is an objective element because it completes the meaning of the action verb. It is a direct object because it tells us *what* children climbed." (Write *do* in lowercase letters underneath the direct object.)

h. "*Stone* tell us *what kind* of wall." (Draw a straight line down from the adjective, then a horizontal line toward the word that it modifies, and then a straight line with an arrow pointing to the word it modifies.)

i. "So, *stone* is an adjectival element because it modifies a noun. It is an adjective." (Write *adj* in lowercase letters in the elbow opposite the line with the arrow.)

j. "*The* tells us *which* wall." (Draw a straight line down from the adjective, then a horizontal line toward the word that it modifies, and connect this modifier line with the modifier line for *stone* since both adjectival elements are modifying *wall.*)

k. "So, *the* is an adjectival element because it modifies a noun. It is an adjective." (Write *adj* in lowercase letters in the elbow opposite the line with the arrow.)

l. "*Neighbor* tells us *what kind* of children." (Draw a straight line down from the adjective, then a horizontal line toward the word that it modifies, and then a straight line with an arrow pointing to the word it modifies.)

m. "So, *neighbor* is an adjectival element because it modifies a noun. It is an adjective." (Write *adj* in lowercase letters in the elbow opposite the line with the arrow.)

n. "*The* tells us *which* children." (Draw a straight line down from the adjective, then a horizontal line toward the word that it modifies, and connect this modifier line with the modifier line for *neighbor* since both adjectival elements are modifying *children.*)

o. "So, *the* is an adjectival element because it modifies a noun. It is an adjective." (Write *adj* in lowercase letters in the elbow opposite the line with the arrow.)

Lesson to Learn
Direct Objects

C

1. Analyze the following sentences.

   S PV
   a. The neighbor children climbed the stone (wall).
   adj adj ↑ adj adj ↑do

   S PV
   b. One parent called the active (children) back.
   adj ↑ ↑ adj adj ↑ do
   adv

   S PV
   c. The six anxious kids quickly jumped down.
   adj adj adj ↑ adv ↑ ↑ adv

   S PV
   d. Suddenly, yellow flashes lit the dark, stormy (sky).
   adj ↑ ↑ adj adj adj ↑do
   adv

2. On the lines provided, list all the *adjectives* from the above sentences. (Do not include article adjectives.)

   a. neighbor
   b. stone
   c. one
   d. active
   e. six
   f. anxious
   g. yellow
   h. dark
   i. stormy

3. Consider what happened when the children were outside watching a storm come. Supply subjects and direct objects for the following sentences. You may need to include article adjectives (*a/an* or *the*) to complete your sentences.

   a. **The boys** saw **the lightning**.

   b. **Winston** called **the boys**.

   c. **Fritz** heard **the thunder**.

   d. **The boys** closed **the door**.

4. What questions does a *direct object* answer? (Answer using a complete sentence.)

   Direct objects answer the questions *what* or *whom*.

5. Imagine wet neighbor children coming inside for cocoa and cookies, and then write a sentence about it, being sure to include a *direct object* in it.

   The children drank cocoa.

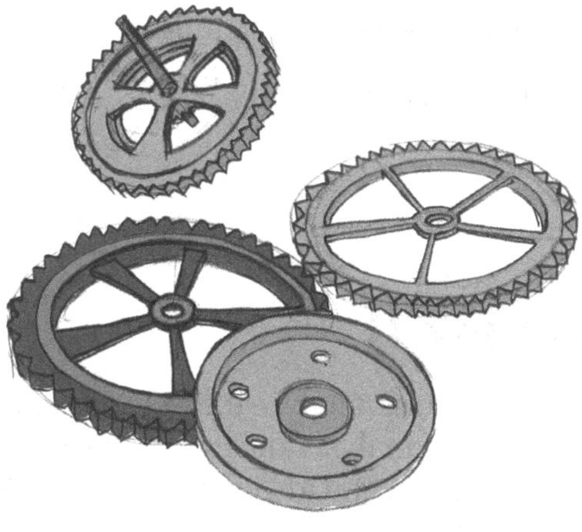

Well-Ordered Notes D

Review It

Review the following:

What is a sentence?
What is a noun?
What is a direct object?
What are the four kinds of sentences?
What are the principal elements?

Practice It

Lead the students in What or Whom, an oral activity in which they complete sentences using direct objects. Have the students stand behind their desks. To the first student, read a sentence with a missing direct object (e.g., "The parents watched *what*?"). The student supplies a direct object that can complete the meaning of the action verb (e.g., *game*), and restates the sentence (e.g., "The parents watched the game."). Then ask the next student to fill in the same sentence but with a person or people (e.g., "The parents watched *whom*?"). The student supplies a direct object (e.g., players), and restates the sentence (e.g., "The parents watched the players.").

Example:
Teacher: "The parents watched *what*?"
Student 1: "What, *game*: The parents watched the *game*."
Teacher: "The parents watched *whom*?"
Student 2: "Whom, *players*: The parents watched the *players*."

1. The soccer coach chose __________ (what: *the mascot*; whom: *Theo*).
2. One player brought extra __________ (what: *water*; whom: *fans*).
3. Several players have __________ (what: *knee pads*; whom: *siblings*).
4. Theo kicks __________ (what: *the ball*; whom: *another player*),
5. Winston was not watching __________ (what: *the game*; whom: *the coach*).
6. The referee signaled __________ (what: *the goal*; whom: *the goalie*).

Analyze It

Now, as a class, analyze the four sentences in the lesson. Here is the script for the first one to help you lead the choral analysis and model the markings on the board. The words in parentheses are like stage directions to guide you and are not to be spoken. The words in gray and enclosed in quotation marks are for you and the students to speak in chorus.

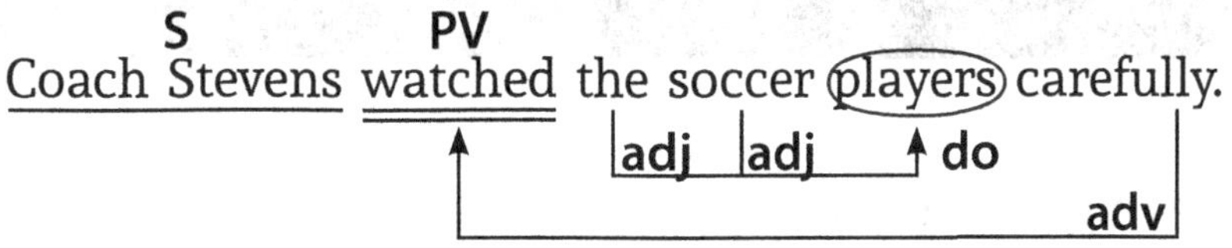

a. (First, read the sentence aloud.) "Coach Stevens watched the soccer players carefully."

b. "This is a sentence and it is declarative."

c. "This sentence is about *Coach Stevens.*" (Underline the subject.) "So, *Coach Stevens* is the subject because it is what the sentence is about." (Place a capital letter *S* above the subject.)

d. "This sentence tells us that Coach Stevens *watched.*" (Double underline the predicate.) "So, *watched* is the predicate because it is what the sentence tells us about *Coach Stevens.*" (Place a capital letter *P* above the action verb.)

e. "It is a predicate verb because it shows action. There is no linking verb because predicate verbs do not need linking verbs." (Place a capital letter *V* to the right of the *P.*)

f. (Before identifying the objective element, pause and think about *what* or *whom* would complete the verb.) "*Players* tells us *what* Coach Stevens watched." (Draw a circle around the word.)

g. "So, *players* is an objective element because it completes the meaning of the action verb. It is a direct object because it tells us *what* Coach Stevens watched." (Write *do* in lowercase letters beneath the direct object.)

h. "*Carefully* tells us *how* Coach Stevens watched." (Draw a straight line down from the adverb, then a horizontal line toward the word that it modifies, and then a straight line with an arrow pointing to the word it modifies.)

i. "So, *carefully* is an adverbial element because it modifies a verb. It is an adverb." (Write *adv* in lowercase letters in the elbow opposite the line with the arrow.)

j. "*Soccer* tells us *what kind* of players." (Draw a straight line down from the adjective, then a horizontal line toward the word that it modifies, and then a straight line with an arrow pointing to the word it modifies.)

k. "So, *soccer* is an adjectival element because it modifies a noun. It is an adjective." (Write *adj* in lowercase letters in the elbow opposite the line with the arrow.)

l. "*The* tells us *which* players." (Draw a straight line down from the adjective, then a horizontal line toward the word that it modifies, and connect this modifier line with the modifier line for *soccer* since both adjectival elements are modifying *players.*)

m. "So, *the* is an adjectival element because it modifies a noun. It is an adjective." (Write *adj* in lowercase letters in the elbow opposite the line with the arrow.)

Lesson to Learn
Direct Objects

1. Analyze the following sentences.

   a. Coach Stevens watched the soccer players carefully.

   S: Coach Stevens; PV: watched; adj: the; adj: soccer; do: players; adv: carefully

   b. The goalie threw the ball overhand.

   S: goalie; PV: threw; adj: The; adj: the; do: ball; adv: overhand

   c. One teammate quickly kicked the ball.

   S: teammate; PV: kicked; adj: One; adv: quickly; adj: the; do: ball

   d. Skillfully, the blue team scored a goal!

   S: team; PV: scored; adv: Skillfully; adj: the; adj: blue; adj: a; do: goal

2. On the lines provided, list all the *nouns* from the above sentences.

   a. Coach Stevens
   b. players
   c. goalie
   d. ball
   e. teammate
   f. ball
   g. team
   h. goal

3. Consider what you would see at the ice cream stand after the soccer game. Supply subjects and direct objects for the following sentences. You may need to include article adjectives (*a*/*an* or *the*) to complete your sentences.

   a. **Winston** chose **a chocolate cone**.

   b. **The man** scooped **the ice cream**.

   c. **Heidi** slurped **a milkshake**.

   d. **Dad** sampled **a Popsicle**.

4. What questions does a *direct object* answer? (Answer using a complete sentence.)

   Direct objects answer the questions *what* or *whom*.

5. Imagine what Winston did during a soccer game, and then write a sentence about it, being sure to include a *direct object* in it. Analyze your sentence.

   Winston dribbled the soccer ball.

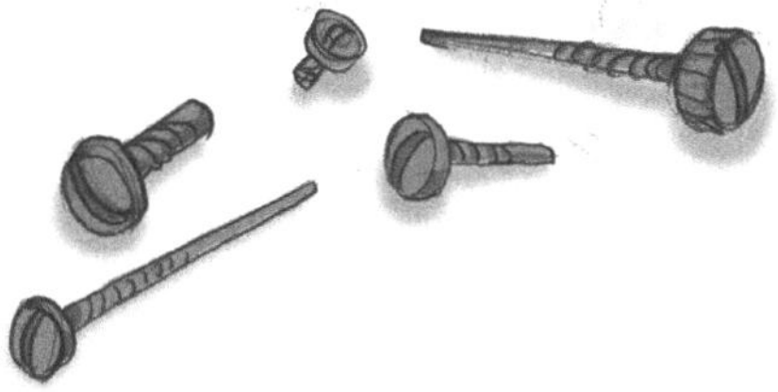

Sentences for Practice
Direct Objects

Analyze the following sentences.

S PV
1. Three filthy children slammed the front door.
adj adj adj adj do

S PV
2. Shoes cluttered the tiny hallway.
adj adj do

S PV
3. Then, Mom followed the muddy trail upward.
adv adj adj do adv

S hv PV
4. The kids were washing the grime off.
adj adj do adv

S PV
5. Brown suds filled the upstairs bathtub.
adj adj adj do

From the Sideline: In each chapter, an extra practice sheet provides more sentences for analysis to use as needed—perhaps for review as a class, for individual students requiring more practice, or even as a refresher for students later in the year.

grime: dirt

6. Winston could not find the laundry basket.
S: Winston; hv: could; PV: find; adv: not; adj: the; adj: laundry; do: basket

7. Dad found smelly, dirty socks everywhere.
S: Dad; PV: found; adj: smelly; adj: dirty; do: socks; adv: everywhere

8. Quickly, the children hung the wrinkly towels.
S: children; PV: hung; adv: Quickly; adj: the; adj: the; adj: wrinkly; do: towels

9. Mom stirred the hot chocolate.
S: Mom; PV: stirred; adj: the; adj: hot; do: chocolate

10. Fritz wanted graham crackers too.
S: Fritz; PV: wanted; adj: graham; do: crackers; adv: too

Lesson to Enjoy—Poem
Direct Objects

Christina Rossetti was a nineteenth-century poet who loved to play with language to delight her readers. Can you find all the puns she packs into "A Pin Has a Head"? A pun is a joking use of a word that possibly has a meaning different from the one you first think of. It's also called a *play on words*. See if you can figure out all of Rossetti's double meanings in this playful poem.

A Pin Has a Head

by Christina Rossetti (1830–1894)

A pin has a head, but has no hair;
A clock has a face, but no mouth there;
Needles have eyes, but they cannot see;
A fly has a trunk without lock or key;
A timepiece may lose, but cannot win;
A corn-field dimples without a chin;
A hill has no leg, but has a foot;
A wine-glass a stem, but not a root;
A watch has hands, but no thumb or finger;
A boot has a tongue, but is no singer;
Rivers run, though they have no feet;
A saw has teeth, but it does not eat;
Ash-trees have keys, yet never a lock;
And baby crows, without being a cock.[2]

dimples: furrows or grooves between rows

ash tree keys: the seeds of ash trees grow in bunches and are commonly called "keys"

cock: rooster

2. Christina G. Rossetti, "A Pin," *Rossetti Poems* (New York: Alfred A. Knopf, 1995), 136.

Questions to Ponder

1. What does "A pin has a head, but has no hair" mean?
2. What is the subject noun in each line of the poem? Many of the subjects are followed by a verb and direct object. Which word is usually the pun—the subject, verb, or direct object?
3. How is the last subject—*baby*—different from the others?

Well-Ordered Notes—Poem

Read

- Have students enjoy the poem as you read it aloud. You may want to collect the items (or photos of these items) mentioned in the poem (pin, clock, needles, fly, timepiece, field of corn, hill, wineglass, watch, boot, river, saw, ash tree, baby) and hold each of them up as you come to them in the poem.

Retell

- Use the Questions to Ponder as discussion starters:

1. **What does "A pin has a head, but has no hair" mean?**
The top of the pin is called its head. Ask the students how it is like a person's head—round and at the top. But unlike a person's head, it has no hair. The pun is on the two meanings of the word *head*. When we say a pin has a head, we are also using a metaphor—a comparison between the thing and something else that is not literally like it but that has a certain resemblance.

2. **What is the subject noun in each line of the poem? Many of the subjects are followed by a verb and direct object. Which word is usually the pun—the subject, verb, or direct object?**
Here is a chart that shows the noun, verb, and direct object in each line. The punning words are in bold. You can see that most of them are the direct objects, which is why this poem was chosen for this chapter:

Line	Subject	Verbs	Direct Object
1	pin	has	**head**
2	clock	has	**face**
3	needles	have	**eyes**
4	fly	has	**trunk**
5	timepiece	may **lose**	---
6	corn-field	**dimples**	---
7	hill	has	**foot**
8	wine-glass	(has)	**stem**
9	watch	has	**hands**
10	boot	has	**tongue**
11	rivers	**run**	---
12	saw	has	**teeth**
13	Ash-tree	has	**keys**
14	Baby	**crows**	---

3. **How is the last subject—*baby*—different from the others?**
   All the other subject nouns are things, but *baby* is a person. The list of things has built up to this one, as if it is the climax of a story. Encourage the students to think of this poem as one a mother might chant to a toddler as she bounces him on her knee. When she gets to the last line, she might tickle him to make him "crow" or laugh loudly. They may like sharing about such games their parents played with them. Point out that these games are poetry, full of rhythm and rhymes and interesting images.

Record

◇ Have the students write a poem together, with each student writing a line. You can use the template below if the class needs assistance rewriting Rossetti's poem with new subject nouns.

A ___cabbage___ has a head, but has no hair;

A ___cliff___ has a face, but no mouth there;

___Potatoes___ have eyes, but they cannot see;

A(n) ___elephant___ has a trunk without lock or key;

A ___hair___ may lose, but cannot win;

A ___golf ball___ dimples without a chin;

A ___slug___ has no leg, but has a foot;

A ___pipe___ a stem, but not a root;

A ___compass___ has hands, but no thumb or finger;

A ___fire___ has a tongue, but is no singer;

___Faucets___ run, though they have no feet;

A ___comb___ has teeth, but it does not eat;

___Pianos___ have keys, yet never a lock;

And baby crows, without being a cock.

Review
Direct Objects

ANSWERS

1. Analyze the following sentences.

   a. Yesterday, Heidi was given a special present.
   S: Heidi; hv: was; PV: given; Yesterday: adv; a: adj; special: adj; present: do

   b. The little girl had never received a pet bird before.
   S: girl; hv: had; PV: received; The: adj; little: adj; never: adv; a: adj; pet: adj; bird: do; before: adv

   c. The birthday canary has two blue wings.
   S: canary; PV: has; The: adj; birthday: adj; two: adj; blue: adj; wings: do

   d. Now, Grandpa Fred is building a sturdy birdhouse.
   S: Grandpa Fred; hv: is; PV: building; Now: adv; a: adj; sturdy: adj; birdhouse: do

From the Sideline: The material in the following pages is not included in the student edition. You can find the Review lesson, the Quiz, the extra Sentences for Practice, and the second Lesson to Enjoy in reproducible form in the Extra Practice & Assessments PDF, available for purchase at ClassicalAcademicPress.com.

2. On the lines provided, list all the *nouns* from the above sentences.

   a. Heidi
   b. present
   c. girl
   d. bird
   e. canary
   f. wings
   g. Grandpa Fred
   h. birdhouse

3. Consider what you would see if you were at the birthday party. Supply subjects and direct objects for the following sentences. You may need to include article adjectives (*a/an* or *the*) to complete your sentences.

   a. **The friends** brought **presents**.

   b. **Mom** frosted **the cake**.

   c. **Fritz** licked **the spoon**.

   d. **The kids** played **games**.

4. What questions does a *direct object* answer? (Answer using a complete sentence.)

   Direct objects answer the questions *what* or *whom*.

5. Imagine a family is buying a bird or a birdcage, and then write a sentence about it, being sure to include a *direct object* in it.

   The family chooses a noisy canary.

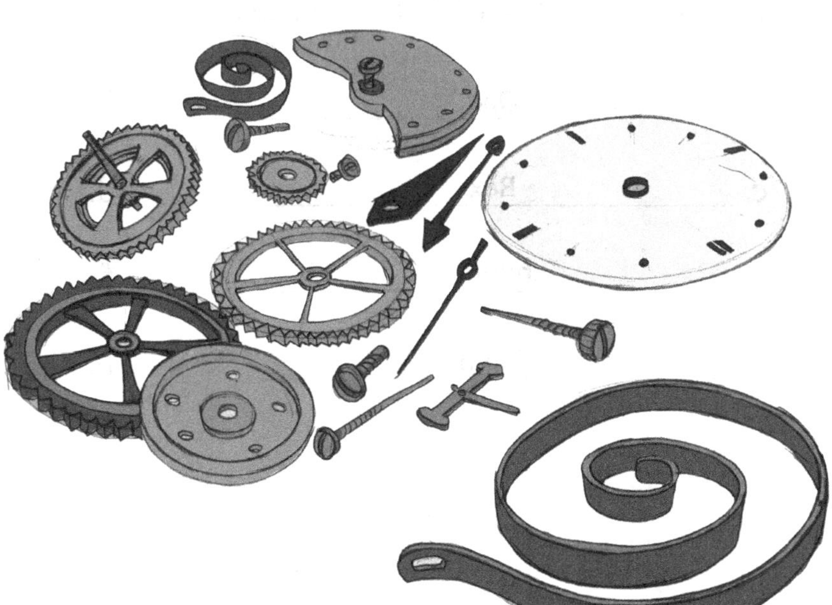

Quiz
Direct Objects
ANSWERS

1. Analyze the following sentences.

   S hv PV
   a. Dad has organized a cleanup (day.)
   adj adj do

   S hv hv PV
   b. Rex has been digging backyard (holes) again.
   adj do adv

   S hv PV
   c. The three children had never shoveled (dirt) before.
   adj adj adv do adv

   S PV
   d. Mom raked the muddy (clumps) together.
   adj adj do adv

2. On the lines provided, list all the *nouns* from the above sentences.

a. Dad	b. day
c. Rex	d. holes
e. children	f. dirt
g. Mom	h. clumps

3. Consider what you would see if you were watching cleanup day. Supply subjects and direct objects for the following sentences. You may need to include article adjectives (*a/an* or *the*) to complete your sentences.

   a. **Dad** waters **the plants**.

   b. **Winston** sweeps **the stairs**.

   c. **Heidi** washes **the windows**.

   d. **Rex** chases **the birds**.

4. What questions does a *direct object* answer? (Answer using a complete sentence.)

   Direct objects answer the questions *what* or *whom*.

5. Imagine what Rex found while he was digging in the backyard, and then write a sentence about it, being sure to include a *direct object* in it.

   Rex found a bone.

Sentences for Practice—Fable
Direct Objects

Analyze the following sentences.

1. The hot sun dried the ground.
   (S: sun; PV: dried; adj: The, hot; adj: the; do: ground)

2. A thirsty Crow found a tall pitcher.
   (S: Crow; PV: found; adj: A, thirsty; adj: a, tall; do: pitcher)

3. A small puddle filled the bottom.
   (S: puddle; PV: filled; adj: A, small; adj: the; do: bottom)

4. The eager Crow wanted the water.
   (S: Crow; PV: wanted; adj: The, eager; adj: the; do: water)

5. Unfortunately, the Crow could not reach the water.
   (S: Crow; hv: could; PV: reach; adj: the; adv: Unfortunately; adv: not; adj: the; do: water)

From the Sideline: These extra practice sentences are a synopsis of the fable "The Crow and the Pitcher." The fable and the extended lesson notes are on the following pages.

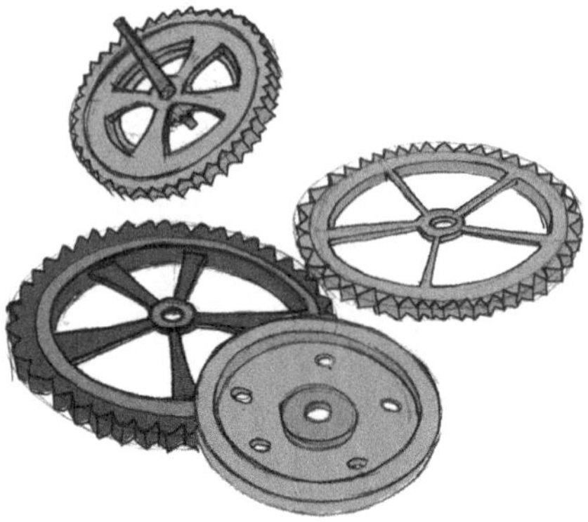

Sentences for Practice—Fable
Direct Objects

S PV
6. The clever Crow pondered an idea.
adj adj do

S PV
7. The Crow gathered small pebbles.
adj adj do

S PV
8. Methodically, the Crow dropped the tiny rocks inside.
adj adj adj do
adv adv

methodically: in an orderly way

S PV
9. The water rose high.
adj adv

S PV
10. The Crow sipped the cool water joyfully.
adj adj adj do
adv

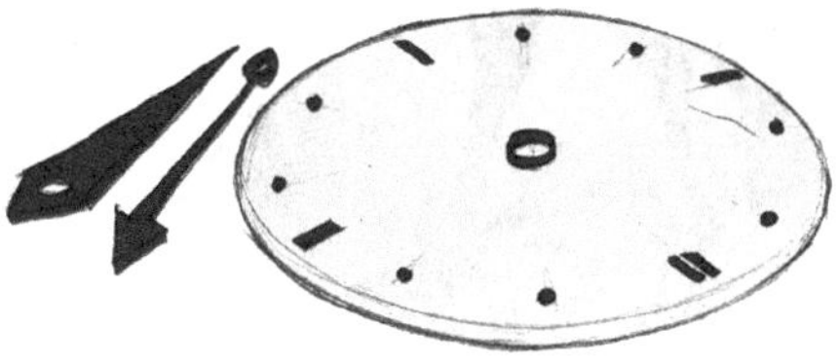

Lesson to Enjoy—Fable
Direct Objects

When you want something badly enough, you can usually figure out a way to get it, can't you? Sometimes it is a ball caught high up in branches and sometimes it is quarter wedged deep in a crevice. The power of desire can be a good source of invention. This fable tells of a Crow that wants something very badly and creatively thinks of a way to get it.

The Crow and the Pitcher

by Aesop

The weather was burning hot, and the birds could find nothing to drink. Even the creek beds carried only sand. A thirsty Crow found a pitcher with a little water in the bottom. But the pitcher was tall and had a narrow neck, and no matter how hard she tried, the Crow could not reach the water. "Oh, I will surely die of thirst!" the poor bird groaned.

despair: hopelessness

plunked: dropped

In despair, she came up with an idea. She gathered a pile of small pebbles; and then, one by one, she dropped them into the pitcher. As each pebble plunked to the bottom, the water rose a little higher. Soon the water was high enough for the Crow to dip her beak into it. How sweet and cool it tasted! By using her wits, the Crow had saved her life.

Moral: Necessity is the mother of invention.[1]

1. Aesop, "The Crow and the Pitcher," from *Writing & Rhetoric Book 1: Fable* by Paul Kortepeter (Camp Hill, PA: Classical Academic Press, 2013), 26.

Questions to Ponder

1. What does it mean, "I will surely die of thirst?"
2. How does the Crow solve her problem?
3. What does "Necessity is the mother of invention" mean?

Well-Ordered Notes—Fable

Read

- Read the fable out loud and help the students to enjoy it. Using a narrow-necked pitcher of water and a dish of pebbles, demonstrate how the water level can increase from the displacement of the water caused by the stones.
- Have students sing the definition of a fable (audio track 1–14; see page 194 for lyrics).

Retell

- Use the Questions to Ponder as discussion starters:

  1. **What does it mean, "I will surely die of thirst?"**
     The crow is tortured by how close the water is, yet how unreachable. Encourage the students to think about a time when they were extremely thirsty and how miserable it was. They may have said something like "I will surely die of thirst," but it is unlikely that they were truly in danger of dying. The crow, however, is. Emphasize the crow's dire *necessity* to help the students better understand the moral.
  2. **How does the Crow solve her problem?**
     She very cleverly displaces the water with pebbles so she can reach it . . . and live!
  3. **What does "Necessity is the mother of invention" mean?**
     It means that sometimes strong need encourages "thinking outside of the box" to solve a problem. For instance, if the crow had not been in such need, she may not have thought of the clever plan to elevate the water so she could reach it. Ask students to give examples of the moral from their own lives.

- Have the students act out the fable. Have one student narrate the tale while each student files by and drops a pebble into the narrow-necked pitcher.

Record

- Have students write another version of this fable using another bird (e.g., pigeon). They can illustrate their version of the fable or decorate the borders of the page.

Notes

Sentence Bank

These four additional sentences are for extra practice if needed. The scripts are provided for your reference as you model the marking on the board while the students analyze the sentences aloud.

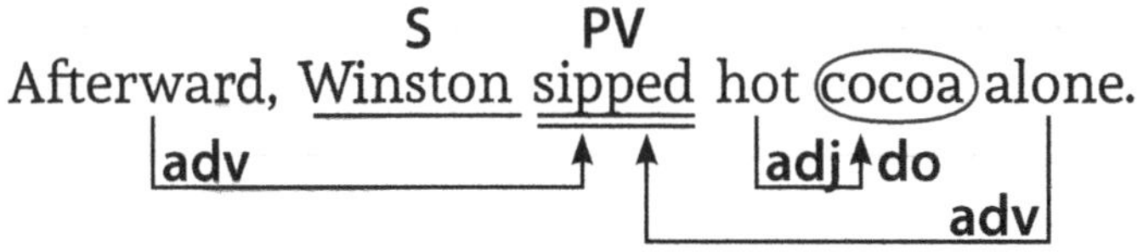

a. (First, read the sentence aloud.) "Afterward, Winston sipped hot cocoa alone."

b. "This is a sentence and it is declarative."

c. "This sentence is about *Winston*." (Underline the subject.) "So, *Winston* is the subject because it is what the sentence is about." (Place a capital letter *S* above the subject.)

d. "This sentence tells us that Winston *sipped*." (Double underline the predicate.) "So, *sipped* is the predicate because it is what the sentence tells us about *Winston*." (Place a capital letter *P* above the action verb.) "It is a predicate verb because it shows action." (Place a capital letter *V* to the right of the *P*.) "There is no linking verb because predicate verbs do not need linking verbs."

e. (Pause and think about what or whom would complete the verb before identifying the objective element.) "*Cocoa* tells us *what* Winston sipped." (Draw a circle around the word.)

f. "So, *cocoa* is an objective element because it completes the meaning of the action verb. It is a direct object because it tells *what* Winston sipped." (Write *do* in lowercase letters beneath the direct object.)

g. "*Alone* tells us *how* Winston sipped." (Draw a straight line down from the adverb, then a horizontal line toward the word that it modifies, and then a straight line with an arrow pointing to the word it modifies.)

h. "So, *alone* is an adverbial element because it modifies a verb. It is an adverb." (Write *adv* in lowercase letters in the elbow opposite the line with the arrow. *Do not* connect this adverbial modifying line with the adjective modifying line.)

i. "*Hot* tells us *what kind* of cocoa." (Draw a straight line down from the adjective, then a horizontal line toward the word that it modifies, and then a straight line with an arrow pointing to the word it modifies.)

j. "So, *hot* is an adjectival element because it modifies a noun. It is an adjective." (Write *adj* in lowercase letters in the elbow opposite the line with the arrow.)

k. "*Afterward* tells us *when* Winston sipped." (Draw a straight line down from the adverb, then a horizontal line toward the word that it modifies, and then a straight line with an arrow pointing to the word it modifies.)

l. "So, *afterward* is an adverbial element because it modifies a verb. It is an adverb." (Write *adv* in lowercase letters in the elbow opposite the line with the arrow.)

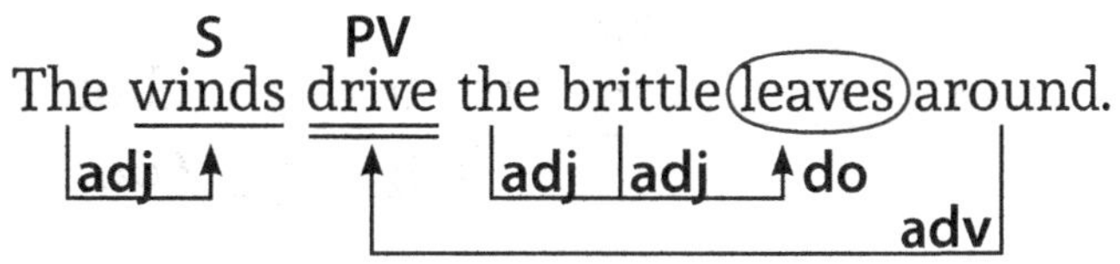

a. (First, read the sentence aloud.) "The winds drive the brittle leaves around."

b. "This is a sentence and it is declarative."

c. "This sentence is about *winds*." (Underline the subject.) "So, *winds* is the subject because it is what the sentence is about." (Place a capital letter *S* above the subject.)

d. "This sentence tells us that winds *drive*." (Double underline the predicate.) "So, *drive* is the predicate because it is what the sentence tells us about *winds*." (Place a capital letter *P* above the action verb.) "It is a predicate verb because it shows action." (Place a capital letter *V* to the right of the *P*.) "There is no linking verb because predicate verbs do not need linking verbs."

e. (Pause and think about what or whom would complete the verb.) "*Leaves* tells us *what* winds drive." (Draw a circle around the word.)

f. "So, *leaves* is an objective element because it completes the meaning of the action verb. It is a direct object because it tells *what* winds drive." (Write *do* in lowercase letters beneath the direct object.)

g. "*Around* tells us *where* winds drive." (Draw a straight line down from the adverb, then a horizontal line toward the word that it modifies, and then a straight line with an arrow pointing to the word it modifies.)

h. "So, *around* is an adverbial element because it modifies a verb. It is an adverb." (Write *adv* in lowercase letters in the elbow opposite the line with the arrow.)

i. "*Brittle* tells us *what kind* of leaves." (Draw a straight line down from the adjective, then a horizontal line toward the word that it modifies, and then a straight line with an arrow pointing to the word it modifies.)

j. "So, *brittle* is an adjectival element because it modifies a noun. It is an adjective." (Write *adj* in lowercase letters in the elbow opposite the line with the arrow.)

k. "*The* tells us *which* leaves." (Draw a straight line down from the adjective, then a horizontal line toward the word that it modifies and connect the line to the modifying line of the word *brittle*. The two modifying lines are joined and point, with a straight line, toward the word they modify.)

l. "So, *the* is an adjectival element because it modifies a noun. It is an adjective." (Write *adj* in lowercase letters in the elbow opposite the line with the arrow.)

m. "*The* tells us *which* winds." (Draw a straight line down from the adjective, then a horizontal line toward the word that it modifies, and then a straight line with an arrow pointing to the word it modifies.)

n. "So, *the* is an adjectival element because it modifies a noun. It is an adjective." (Write *adj* in lowercase letters in the elbow opposite the line with the arrow.)

S PV
The captain lowered the heavy anchor.
adj adj adj do

a. (First, read the sentence aloud.) "The captain lowered the heavy anchor."

b. "This is a sentence and it is declarative."

c. "This sentence is about *captain*." (Underline the subject.) "So, *captain* is the subject because it is what the sentence is about." (Place a capital letter *S* above the subject.)

d. "This sentence tells us that captain *lowered*." (Double underline the predicate.) "So, *lowered* is the predicate because it is what the sentence tells us about *captain*." (Place a capital letter *P* above the action verb.) "It is a predicate verb because it shows action." (Place a capital letter *V* to the right of the *P*.) "There is no linking verb because predicate verbs do not need linking verbs."

e. (Pause and think about what or whom would complete the verb.) "*Anchor* tells us *what* captain lowered." (Draw a circle around the word.)

f. "So, *anchor* is an objective element because it completes the meaning of the action verb. It is a direct object because it tells *what* captain lowered." (Write *do* in lowercase letters beneath the direct object.)

g. "*Heavy* tells us *what kind* of anchor." (Draw a straight line down from the adjective, then a horizontal line toward the word that it modifies, and then a straight line with an arrow pointing to the word it modifies.)

h. "So, *heavy* is an adjectival element because it modifies a noun. It is an adjective." (Write *adj* in lowercase letters in the elbow opposite the line with the arrow.)

i. "*The* tells us *which* anchor." (Draw a straight line down from the adjective, then a horizontal line toward the word that it modifies and connect the line to the modifying line of the word *heavy*. The two modifying lines are joined and point, with a straight line, toward the word they modify.)

j. "So, *the* is an adjectival element because it modifies a noun. It is an adjective." (Write *adj* in lowercase letters in the elbow opposite the line with the arrow.)

k. "*The* tells us *which* captain." (Draw a straight line down from the adjective, then a horizontal line toward the word that it modifies, and then a straight line with an arrow pointing to the word it modifies.)

l. "So, *the* is an adjectival element because it modifies a noun. It is an adjective." (Write *adj* in lowercase letters in the elbow opposite the line with the arrow.)

S PV
Aunt Gabby cheerfully planted beautiful mums.
adv adj do

a. (First, read the sentence aloud.) "Aunt Gabby cheerfully planted beautiful mums."

b. "This is a sentence and it is a declarative."

c. "This sentence is about *Aunt Gabby*." (Underline the subject.) "So, *Aunt Gabby* is the subject because it is what the sentence is about." (Place a capital letter *S* above the subject.)

d. "This sentence tells us that Aunt Gabby *planted*." (Double underline the predicate.) "So, *planted* is the predicate because it is what the sentence tells us about *Aunt Gabby*." (Place a capital letter *P* above the action verb.) "It is a predicate verb because it shows action." (Place a capital letter *V* to the right of the *P*.) "There is no linking verb because predicate verbs do not need linking verbs."

e. (Pause and think about what or whom would complete the verb.) "*Mums* tells us *what* Aunt Gabby planted." (Draw a circle around the word.)

f. "So, *mums* is an objective element because it completes the meaning of the action verb. It is a direct object because it tells *what* Aunt Gabby planted." (Write *do* in lowercase letters beneath the direct object.)

g. "*Beautiful* tells us *what kind* of mums." (Draw a straight line down from the adjective, then a horizontal line toward the word that it modifies, and then a straight line with an arrow pointing to the word it modifies.)

h. "So, *beautiful* is an adjectival element because it modifies a noun. It is an adjective." (Write *adj* in lowercase letters in the elbow opposite the line with the arrow.)

i. "*Cheerfully* tells us *how* Aunt Gabby planted." (Draw a straight line down from the adverb, then a horizontal line toward the word that it modifies, and then a straight line with an arrow pointing to the word it modifies.)

j. "So, *cheerfully* is an adverbial element because it modifies a verb. It is an adverb." (Write *adv* in lowercase letters in the elbow opposite the line with the arrow.)

From the Sideline: Expect respect. Teach students to give proper responses while making eye contact. Don't allow grunts for answers. We have the students say, "Yes, ma'am" or "No, sir."

[A]Bring in an umbrella to hold as a prop while you read aloud the weather report in the first paragraph, exaggerating the monotonous repetition of "these storms." Discuss how using pronouns can improve the report, if not the stormy forecast.

Chapter 7

Subject Pronouns[A]

Hearing the same word used over and over again can be boring. Imagine if you are watching the weather report on television, and the newscaster says, "Expect the first line of storms to hit later tonight. These storms pose the most serious weather threat in Dane and Butler counties. These storms are the tail end of a storm system. These storms have caused severe problems along the valley over the past several hours. These storms snarled air traffic. These storms slowed highways. These storms have even stopped soccer games." It would be strange to hear so many *storms* in a row, wouldn't it? In fact, you might tune out after the first few *storms* and not hear that your own soccer game is canceled. Using pronouns instead of repeating the same nouns can break the monotony (dullness) and make sentences more lively and even more clear.

This meteorologist needs to learn that a **pronoun**■ is a word that is used in place of a noun. There are a number of pronouns that substitute for designated nouns. Certain pronouns are used as subjects and certain pronouns are used as objects. This chapter of your guide to grammar focuses on personal **subject pronouns**, saving personal object pronouns for *Well-Ordered Language Level 1B*.

To the Source:

■ **pronoun**

The word *pronoun* comes from the Latin word *pronomen,* which literally means "in place of a noun." *Pro* means "in place of" and *nomen* means "name" or "noun."

Ideas to Understand

Pick up almost any book and you will find pronouns on every page. Look at the pronouns in this passage from *The Cricket in Times Square* in which Chester first chirps for Tucker Mouse and Harry Cat shortly after they meet the poor lost cricket:

Off the Shelf: Have you read the novel *The Cricket in Times Square*, by George Selden? In it, a cricket named Chester ends up in a New York subway station, where he makes three unlikely friends: a boy named Mario, a mouse named Tucker, and Harry the cat. Spoiler alert! Chester's crickety chirping leads to some very interesting escapades (wild adventures). You can read a longer passage from the novel in the back of this book or you can check out the novel at your library.

To the Source:

■ antecedent

The word *antecedent* comes from the Latin roots *cede*, meaning "go," and *ante*, meaning "before" or "in front of." An antecedent goes before the pronoun that refers to it.

> "Yes," said Chester. "These wings aren't much good for flying, but I prefer music anyhow." He made three rapid chirps. . . .
>
> "It sounds to me as if you were going 'crik crik crik,'" said Harry.
>
> "Maybe that's why they call him a 'cricket,'" said Tucker.
>
> They all laughed. Tucker had a squeaky laugh that sounded as if he were hiccuping. Chester was feeling much happier now. The future did not seem nearly as gloomy as it had over in the pile of dirt in the corner.[1]

The story flows because the author George Selden uses the subject pronouns *I*, *he*, *it*, *you*, and *they*. Notice how Selden uses the pronouns. *I* refers to Chester the cricket when he speaks about himself. *He* refers to Chester when he is spoken about. *It* refers to the sound Chester makes. *You* refers to Chester when Harry speaks to him. In "They all laughed," *they* refers to Harry, Tucker, and Chester. Another *he* refers to Tucker, the mouse, when he laughs as if hiccuping. Without pronouns, the reader would be tripping over extra nouns.

Although a pronoun stands for a noun, it does not actually name the person, place, or thing that it represents. In grammar, that noun to which the pronoun refers is called an **antecedent**.■ In the passage you just read, the antecedents of the subject pronouns were the proper names of the characters.

When we study grammar, we classify pronouns in different ways, which means we organize them or group them according to how they function in a sentence. You've already experienced in this chapter one way to group pronouns, either as subject pronouns or object pronouns. All the pronouns we've examined in *A Cricket in Times Square* so far have been subject pronouns. They all function as subjects. (Remember, we're saving object pronouns for the next book.)

Now, we will look at two other ways to classify pronouns: **person** and **number**. Classifying subject pronouns by *person* helps us distinguish between the person speaking, the person being spoken to, and all others. For subject pronouns, these three grammatical persons are organized into the following:

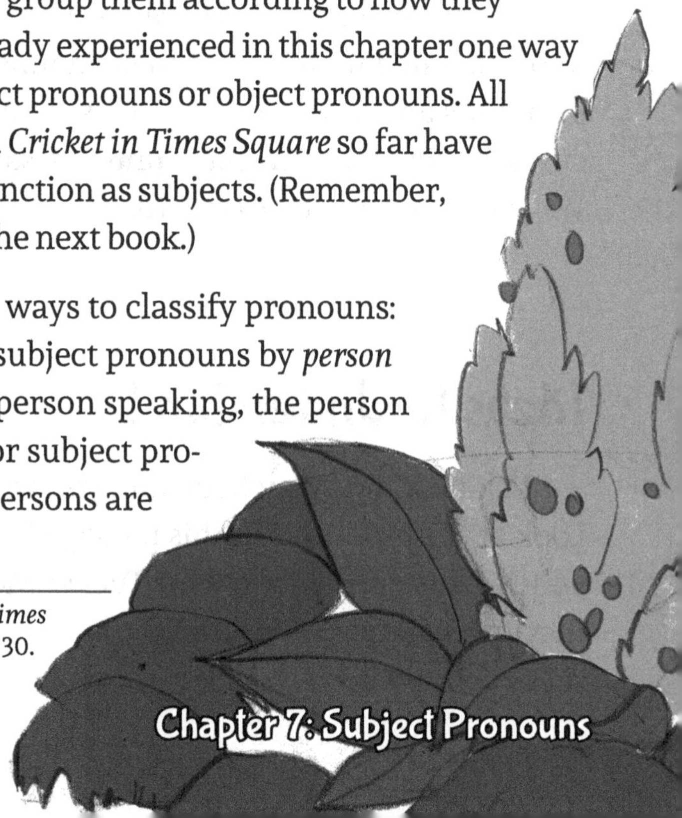

1. George Selden Thompson, *The Cricket in Times Square* (New York: A Yearling Book, 1960), 30.

1. **First person:** The subject is speaking about itself (I or we).

2. **Second person:** The subject is being spoken *to* (you).

3. **Third person:** The subject is being spoken *about* (he, she, it, they).

Look at the illustration in this chapter. Heidi is talking to her mother about Fritz, who has climbed dangerously high up in a tree (at least Heidi thinks so!). If you were Heidi, you would be the first person—the one speaking. Do you see to whom Heidi is directly speaking? She is speaking to her mom. Her mom is the second person. Can you tell about whom Heidi is speaking (look at where she is pointing)? She is speaking about Fritz! Since Fritz is the one being spoken about, he is the third person. Heidi would be using subject pronouns in all three persons if she said, "*I* see Fritz climbing too high! *You* should do something! *He* might fall!"

From the Sideline: To reinforce the three types of persons, have the students chant:

First: speaking (Use your thumbs and point to yourself.)

Second: spoken to (Point your index fingers straight out.)

Third: spoken of (Point your thumbs over your right shoulder.)

A personal subject pronoun is also identified and classified using its number, which is what tells us whether it is singular or plural. *Singular* means the pronoun represents only one person, place, or thing, while *plural* means the pronoun represents more than one person, place, or thing. The subject pronoun's antecedent determines which pronoun should be used. If the antecedent is singular, the pronoun must also be singular. For example, in the sentence "*Tucker* laughed, and then *he* squeaked," the singular pronoun *he* replaces the singular antecedent *Tucker*. If the antecedent is plural, however, then the pronoun must be plural. In the sentence "The three *friends* laughed, and *they* felt better," the plural pronoun *they* refers to the plural antecedent *friends*.

The following chart helps to organize these subject pronouns according to person and number:

Subject Pronouns

	Singular	Plural
First Person	I	we
Second Person	you	you
Third Person	he, she, it	they

When studying grammar, you will find other words besides *person* and *number* to describe a pronoun. Subject pronouns are in the **nominative case** (also called the **subjective case**), and in *Well-Ordered Language Level 1B*, you will learn that object pronouns are in the **objective case**.

Moment for Mechanics

Subject-verb agreement means that singular subjects have singular verbs, and plural subjects have plural verbs. This rule also applies to subject pronouns and their verbs, with two exceptions: the first-person singular *I* and the second-person singular *you* are followed by the plural form of the verb.

Look at the following chart to see how only the third-person singular pronouns—*he, she, it*—end up with the singular form of the verb!

Person	Singular	Plural
First Person	I *have* a cricket.	We *have* a cricket.
Second Person	You *have* a cricket.	You *have* a cricket.
Third Person	He *has*; She *has*; It *has* a cricket.	They *have* a cricket.

[B]For the lyrics to all of the songs, please see the Song Lyrics section on page 191. Play the appropriate audio tracks and have students sing/chant along. Students should commit the songs to memory.

Terms to Remember[B]

If you have been practicing, you already remember the definition for the eight parts of speech. Now, you can add three new definitions to your repertoire (the whole collection of musical pieces that a musician is able to perform). Imagine Chester the musical cricket chirping along with you.

Eight Parts of Speech *(1–1)*

NEW! **Pronoun** *(1–11)*

NEW! **Subject Pronouns** *(1–12)*

NEW! **Antecedent** *(1–13)*

A Sentence to Analyze

Pronouns are easy to analyze because they behave like nouns. Follow these steps to analyze the following sentence with your teacher's guidance. If you pay careful attention and participate enthusiastically, you will be ready to take the lead for the sentences that you will analyze in the rest of the chapter.

S hv PV
He was making (chirps.)
do

a. (First, read the sentence aloud.) "He was making chirps."

b. "This is a sentence, and it is declarative."

c. "This sentence is about *he*. So, *he* is the subject because it is what the sentence is about." (Since *he* is the subject, underline it and place a capital letter *S* above it.)

d. "This sentence tells us that he *was making*. So, *was making* is the predicate because it is what the sentence tells us about *he*." (Since *was making* tells us something about *he*, double underline the predicate, including the helping verb, and place a capital letter *P* above the action verb.) "It is a predicate verb because it shows action." (Place a capital letter *V* to the right of the *P*.) "There is no linking verb because predicate verbs do not need linking verbs. *Was* is the helping verb because it helps a verb." (Place the lowercase letters *hv* above the helping verb *was*.)

e. "*Chirps* tells us *what* he is making." (Since *chirps* tells what he is making, draw a circle around the word *chirps*.) "So, *chirps* is an objective element because it completes the meaning of an action verb. It is a direct object because it tells *what* he was making." (Write *do* in lowercase letters beneath the direct object.)

From the Sideline: Write the sentence on the board and model the steps of the analysis for the students. Remember that repetition is important for learning the relationships among the words in the sentences. Because the students already have the marked sentence in their books, they can pay full attention to your markings on the board. As you progress through the chapters' lessons, you should do less of the "work," allowing the students, in chorus, to lead the analysis themselves.

Analyzing pronouns is like being able to recognize whether or not a bug is an insect by the number of its legs and body parts. (Insects have six legs and three body parts, by the way.) With that knowledge, you can then classify it more exactly according to other characteristics. You already use pronouns often in speech and writing without thinking about them, but being able to recognize them as subject pronouns and to choose which ones to use according to person and number is a very handy skill that increases your language powers. It is a skill that our weather forecaster should have mastered before reporting on those storms, storms, storms.

Study the illustration at the beginning of this chapter. Did you notice the storm clouds in the sky? What is Rex (the dog) doing? What is Heidi's mom doing?

Well-Ordered Notes A

Review It

Review the following:

What are the eight parts of speech?
What is a direct object?
What is a noun?
What are the four kinds of sentences?

Practice It

Lead the students in Name That Subject Pronoun. The goal of this exercise is mastery of the subject pronouns. Write the following chart on the board with blanks for the pronouns. Before you begin the activity, remind the students that pronouns are organized using person and number. To reinforce the three types of persons, have the students chant:

First: speaking (Use your thumbs and point to yourself.)
Second: spoken to (Point your index fingers straight out.)
Third: spoken of (Point your thumbs over your right shoulder.)

During the activity, the students will sing/chant the Subject Pronouns lyrics repeatedly. While the class chants, volunteers will fill in the blanks in the chart, starting with the singular pronouns in order of person (first, second, and third). Next, have them fill in the plural pronouns in order of person.

Variation: After the chart is completely filled in, have volunteers systematically erase each pronoun as the students repeat the chant.

Subject Pronouns

	Singular	Plural
First person	I	we
Second person	you	you
Third person	he, she, it	they

Analyze It

From the Sideline: Visit http://capress.link/wol1att for a video demonstration of analysis.

Now, as a class, analyze the four sentences in the lesson. Here is the script for the first one to help you lead the choral analysis and model the markings on the board. The words in parentheses are like stage directions to guide you and are not to be spoken. The words in gray and enclosed in quotation marks are for you and the students to speak in chorus.

S PV
They slowly opened the wooden door.
adv adj adj do

a. (First, read the sentence aloud.) "They slowly opened the wooden door."

b. "This is a sentence and it is declarative."

c. "This sentence is about *they*." (Underline the subject.) "So, *they* is the subject because it is what the sentence is about." (Place a capital letter *S* above the subject.)

d. "This sentence tells us that they *opened*." (Double underline the predicate.) "So, *opened* is the predicate because it is what the sentence tells us about *they*." (Place a capital letter *P* above the action verb.) "It is a predicate verb because it shows action." (Place a capital letter *V* to the right of the *P*.) "There is no linking verb because predicate verbs do not need linking verbs."

e. "*Door* tells us *what* they opened." (Draw a circle around the word.) "So, *door* is an objective element because it completes the meaning of the action verb. It is a direct object because it tells *what* they opened." (Write *do* in lowercase letters beneath the direct object.)

f. "*Wooden* tells us *what kind* of door." (Draw a straight line down from the adjective, then a horizontal line toward the word that it modifies, and then a straight line with an arrow pointing to the word it modifies.) "So, *wooden* is an adjectival element because it modifies a noun. It is an adjective." (Write *adj* in lowercase letters in the elbow opposite the line with the arrow.)

g. "*The* tells us *which* door." (Draw a straight line down from the adjective, then a horizontal line toward the word that it modifies and connect the line to the modifying line of the word *wooden*. The two modifying lines are joined and point, with a straight line, toward the word they modify.) "So, *the* is an adjectival element because it modifies a noun. It is an adjective." (Write *adj* in lowercase letters in the elbow opposite the line with the arrow.)

h. "*Slowly* tells us *how* they opened the door." (Draw a straight line down from the adverb, then a horizontal line toward the word that it modifies, and then a straight line with an arrow pointing to the word it modifies.) "So, *slowly* is an adverbial element because it modifies a verb. It is an adverb." (Write *adv* in lowercase letters in the elbow opposite the line with the arrow.)

From the Sideline: For extra guided practice, refer to the Sentence Bank at the end of this chapter.

Lesson to Learn
Subject Pronouns

A

1. Analyze the following sentences.

> **From the Sideline:** Remember that when you see the word *analyze* in instructions throughout this book, we mean both choral analysis and written notations. Thc two go hand in hand as a prediagramming system.

S PV
a. They slowly opened the wooden door.
adv adj adj do

S PV
b. Quickly, he crossed the glossy floor.
adv adj adj do

S PV
c. She eagerly watched Winston.
adv do

S PV
d. Then, she tiptoed silently across.
adv adv adv

2. Fill in the following chart with the correct subject pronouns.

Subject Pronouns

	Singular	Plural
First Person	I	we
Second Person	you	you
Third Person	he, she, it	they

A Lesson to Learn
Subject Pronouns

3. What is a *pronoun*?

   A pronoun is a part of speech used in place of a noun or of more than one noun.

4. In the following sentences, write in the blanks provided the correct pronoun that goes with the underlined antecedent. Remember, if the antecedent is singular, the pronoun must be singular. Similarly, plural antecedents require plural pronouns.

   a. Winston wandered over to the sports section. ___He___ chose many books about baseball.

   b. Heidi walked to the animal section. ___She___ selected six books on crickets.

   c. Mom and I went downstairs to the fiction section. ___We___ were looking for the book *The Cricket in Times Square* by George Selden.

   d. Lucy and Fritz sat in the rocking chairs. ___They___ read picture books together.

   e. Then, a rocking chair fell over. ___It___ knocked over the stack of books.

5. Imagine that you're at the library. Using a subject pronoun and a direct object, write a sentence about what you do at the library.

   I read books.

Well-Ordered Notes B

Review It

Review the following:

What is a verb?
What is a pronoun?
What are the twenty-three helping verbs?
What are the subject pronouns?

Practice It

Lead the students in Which Pronoun Is It? Write the following phrases on cards or make up your own and place them in an envelope. Put the subject pronoun chart (see page 123) on the board and review the subject pronoun chant. Then, have the first student select a card from the envelope (e.g., "A pirate on a ship"), change the subject noun into a subject pronoun (e.g., *he*), and describe the person and number of the pronoun (e.g., "he is a third-person, singular subject pronoun"). Review the subject pronoun chant after each student. Continue with the next student, giving each student a chance.

Example: A pirate on a ship.
Student: "*He. He* is a third-person, singular subject pronoun."

1. Four cannonballs (they: third-person, plural)
2. One parrot (it: third-person, singular)
3. The one speaking (I: first-person, singular)
4. You and I (we: first-person, plural)
5. Blackbeard (he: third-person, singular)
6. The one spoken to (you: second-person, singular)
7. One maiden (she: third-person, singular)
8. Five sailors in a boat (they: third-person, plural)
9. A desert island (it: third-person, singular)
10. The man spoken about (he: third-person, singular)

Analyze It

Now, as a class, analyze the four sentences in the lesson. Here is the script for the first one to help you lead the choral analysis and model the markings on the board. The words in parentheses are like stage directions to guide you and are not to be spoken. The words in gray and enclosed in quotation marks are for you and the students to speak in chorus.

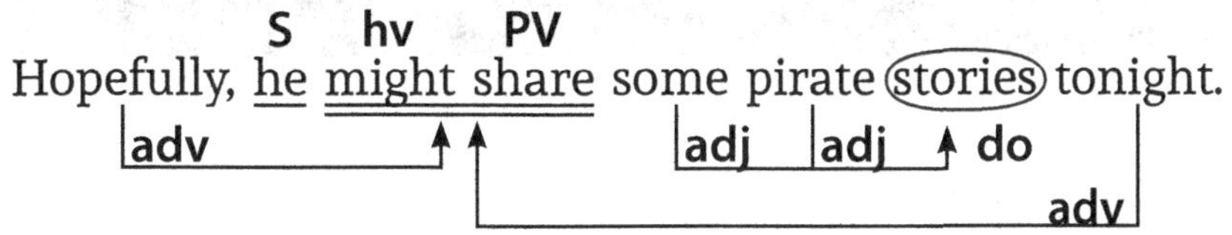

a. (First, read the sentence aloud.) "Hopefully, he might share some pirate stories tonight."

b. "This is a sentence and it is declarative."

c. "This sentence is about *he*." (Underline the subject.) "So, *he* is the subject because it is what the sentence is about." (Place a capital letter *S* above the subject.)

d. "This sentence tells us that he *might share*." (Double underline the predicate.) "So, *might share* is the predicate because it is what the sentence tells us about *he*." (Place a capital letter *P* above the action verb.) "It is a predicate verb because it shows action. There is no linking verb because predicate verbs do not need linking verbs." (Place a capital letter *V* to the right of the *P*.)

e. "*Might* is the helping verb because it helps the verb." (Place a lowercase *hv* above the helping verb.)

f. "*Stories* tells us *what* he might share." (Draw a circle around the word.) "So, *stories* is an objective element that completes the meaning of the action verb. It is a direct object because it tells us *what* he might share." (Write *do* in lowercase letters underneath the direct object.)

g. "*Tonight* tells us *when* he might share." (Draw a straight line down from the adverb, then a horizontal line toward the word that it modifies, and then a straight line with an arrow pointing to the word it modifies.) "So, *tonight* is an adverbial element because it modifies a verb. It is an adverb." (Write *adv* in lowercase letters in the elbow opposite the line with the arrow.)

h. "*Pirate* tells us *what kind* of stories." (Draw a straight line down from the adjective, then a horizontal line toward the word that it modifies, and then a straight line with an arrow pointing to the word it modifies.) "So, *pirate* is an adjectival element because it modifies a noun. It is an adjective." (Write *adj* in lowercase letters in the elbow opposite the line with the arrow.)

i. "*Some* tells us *how many* stories." (Draw a straight line down from the adjective, then a horizontal line toward the word that it modifies, and connect this modifier line with the modifier line for *pirate* since both adjectival elements are modifying *stories*.) "So, *some* is an adjectival element because it modifies a noun. It is an adjective." (Write *adj* in lowercase letters in the elbow opposite the line with the arrow.)

j. "*Hopefully* tells us *how* he might share." (Draw a straight line down from the adverb, then a horizontal line toward the word that it modifies, and then a straight line with an arrow pointing to the word it modifies.) "So, *hopefully* is an adverbial element because it modifies a verb. It is an adverb." (Write *adv* in lowercase letters in the elbow opposite the line with the arrow.)

Lesson to Learn B
Subject Pronouns

1. Analyze the following sentences.

S hv PV
a. Hopefully, he might share some pirate stories tonight.
adv adj adj do adv

S hv PV
b. Earlier, she had cooked a special supper.
adv adj adj do

S hv PV
c. They had brought a homemade pie along.
adj adj do adv

S PV
d. Afterward, we listened carefully together.
adv adv adv

2. Fill in the following chart with the correct subject pronouns.

Subject Pronouns

	Singular	Plural
First Person	I	we
Second Person	you	you
Third Person	he, she, it	they

B

Lesson to Learn
Subject Pronouns

3. What is a *pronoun*?

   A pronoun is a part of speech used in place of a noun or of more than one noun.

4. In the following sentences, write in the blanks provided the correct pronoun that goes with the underlined antecedent. Remember, if the antecedent is singular, the pronoun must be singular. Similarly, plural antecedents require plural pronouns.

   a. The dinner guest told stories to the <u>kids</u>. They loved pirate tales.

   b. Once, a <u>pirate</u> dragged a heavy chest on shore. He collapsed on the beach.

   c. Surprisingly, the dark <u>cave</u> was dry. It provided a secret shelter.

   d. A sneaky sea <u>bandit</u> stole the treasure. He was hiding in the dark.

   e. <u>Lucy</u> wanted another story. She could listen all night to the pirate tales.

5. Imagine that you were in the pirate cave. Using a subject pronoun and a direct object, write a sentence about what happens in the cave.

   He dragged the chest away.

Well-Ordered Notes C

Review It

Review the following:

What are the principal elements?
What is an adverb?
What is an adjective?
What are the three parts of speech an adverb modifies?
What are the two parts of speech an adjective modifies?

Practice It

Lead the students in the activity Quick Draw. Draw the structure (the lines and the column and row headings) of the following chart on the board. Divide the class into two teams, with one student from each team at the board with a marker. Point out to students that subject pronouns must agree with their predicates. Tell them that they'll be working with the verbs *have* and *has.* Call out a pronoun at random (*I, you [s.], you [pl.], he, she, it, we,* or *they*) and the students with markers will write the pronoun and its appropriate matching predicate in the correct place on the chart. The first student to write the correct pronoun and predicate wins a point for his team.

Subject Pronouns

	Singular	Plural
First person	I have	we have
Second person	you have	you have
Third person	he has, she has, it has	they have

Analyze It

Now, as a class, analyze the four sentences in the lesson. Here is the script for the first one to help you lead the choral analysis and model the markings on the board. The words in parentheses are like stage directions to guide you and are not to be spoken. The words in gray and enclosed in quotation marks are for you and the students to speak in chorus.

S PV
Carelessly, they carried the old glass tubes.
adv adj adj adj do

a. (First, read the sentence aloud.) "Carelessly, they carried the old glass tubes."

b. "This is a sentence and it is declarative."

c. "This sentence is about *they*." (Underline the subject.) "So, *they* is the subject because it is what the sentence is about." (Place a capital letter *S* above the subject.)

d. "This sentence tells us that they *carried*." (Double underline the predicate.) "So, *carried* is the predicate because it is what the sentence tells us about *they*." (Place a capital letter *P* above the action verb.) "It is a predicate verb because it shows action. There is no linking verb because predicate verbs do not need linking verbs." (Place a capital letter *V* to the right of the *P*.)

e. "*Tubes* tells us *what* they carried." (Draw a circle around the word.) "So, *tubes* is an objective element because it completes the meaning of the action verb. It is a direct object because it tells us *what* they carried." (Write ***do*** in lowercase letters underneath the direct object.)

f. "*Glass* tells us *what kind* of tubes." (Draw a straight line down from the adjective, then a horizontal line toward the word that it modifies, and then a straight line with an arrow pointing to the word it modifies.) "So, *glass* is an adjectival element because it modifies a noun. It is an adjective." (Write ***adj*** in lowercase letters in the elbow opposite the line with the arrow.)

g. "*Old* tells us *what kind* of tubes." (Draw a straight line down from the adjective, then a horizontal line toward the word that it modifies, and connect this modifier line with the modifier line for ***glass*** since both adjectival elements are modifying ***tubes***.) "So, *old* is an adjectival element because it modifies a noun. It is an adjective." (Write ***adj*** in lowercase letters in the elbow opposite the line with the arrow.)

h. "*The* tells us *which* tubes." (Draw a straight line down from the adjective, then a horizontal line toward the word that it modifies, and connect this modifier line with the modifier lines for ***old*** and ***glass*** since they are adjectival elements modifying ***tubes***.) "So, *the* is an adjectival element because it modifies a noun. It is an adjective." (Write ***adj*** in lowercase letters in the elbow opposite the line with the arrow.)

i. "*Carelessly* tells us *how* they carried." (Draw a straight line down from the adverb, then a horizontal line toward the word that it modifies, and then a straight line with an arrow pointing to the word it modifies.) "So, *carelessly* is an adverbial element because it modifies a verb. It is an adverb." (Write ***adv*** in lowercase letters in the elbow opposite the line with the arrow.)

Lesson to Learn

Subject Pronouns

C

1. Analyze the following sentences.

   S PV
   a. Carelessly, they carried the old glass (tubes.)
   adv adj adj adj do

   S hv PV
   b. They did not like the (smell.)
   adv adj do

   S PV
   c. He unfortunately dropped the empty (containers.)
   adv adj adj do

   S hv hv PV
   d. Shortly, he will be sweeping up (glass.)
   adv adv do

2. Fill in the following chart with the correct subject pronouns.

Subject Pronouns

	Singular	Plural
First Person	I	we
Second Person	you	you
Third Person	he, she, it	they

3. What is a *pronoun*?

   A pronoun is a part of speech used in place of a noun or of more than one noun.

4. For each of the following sentences, write in the blank provided the correct predicate—either *has* or *have*.

   a. He **has** the wobbly chair again.

   b. You **have** a new lab partner.

   c. She **has** the only orange test tube holder.

   d. We **have** old science books.

   e. Unfortunately, Theo and I **have** a science test now.

5. Imagine that you were in science class. Using a subject pronoun and a direct object, write a sentence about what happens in class.

   Actually, they broke several test tubes.

Well-Ordered Notes D

Review It

Review the following:

What is a sentence?
What is a noun?
What is a direct object?
What are the four kinds of sentences?
What are the principal elements?

Practice It

Lead the students in Ping-Pong. Write the subject pronoun chart (see page 123) on the board. Divide the students into pairs for this oral exercise. Have the first student say a subject pronoun (e.g., *they*). Have the second student describe the pronoun (e.g., *they*: third-person plural) and then volley another subject pronoun to her buddy (e.g., *I*). Then, the first student describes the "volleyed" pronoun (e.g., *I*: first-person singular) and so on. Have the students continue back and forth until you stop the match. For fun, speed up the game to see how quickly the students can "ping-pong" the subject pronouns to one another.

Fewer than Five: Adapt the activity by filling in the subject pronoun chart using a set of subject pronoun cards. Have each student select one card (e.g., *him*). Have the student describe the pronoun (e.g., *him*: third-person singular) and then affix the card in the chart. Continue until the chart is filled.

Example:
Student 1: "*they*"
Student 2: "*they*: third-person plural; *I*"
Student 1: "*I*: first-person singular . . ."

Analyze It

Now, as a class, analyze the four sentences in the lesson. Here is the script for the first one to help you lead the choral analysis and model the markings on the board. The words in parentheses are like stage directions to guide you and are not to be spoken. The words in gray and enclosed in quotation marks are for you and the students to speak in chorus.

S hv PV
Surprisingly, she could not solve the riddle.
adv adv adj do

a. (First, read the sentence aloud.) "Surprisingly, she could not solve the riddle."

b. "This is a sentence and it is declarative."

c. "This sentence is about *she*." (Underline the subject.) "So, *she* is the subject because it is what the sentence is about." (Place a capital letter *S* above the subject.)

d. "This sentence tells us that she *could solve*." (Double underline the predicate.) "So, *could solve* is the predicate because it is what the sentence tells us about *she*." (Place a capital letter *P* above the action verb.) "It is a predicate verb because it shows action. There is no linking verb because predicate verbs do not need linking verbs." (Place a capital letter *V* to the right of the *P*.)

e. "*Could* is a helping verb because it helps the verb." (Place a lowercase *hv* above the helping verb.)

f. "*Riddle* tells us *what* she could solve." (Draw a circle around the word.) "So, *riddle* is an objective element because it completes the meaning of the action verb. It is a direct object because it tells us *what* she could solve." (Write *do* in lowercase letters beneath the direct object.)

g. "*The* tells us *which* riddle." (Draw a straight line down from the adjective, then a horizontal line toward the word that it modifies, and then a straight line with an arrow pointing to the word it modifies.) "So, *the* is an adjectival element because it modifies a noun. It is an adjective." (Write *adj* in lowercase letters in the elbow opposite the line with the arrow.)

h. "*Not* tells us *how* she could solve." (Draw a straight line down from the adverb, then a horizontal line toward the word that it modifies, and then a straight line with an arrow pointing to the word it modifies.) "So, *not* is an adverbial element because it modifies a verb. It is an adverb." (Write *adv* in lowercase letters in the elbow opposite the line with the arrow.)

i. "*Surprisingly* tells us *how* she could solve." (Draw a straight line down from the adverb, then a horizontal line toward the word that it modifies, and connect this modifier line with the modifier line for *not* since both adverbial elements are modifying *solve*.) "So, *surprisingly* is an adverbial element because it modifies a verb. It is an adverb." (Write *adv* in lowercase letters in the elbow opposite the line with the arrow.)

Lesson to Learn
Subject Pronouns

1. Analyze the following sentences.

   S hv PV
   a. Surprisingly, she could not solve the riddle.
   adv adv adj do

   S PV
   b. He asked Heidi repeatedly.
   do adv

   S PV
   c. Finally, she successfully gave an answer.
   adv adv adj do

   S PV
   d. Afterward, they wrote word puzzles together.
   adv adj do adv

2. Fill in the following chart with the correct subject pronouns.

Subject Pronouns

	Singular	Plural
First Person	I	we
Second Person	you	you
Third Person	he, she, it	they

Lesson to Learn
Subject Pronouns

3. What is a *pronoun*?

   A pronoun is a part of speech used in place of a noun or of more than one noun.

4. In the following sentences, write in the blanks provided the correct pronoun that goes with the underlined antecedent. Remember, if the antecedent is singular, the pronoun must be singular. Similarly, plural antecedents require plural pronouns.

   a. Heidi loves puzzle books. ____She____ studies riddles.

   b. A riddle book can be tricky. ____It____ has many clever questions.

   c. Winston and Heidi actually collect word puzzles. ____They____ save them.

   d. Uncle Ulysses creates brainteasers. ____He____ likes mysteries too.

   e. The kids are often stumped. ____They____ cannot answer the riddles.

5. Imagine that you were sharing riddles with a friend. Using a subject pronoun and a direct object, write a sentence about what happens when you share.

   He could not answer the hard riddle.

Sentences for Practice
Subject Pronouns

Analyze the following sentences.

S hv PV
1. They are eating chili tonight.
do adv

S PV
2. I wanted some hot chili too.
adj adj do adv

S PV
3. Occasionally, we eat spicy foods.
adv adj do

S hv PV
4. Unfortunately, he will not make chili anymore.
adv adv do adv

S PV
5. It burned yesterday.
adv

From the Sideline: In each chapter, an extra practice sheet provides more sentences for analysis to use as needed—perhaps for review as a class, for individual students requiring more practice, or even as a refresher for students later in the year.

6. Earlier, he forgot the chili pot.
   S: he; PV: forgot; Earlier (adv → forgot); the (adj), chili (adj) → pot (do)

7. She will never clean the icky, sticky chili pot again.
   S: She; hv: will; PV: clean; never (adv → will clean); the (adj), icky (adj), sticky (adj), chili (adj) → pot (do); again (adv → clean)

8. Sadly, I hungrily left the table.
   S: I; PV: left; Sadly (adv), hungrily (adv) → left; the (adj) → table (do)

9. Fortunately, they brought dinner over.
   S: they; PV: brought; Fortunately (adv → brought); dinner (do); over (adv → brought)

10. We are having spicy tacos instead!
    S: We; hv: are; PV: having; spicy (adj) → tacos (do); instead (adv → are having)

Critter Riddles
Subject Pronouns

From the Sideline: Guess the Antecedent is included as an enjoyable extra, which you can do as a class or assign to individuals who finish their work early. You could also have the class write more riddles like these.

See if you can guess the antecedent for each of the following riddles. Read the three clues with their subject pronouns, and then on the line provided write the answer. Make sure your answer is a complete sentence. Create your own critter riddles and share them with your friends!

It is a house for eggs to be safe.

It is tightly woven, yet fragile.

It is stored in bushes and trees.

What is it?

It is a bird's nest.

They often make their own hills.

They have three body parts and six legs.

They have one queen, but many workers.

What are they?

They are ants.

She is busy in spring.

She cares for her fledglings.

She teaches her young to swim.

What is she?

She is a duck.

Critter Riddles
Subject Pronouns

He can fit in my pocket, if I can catch him.

He is brown, gray, or green.

He uses his back legs to jump really high and to make chirping sounds.

What is he?

He is a grasshopper or cricket.

We chatter in trees.

We hide nuts in the ground.

We scurry from branch to branch.

What are we?

We are squirrels.

I spin webs in corners of rooms.

I have eight legs and a plump body.

I look like an insect, but I am not one.

What am I?

I am a spider.

Lesson to Enjoy—Poem
Subject Pronouns

Did you have a special stuffed animal when you were little? Christopher Robin has one named Winnie the Pooh, the beloved Pooh Bear. They have an adventure together in the poem "Us Two" by A.A. Milne. As you read the poem, keep in mind that Christopher Robin is *I* in the poem because he is the one speaking. When he talks *about* Pooh Bear he uses *he*, but when he quotes his best friend, Pooh Bear calls him *you*. Look for the first-, second-, and third-person subject pronouns in this poem.

Us Two

by A.A. Milne (1882–1956)

Wherever I am, there's always Pooh,
There's always Pooh and Me.
Whatever I do, he wants to do,
"Where are you going today?" says Pooh:
"Well, that's very odd 'cos I was too.
Let's go together," says Pooh, says he,
"Let's go together," says Pooh.

"What's twice eleven?" I said to Pooh.
("Twice what?" said Pooh to Me.)
"I think it ought to be twenty-two."
"Just what I think myself," said Pooh.
"It wasn't an easy sum to do,
But that's what it is," said Pooh, said he.
"That's what it is," said Pooh.

"Let's look for dragons," I said to Pooh.
"Yes, let's," said Pooh to Me.
We crossed the river and found a few—
"Yes, those are dragons all right," said Pooh.
"As soon as I saw their beaks I knew.
That's what they are," said Pooh, said he.
"That's what they are," said Pooh.

"Let's frighten the dragons," I said to Pooh.
"That's right," said Pooh to Me.
"I'm not afraid," I said to Pooh,
And I held his paw and I shouted "Shoo!
Silly old dragons!" and off they flew.
"I wasn't afraid," said Pooh, said he,
"I'm never afraid with you."

So wherever I am, there's always Pooh,
There's always Pooh and Me.
"What would I do?" I said to Pooh,
"If it wasn't for you," and Pooh said: "True,
It isn't much fun for One, but Two,
Can stick together," says Pooh, says he.
"That's how it is," says Pooh.[2]

Questions to Ponder

1. What does "Well, that's very odd 'cos I was too" mean?
2. Who solves the math problem in the second stanza (or group of lines), and who just goes along with the answer?
3. What happens to the dragons they find?

2. A.A. Milne, "Us Two," *There's Always Pooh and Me* (New York: Dutton Children's Books, 1998), 143.

Well-Ordered Notes—Poem

Read

- Have students enjoy the poem while drinking cocoa with marshmallows in it.
- Have three volunteers read the poem: one as Christopher Robin, one as Pooh, and one as the narrator. It might be helpful if you highlight each part in different colors to make it easier for the volunteers to read.

Retell

- Use the Questions to Ponder as discussion starters:

1. **What does "Well, that's very odd 'cos I was too" mean?**
   The word *'cos* captures a child's pronunciation of *because*. Pooh asks Christopher where he's going. The poem does not include Christopher's answer, but it doesn't matter. Whatever Christopher would say, Pooh is agreeable: "Well, that's odd because I was going there too." Calling it "odd" is just Pooh's typical manner of speaking, as we know from Milne's stories.
2. **Who solves the math problem in the second stanza (or group of lines), and who just goes along with the answer?**
   This question gives you the opportunity to show how the quotation marks are working in the poem. Christopher asks the question in line one; Pooh seems a little confused by it in line two; Christopher solves it himself in line three; then Pooh agrees but points out that even though it was difficult, Christopher got it right. Pooh has been a very supportive friend in this matter.
3. **What happens to the dragons they find?**
   They fly away! And what are the dragons? Perhaps birds or ducks or maybe even chickens . . . decidedly not dragons. However, this is a poem that celebrates children's imaginations. After all, Pooh isn't real either—just a silly old stuffed bear. Or is he?

- Divide the students into pairs and have them retell in their own words what happens in the poem. Have a few pairs share their version with the others.

Record

- Have students copy the first stanza into their copybooks and add a drawing of the dragons.

Notes

1. Analyze the following sentences.

   S hv PV
   a. She did not run the (ball) aggressively.
   adv, adj, do, adv

   S PV
   b. He slowly approached the soccer (ball)
   adv, adj, adj, do

   S PV
   c. Accidentally, it hit the wrong (goal)
   adv, adj, adj, do

   S PV
   d. They never disobeyed the (coach) again.
   adv, adj, do, adv

2. Fill in the following chart with the correct subject pronouns.

Subject Pronouns

	Singular	Plural
First Person	I	we
Second Person	you	you
Third Person	he, she, it	they

3. What is a *pronoun*?

A pronoun is a part of speech used in place of a noun or of more than one noun.

4. In the following sentences, write in the blanks provided the correct pronoun that goes with the underlined antecedent. Remember, if the antecedent is singular, the pronoun must be singular. Similarly, plural antecedents require plural pronouns.

   a. The referee stopped the game. He OR She saw two geese on the field.

   b. One bird paraded to the midfield. It honked for the other.

   c. The first goose hissed at Winston. He hid behind the other players.

   d. Oddly, the players made two lines. They made a path for the geese.

   e. The two geese calmly waddled through. They left for another field.

5. Imagine that you saw the geese on the soccer field. Using a subject pronoun and a direct object, write a sentence about what happens with the geese.

They chased one player.

Quiz
Subject Pronouns — ANSWERS

1. Analyze the following sentences.

   S hv PV
   a. Earlier, they were paddling the wooden (canoe.)
   adv → were paddling; adj, adj → do

   S hv PV
   b. I was watching the two (kids) closely.
   adj, adj → do; adv → was watching

   S PV
   c. He gently rocked the tiny (boat.)
   adv → rocked; adj, adj → do

   S PV
   d. Suddenly, she fell in.
   adv → fell; adv → fell

2. Fill in the following chart with the correct subject pronouns.

Subject Pronouns

	Singular	Plural
First Person	I	we
Second Person	you	you
Third Person	he, she, it	they

3. What is a *pronoun*?

A pronoun is a part of speech used in place of a noun or of more than one noun.

4. In the following sentences, write in the blanks provided the correct pronoun that goes with the underlined antecedent. Remember, if the antecedent is singular, the pronoun must be singular. Similarly, plural antecedents require plural pronouns.

a. The guy explained the rule. Then he lifted a yellow paddle.

b. Yesterday, a lady lost this paddle. She accidentally let it go.

c. The paddle drifted downstream. It floated away.

d. The other instructor and I saw it. We grabbed the paddle.

e. Now, the kids understood the rule. They should not let go of their paddles.

5. Imagine that you saw a yellow paddle drift by on a river. Using a subject pronoun and a direct object, write a sentence about what happens with the paddle.

She saw a lost yellow paddle.

Sentences for Practice—Fable
Subject Pronouns

Analyze the following sentences.

1. It held sweet, juicy grapes.
   (S: It; PV: held; adj: sweet; adj: juicy; do: grapes)

2. They hung high.
   (S: They; PV: hung; adv: high)

3. Early, he watched the plump grapes.
   (S: he; PV: watched; adv: Early; adj: the; adj: plump; do: grapes)

4. First, he jumped up.
   (S: he; PV: jumped; adv: First; adv: up)

5. He carefully jumped again.
   (S: He; PV: jumped; adv: carefully; adv: again)

From the Sideline: These extra practice sentences are a synopsis of the fable "The Fox and the Grapes." The fable and the extended lesson notes are on the following pages.

Sentences for Practice—Fable

Subject Pronouns

S PV
6. Frantically, he wanted those delicious grapes.
adv adj adj do

S PV
7. Again, he jumped high.
adv adv

S PV
8. They clung tightly.
adv

S PV
9. He even took one last leap.
adv adj adj do

S PV
10. Finally, he scornfully left.
adv adv

Lesson to Enjoy—Fable
Subject Pronouns

Have you ever heard of something being "sour grapes"? It is a saying that is used when a person scorns (mocks) something because it can't be obtained. This expression comes from "The Fox and the Grapes," a fable written by Aesop. As you read, notice how the Fox changes his feelings about those grapes at the end of the fable.

The Fox and the Grapes

by Aesop

A Fox one day spied a beautiful bunch of ripe grapes hanging from a vine twisting around the branches of a tree. The grapes seemed ready to burst with juice, and the Fox's mouth watered as he gazed longingly at them. "That's just what I need to quench my thirst," he thought.

quench: satisfy

The bunch hung from a lofty branch, and the Fox had to jump for it. The first time he jumped, he missed it by a long way. "I'll have to do better than that," said he. "Those are probably the sweetest, most delicious grapes in all of Greece." So he walked off a short distance and took a running leap at the bunch, only to fall short once more. Again and again he tried, but in vain.

"What a fool I am," he said. "Here I am wearing myself out to get a bunch of grapes that are probably sour anyway. I wouldn't bother to eat them if they were an inch off the ground." Away he walked very, very scornfully.

Moral: It is easy to despise what you cannot have.[1]

despise: be disgusted by

1. Aesop, "The Fox and the Grapes," taken from *Writing & Rhetoric Book 1: Fable* by Paul Kortepeter (Camp Hill, PA: Classical Academic Press, 2013), 36.

Questions to Ponder

1. What does the Fox want?
2. What does "to quench my thirst" mean?
3. What does the Fox do at the end of the fable?

Well-Ordered Notes—Fable

Read

- Have students enjoy reading the fable while eating plump green and purple grapes.
- Have students sing the definition of a fable (audio track 1–14; see page 194 for lyrics).

Retell

- Use the Questions to Ponder as discussion starters:
    1. **What does the Fox want?**
    He wants grapes—but not just any grapes. These look particularly succulent, sweet, and delicious. He tries hard to get them, jumping again and again. He gives himself a little pep talk. He tries different approaches. But in the end, the grapes are impossibly high off the ground.
    2. **What does "to quench my thirst" mean?**
    To quench your thirst is to satisfy your desire for a drink. Encourage the children to think of sometime when they were really thirsty. What did it feel like? What did they long for? Have they ever quenched their thirst by eating something juicy?
    3. **What does the Fox do at the end of the fable?**
    After being so persistent, patient, and clever in his attempt to get the grapes, the fox gives up. That seems understandable. His fault lies in his revised attitude toward the grapes. Instead of admitting his shortcomings, he scorns the grapes. Ask the students if they know of any real life examples of "sour grapes."
- Have students pantomime the fable using a bunch of grapes.

Record

- Have students rewrite the fable using another animal and another fruit, such as a pig and an apple tree.
- Have students draw a poster of the Fox and the grapes and copy the moral onto it.

Notes

Sentence Bank

These four additional sentences are for extra practice if needed. The scripts are provided for your reference as you model the marking on the board while the students analyze the sentences aloud.

S PV
Earlier, we simply watched the two wild geese.
adv adv adj adj adj do

a. (First, read the sentence aloud.) "Earlier, we simply watched the two wild geese."

b. "This is a sentence and it is declarative."

c. "This sentence is about *we*." (Underline the subject.) "So, *we* is the subject because it is what the sentence is about." (Place a capital letter *S* above the subject.)

d. "This sentence tells us that we *watched*." (Double underline the predicate.) "So, *watched* is the predicate because it is what the sentence tells us about *we*." (Place a capital letter *P* above the action verb.) "It is a predicate verb because it shows action. There is no linking verb because predicate verbs do not need linking verbs." (Place a capital letter *V* to the right of the *P*.)

e. "*Geese* tells us *what* we watched." (Draw a circle around the word.) "So, *geese* is an objective element because it completes the meaning of the action verb. It is a direct object because it tells us *what* we watched." (Write *do* in lowercase letters underneath the direct object.)

f. "*Wild* tells us *what kind* of geese." (Draw a straight line down from the adjective, then a horizontal line toward the word that it modifies, and then a straight line with an arrow pointing to the word it modifies.) "So, *wild* is an adjectival element because it modifies a noun. It is an adjective." (Write *adj* in lowercase letters in the elbow opposite the line with the arrow.)

g. "*Two* tells us *how many* geese." (Draw a straight line down from the adjective, then a horizontal line toward the word that it modifies, and connect this modifier line with the modifier line for *wild* since both adjectival elements are modifying *geese*.) "So, *two* is an adjectival element because it modifies a noun. It is an adjective." (Write *adj* in lowercase letters in the elbow opposite the line with the arrow.)

h. "*The* tells us *which* geese." (Draw a straight line down from the adjective, then a horizontal line toward the word that it modifies, and connect this modifier line with the modifier line for *two* and *wild* since they are adjectival elements modifying *geese*.) "So, *the* is an adjectival element because it modifies a noun. It is an adjective." (Write *adj* in lowercase letters in the elbow opposite the line with the arrow.)

i. "*Simply* tells us *how* we watched." (Draw a straight line down from the adverb, then a horizontal line toward the word that it modifies, and then a straight line with an arrow pointing to the word it modifies.) "So, *simply* is an adverbial element because it modifies a verb. It is an adverb." (Write *adv* in lowercase letters in the elbow opposite the line with the arrow.)

j. "*Earlier* tells us *when* we watched." (Draw a straight line down from the adverb, then a horizontal line toward the word that it modifies, and connect the line to the modifying line of the word *simply*. The two modifying lines are joined and point, with a straight line, toward the word they modify.) "So, *earlier* is an adverbial element because it modifies a verb. It is an adverb." (Write *adv* in lowercase letters in the elbow opposite the line with the arrow.)

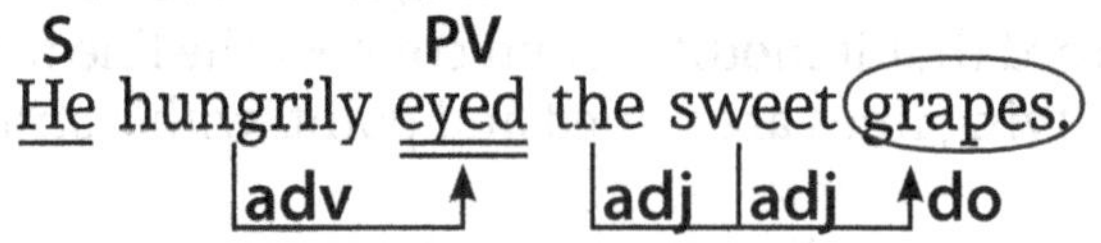

a. (First, read the sentence aloud.) "He hungrily eyed the sweet grapes."

b. "This is a sentence and it is declarative."

c. "This sentence is about *he*." (Underline the subject.) "So, *he* is the subject because it is what the sentence is about." (Place a capital letter *S* above the subject.)

d. "This sentence tells us that he *eyed*." (Double underline the predicate.) "So, *eyed* is the predicate because it is what the sentence tells us about *he*." (Place a capital letter *P* above the action verb.) "It is a predicate verb because it shows action." (Place a capital letter *V* to the right of the *P*.) "There is no linking verb because predicate verbs do not need linking verbs."

e. "*Grapes* tells us *what* he eyed." (Draw a circle around the word.) "So, *grapes* is an objective element because it completes the meaning of the action verb. It is a direct object because it tells *what* he eyed." (Write *do* in lowercase letters beneath the direct object.)

f. "*Sweet* tells us *what kind* of grapes." (Draw a straight line down from the adjective, then a horizontal line toward the word that it modifies, and then a straight line with an arrow pointing to the word it modifies.) "So, *sweet* is an adjectival element because it modifies a noun. It is an adjective." (Write *adj* in lowercase letters in the elbow opposite the line with the arrow.)

g. "*The* tells us *which* grapes." (Draw a straight line down from the adjective, then a horizontal line toward the word that it modifies and connect the line to the modifying line of the word *sweet*. The two modifying lines are joined and point, with a straight line, toward the word they modify.) "So, *the* is an adjectival element because it modifies a noun. It is an adjective." (Write *adj* in lowercase letters in the elbow of the line with the arrow.)

h. "*Hungrily* tells us *how* he eyed." (Draw a straight line down from the adverb, then a horizontal line toward the word that it modifies, and then a straight line with an arrow pointing to the word it modifies.) "So, *hungrily* is an adverbial element because it modifies a verb. It is an adverb." (Write *adv* in lowercase letters in the elbow opposite the line with the arrow.)

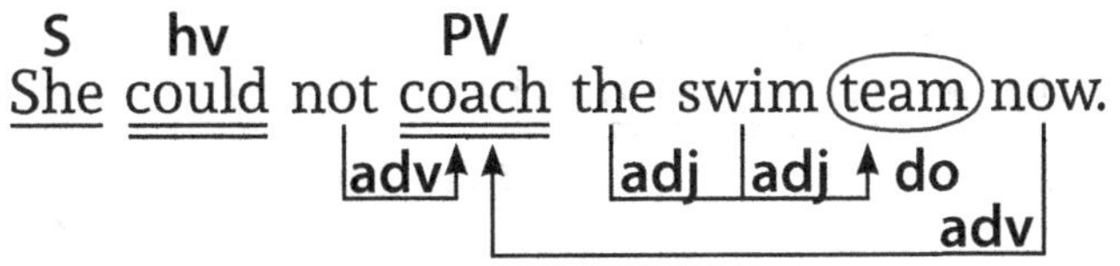

a. (First, read the sentence aloud.) "She could not coach the swim team now."

b. "This is a sentence and it is declarative."

c. "This sentence is about *she*." (Underline the subject.) "So, *she* is the subject because it is what the sentence is about." (Place a capital letter *S* above the subject.)

d. "This sentence tells us that she *could coach*." (Double underline the predicate.) "So, *could coach* is the predicate because it is what the sentence tells us about *she*." (Place a capital letter *P* above the action verb.) "It is a predicate verb because it shows action." (Place a capital letter *V* to the right of the *P*.) "There is no linking verb because predicate verbs do not need linking verbs. *Could* is the helping verb because it helps the verb." (Place a lowercase *hv* above the helping verb.)

e. "*Team* tells us *what* she could coach." (Draw a circle around the word.) "So, *team* is an objective element because it completes the meaning of the action verb. It is a direct object because it tells *what* she could coach." (Write *do* in lowercase letters beneath the direct object.)

f. "*Now* tells us *when* she could coach." (Draw a straight line down from the adverb, then a horizontal line toward the word that it modifies, and then a straight line with an arrow pointing to the word it modifies.) "So, *now* is an adverbial element because it modifies a verb. It is an adverb." (Write *adv* in lowercase letters in the elbow opposite the line with the arrow.)

g. "*Swim* tells us *what kind* of team." (Draw a straight line down from the adjective, then a horizontal line toward the word that it modifies, and then a straight line with an arrow pointing to the word it modifies.) "So, *swim* is an adjectival element because it modifies a noun. It is an adjective." (Write *adj* in lowercase letters in the elbow opposite the line with the arrow.)

h. "*The* tells us *which* team." (Draw a straight line down from the adjective, then a horizontal line toward the word that it modifies, and connect the line to the modifying line of the word *swim*. The two modifying lines are joined and point, with a straight line, toward the word they modify.) "So, *the* is an adjectival element because it modifies a noun. It is an adjective." (Write *adj* in lowercase letters in the elbow opposite the line with the arrow.)

i. "*Not* tells us *how* she could coach." (Draw a straight line down from the adverb, then a horizontal line toward the word that it modifies, and then a straight line with an arrow pointing to the word it modifies.) "So, *not* is an adverbial element because it modifies a verb. It is an adverb." (Write *adv* in lowercase letters in the elbow opposite the line with the arrow.)

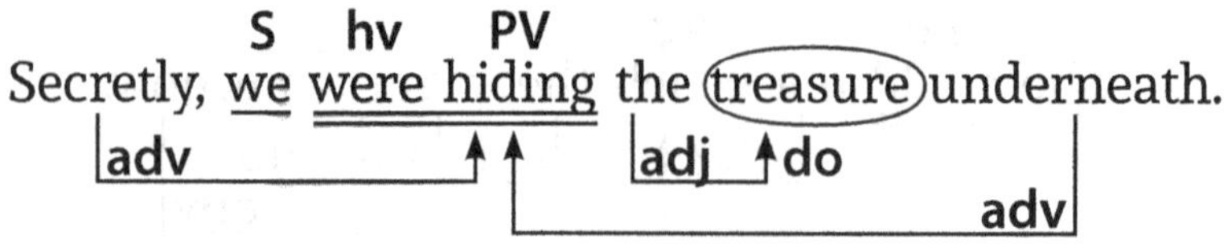

a. (First, read the sentence aloud.) "Secretly, we were hiding the treasure underneath."

b. "This is a sentence and it is declarative."

c. "This sentence is about *we*." (Underline the subject.) "So, *we* is the subject because it is what the sentence is about." (Place a capital letter *S* above the subject.)

d. "This sentence tells us that we *were hiding*." (Double underline the predicate.) "So, *were hiding* is the predicate because it is what the sentence tells us about *we*." (Place a capital letter *P* above the action verb.) "It is a predicate verb because it shows action." (Place a capital letter *V* to the right of the *P*.) "There is no linking verb because predicate verbs do not need linking verbs. *Were* is the helping verb because it helps the verb." (Place a lowercase *hv* above the helping verb.)

e. "*Treasure* tells us *what* we were hiding." (Draw a circle around the word.) "So, *treasure* is an objective element because it completes the meaning of the action verb. It is a direct object because it tells *what* we were hiding." (Write *do* in lowercase letters beneath the direct object.)

f. "*Underneath* tells us *where* we were hiding." (Draw a straight line down from the adverb, then a horizontal line toward the word that it modifies, and then a straight line with an arrow pointing to the word it modifies.) "So, *underneath* is an adverbial element because it modifies a verb. It is an adverb." (Write *adv* in lowercase letters in the elbow opposite the line with the arrow.)

g. "*The* tells us *which* treasure." (Draw a straight line down from the adjective, then a horizontal line toward the word that it modifies, and then a straight line with an arrow pointing to the word it modifies.) "So, *the* is an adjectival element because it modifies a noun. It is an adjective." (Write *adj* in lowercase letters in the elbow opposite the line with the arrow.)

h. "*Secretly* tells us *how* we were hiding." (Draw a straight line down from the adverb, then a horizontal line toward the word that it modifies, and then a straight line with an arrow pointing to the word it modifies.) "So, *secretly* is an adverbial element because it modifies a verb. It is an adverb." (Write *adv* in lowercase letters in the elbow opposite the line with the arrow.)

Notes

From the Sideline: Expect obedience. Teach students to respond quickly and eagerly. We have a saying, "Obey right away, all the way, and with a good attitude."

[A]Bring in pictures that show a happy, an angry, and a sad dog. Discuss how these images reinforce the point that a dog gives clear signals, just as a sentence can start with a hint of what comes next.

Chapter 8

Interrogative Sentences—Subject Pronouns and Helping Verbs[A]

Can you tell when a dog is happy, angry, or guilty? If he is wagging his tail, he's in a happy-go-lucky mood. It is almost as if he is asking you, "Will you play with me?" If he is showing you his teeth and snarling—step back! If his ears are down and his tail is between his legs, he is probably guilty of eating the cake your mom was saving for after dinner!

Words in sentences are a little bit like these signs that we see in the behavior of a dog. If a dog greets you with a wagging tail, you know he is asking to play. If a sentence greets you with a helping verb as its first word, it is a sign that a question is being asked. The first sign in the sentence predicts what is coming next. Consider this sentence:

Did he fetch the ball?

Do you see how it starts with the helping verb *did*? Notice how the pronoun *he* sits in between *did* and *fetch*. When we are not asking a question, the helping verb and action verb are normally together, as in *did fetch*. Be alert! Read the signs. If a helping verb starts the sentence, it means a question is coming. In this chapter, you will learn how to make sentences that ask questions. We will make these interrogative sentences using helping verbs and subject pronouns.

Ideas to Understand

As you have already learned, interrogative■ sentences ask questions. In English, there are several ways to form interrogative sentences. One way to construct a question is to place the helping verb before the subject. This placement separates the verb phrase, creating the following order: *helping verb—subject—main verb.*

To the Source:

■ interrogative
Remember, the word *interrogative* comes from the Latin word *interrogare*, meaning "to ask, to question."

Off the Shelf: You might have seen the animated movie version of *Peter Pan*, but did you know that the first version was a play produced in London in 1904? The playwright, J.M. Barrie, later wrote the novel by the same title. In the final chapter of the novel, which is not in the play or the cartoon, Peter Pan visits Wendy again after she is a grown-up woman. There's a longer passage from *Peter Pan* in The Curious Child's Literary Appendix, or you can check the book out from your library and see what happens.

To the Source:

■ contraction

The word *contraction* comes from the Latin word *contractus*, meaning "to draw together, to combine."

In the novel *Peter Pan* by J.M. Barrie, Wendy tells a story about her own mother to comfort the Lost Boys, but they keep interrupting her with declarations, exclamations, and questions. J.M. Barrie uses the *helping verb—subject—main verb* (*hv-S-PV*) structure for some of his interrogative sentences. For example, the Lost Boy called Twin asks this question:

Did you hear that, John?

The verb phrase is *did hear*. Notice how it is divided by the subject pronoun *you*: *Did—you—hear?* Later, when Wendy gets to the important part about how much a mother loves her children, the Lost Boy called Tootles interrupts with another rather profound question:

Do you like a mother's love, Nibs?[1]

The verb phrase is *do like*. It is also divided by the subject pronoun *you*: *Do—you—like?* If you read these two questions aloud, you hear that the word order signals that they are interrogative sentences before you even get to the question mark at the end.

Do you realize that when you finish this chapter, you are nearly halfway through *WOL Level 1*? You have learned about the four kinds of sentences, principal elements, modifiers, direct objects, and subject pronouns. You will use interrogative sentences, helping verbs, and subject pronouns to apply all that you have learned so far. In this chapter, you also get to learn about the **contraction**,■ which is the combined form of two words. Contractions are shortened versions of words that are created by taking out letters (sounds) and inserting an apostrophe (') in their place.

Often, subject pronouns are written or spoken as contractions with the verbs that follow them. For example, *I am* becomes *I'm* when an apostrophe replaces a space and a letter. Similarly, *it is* becomes *it's*, and *you are* is *you're*. The following chart, organized according to person and number, shows how subject pronouns can form contractions with the verbs *am*, *is*, and *are*:

Person	Singular	Plural
First Person	I am = I'm	we are = we're
Second Person	you are = you're	you are = you're
Third Person	he, she, it is = he's, she's, it's	they are = they're

1. J.M. Barrie, *Peter Pan* (New York: Dover Publications, Inc., 1999), 94–95.

The helping verbs *will* and *would* can also form contractions with subject pronouns. Notice in these sentences how the letters *wi* and *wou* are replaced by an apostrophe:

- *She'll* (she will) tell a story.
- *They'd* (they would) listen intently.

Other common contractions are created when subject pronouns combine with the helping verbs *has, have,* and *had*. For these, the letters *ha* are dropped and replaced by an apostrophe, as in these examples:

- *He's* (he has) never known his mother.
- *We've* (we have) always loved Peter Pan.
- *I'd* (I had) read the book three times before.

Pause for Punctuation

Contractions can also be made with helping verbs and the adverb *not*, which usually negates or nullifies a verb. It makes the verb mean its opposite. We form the contraction by removing the space between the helping verb and *not* and replacing the *o* in *not* with an apostrophe. (Note that the irregular contractions *won't* and *can't* are formed differently.) Contractions with *not* are often used in interrogative sentences: *Haven't* you read *Peter Pan*?

Helping Verb and Adverb	Contraction	Helping Verb and Adverb	Contraction
is not	*isn't*	would not	*wouldn't*
are not	*aren't*	do not	*don't*
was not	*wasn't*	does not	*doesn't*
were not	*weren't*	did not	*didn't*
have not	*haven't*	cannot	*can't*
has not	*hasn't*	could not	*couldn't*
had not	*hadn't*	should not	*shouldn't*
will not	*won't*	might not	*mightn't*

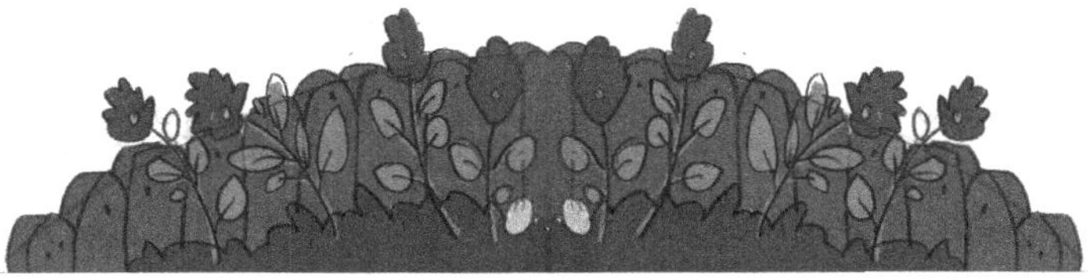

Terms to Remember[B]

All of the terms to practice for this lesson are ones you already know. Do you remember all the words and tunes? Keep practicing!

[B]For the lyrics to all of the songs, please see the Song Lyrics section on page "Song Lyrics" on page 191. Play the appropriate audio tracks and have students sing/chant along. Students should commit the songs to memory.

Principal Elements *(1–3)*

Pronoun *(1–11)*

Subject Pronouns *(1–12)*

Antecedent *(1–13)*

Verb and Helping Verb *(1–6)*

Sentences to Analyze

Let's keep practicing how to take apart sentences, which helps us see how the words work together to make meaning. In this chapter, you're going to learn how to analyze interrogative sentences. Don't worry: Declarative and interrogative sentences are analyzed in a similar way.

From the Sideline: Continue to model how to mark the sentences while the students chorally analyze them.

Analyze the following interrogative sentence. Remember to mark the sentence neatly as you say the analysis with expression.

hv S PV
Will you tell stories?
do

a. (Read the sentence first aloud.) "Will you tell stories?"

b. "This is a sentence because it is a group of words that expresses a complete thought. It is an interrogative sentence because it asks a question."

c. "This sentence is about *you*. So, *you* is the subject because it is what the sentence is about." (Since *you* is the subject, underline it and place a capital letter *S* above it.)

d. "This sentence tells us that you *will tell*. So, *will tell* is the predicate because it is what the sentence tells us about *you*." (Since *will tell* tells us something about *you*, double underline the predicate, including the helping verb, and place a capital letter *P* above the action verb.) "It is a predicate verb because it shows action. There is no linking verb because predicate verbs do not need linking verbs." (Place a capital letter *V* to the right of the *P*.) "*Will* is the helping verb because it helps a verb." (Place the lowercase letters *hv* above the helping verb.)

e. "*Stories* tells us *what* you will tell." (Since *stories* tells *what* you will tell, draw a circle around it.)

f. "So, *stories* is an objective element because it completes the meaning of an action verb. It is a direct object because it tells *what* you will tell." (Write *do* in lowercase letters beneath the direct object.)

Keep in mind that even if a sentence begins with an adverb, the *hv-S-PV* pattern still stands true.

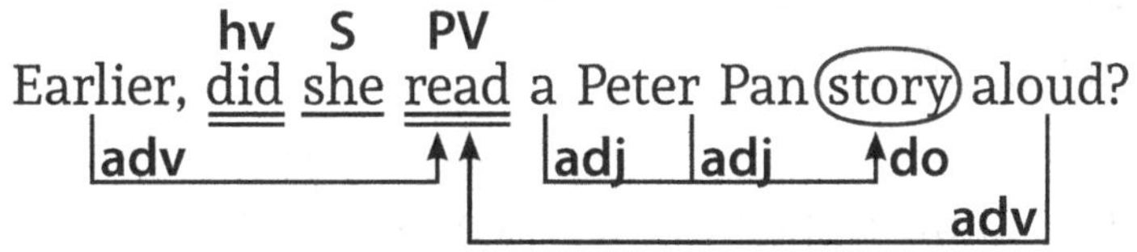

a. (Read the sentence first aloud.) "Earlier, did she read a Peter Pan story aloud?"

b. "This is a sentence because it is a group of words that expresses a complete thought. It is an interrogative sentence because it asks a question."

c. "This sentence is about *she*. So, *she* is the subject because it is what the sentence is about." (Since *she* is the subject, underline it and place a capital letter *S* above the subject.)

d. "This sentence tells us that she *did read*. So, *did read* is the predicate because it is what the sentence tells us about *she*." (Since *did read* tells us something about *she*, double underline the predicate, including the helping verb, and place a capital letter *P* above the action verb.) "It is a predicate verb because it shows action. There is no linking verb because predicate verbs do not need linking verbs." (Since *read* shows action, place a capital letter *V* to the right of the *P*.) "*Did* is the helping verb because it helps the verb." (Place the lowercase letters *hv* above the helping verb.)

e. "*Story* tells us *what* she did read." (Since *story* tells us *what* she did read, draw a circle around the word *story*.) "So, *story* is an objective element because it completes the meaning of an action verb. It is a direct object because it tells us *what* she did read." (Write *do* in lowercase letters beneath the direct object.)

f. "*Aloud* tells us *how* she did read." (Draw a straight line down from the adverb, then a horizontal line toward the word that it modifies, and then a straight line with an arrow pointing to the word it modifies.) "So, *aloud* is an adverbial element because it modifies a verb. It is an adverb." (Write *adv* in lowercase letters in the elbow opposite the line with the arrow.)

g. "*Peter Pan* tells us *what kind* of story." (Draw a straight line down from the adjective, then a horizontal line toward the word that it modifies, and then a straight line with an arrow pointing to the word it modifies.) "So, *Peter Pan* is an adjectival element because it modifies a noun. It is an adjective." (Write *adj* in lowercase letters in the elbow opposite the line with the arrow.)

h. "*A* tells us *how many* stories." (Draw a straight line down from the adjective, then a horizontal line toward the word that it modifies. Connect this modifier line with the modifier line for *Peter Pan* since both are adjectival elements modifying *story*.) "So, *a* is an adjectival element because it modifies a noun. It is an adjective." (Write *adj* in lowercase letters in the elbow opposite the line with the arrow.)

i. "*Earlier* tells us *when* she did read." (Draw a straight line down from the adverb, then a horizontal line toward the word that it modifies, and then a straight line with an arrow pointing to the word it modifies.) "So, *earlier* is an adverbial element because it modifies a verb. It is an adverb." (Write *adv* in lowercase letters in the elbow opposite the line with the arrow.)

You know how to "read" your dog. A wagging tail, snarling teeth, or drooping ears—these signs each mean something specific. As a student of grammar, you use *hv-S-PV* to read the signs in the sentence. When you are greeted with a helping verb at the start of a sentence, you know you have a question.

Flip back to the illustration at the beginning of this chapter. Is Fritz facing forward or backwards on the swing? What game do you think Winston and Rex are playing? Have you ever played with a dog?

Well-Ordered Notes A

Review It

Review the following:

What are the eight parts of speech?
What is a verb?
What are the four kinds of sentences?
What are the twenty-three helping verbs?

Practice It

Lead the students in Roll It to convert words into contractions. Copy the first chart below on the board. Have the students stand behind their desks. Give one die to the first student and let him roll it (e.g., *he rolls a four*). Then he refers to the chart on the board (e.g., *we are*) and converts the words into a contraction (e.g., *we're*). Have him explain what the apostrophe represents. If there is time, change the chart to have only contractions and have the students convert contractions into full words.

Example:
Student rolls #4; Chart #4 = we are
Student: "*We are* becomes *we're*. The apostrophe represents the letter *a* in *are*."

1. I am	4. we are
2. you are	5. you are
3. he/she/it is	6. they are

1. I'm	4. we're
2. you're	5. you're
3. he's/she's/it's	6. they're

Analyze It

From the Sideline: Visit http://capress.link/wol1att for a video demonstration of analysis.

Now, as a class, analyze the four sentences in the lesson. Here is the script for the first one to help you lead the choral analysis and model the markings on the board. The words in parentheses are like stage directions to guide you and are not to be spoken. The words in gray and enclosed in quotation marks are for you and the students to speak in chorus.

hv S PV
Will they arrive later together?
adv adv

a. (First, read the sentence aloud.) "Will they arrive later together?"

b. "This is a sentence and it is interrogative."

c. "This sentence is about *they*." (Underline the subject.) "So, *they* is the subject because it is what the sentence is about." (Place a capital letter *S* above the subject.)

d. "This sentence tells us that they *will arrive*." (Double underline the predicate.) "So, *will arrive* is the predicate because it is what the sentence tells us about *they*." (Place a capital letter *P* above the action verb.) "It is a predicate verb because it shows action. There is no linking verb because predicate verbs do not need linking verbs." (Place a capital letter *V* to the right of the *P*.) "*Will* is a helping verb because it helps the verb." (Place lowercase *hv* above the helping verb.)

e. "*Together* tell us *how* they will arrive." (Draw a straight line down from the adverb, then a horizontal line toward the word that it modifies. Connect this modifier line with the modifier line for *together* since both of the adverbial elements are modifying *arrive*.) "So, *together* is an adverbial element because it modifies a verb. It is an adverb." (Write *adv* in lowercase letters in the elbow opposite the line with the arrow.)

f. "*Later* tell us *when* they will arrive." (Draw a straight line down from the adverb, then a horizontal line toward the word that it modifies, and then a straight line with an arrow pointing to the word it modifies.) "So, *later* is an adverbial element because it modifies a verb. It is an adverb." (Write *adv* in lowercase letters in the elbow opposite the line with the arrow.)

From the Sideline: For extra guided practice, refer to the Sentence Bank at the end of this chapter.

Lesson to Learn
Interrogative Sentences

1. Analyze the following sentences.

   hv S PV
   a. Will they arrive later together?
   adv adv

   hv S PV
   b. Are we getting a new puppy?
   adj adj do

   hv S PV
   c. Did you see that frisky brown Labrador?
   adj adj adj do

   hv S PV
   d. Should he really feed those puppies too?
   adv adj do
   adv

> **From the Sideline:**
> Remember that when you see the word *analyze* in instructions throughout this book, we mean both choral analysis and written notations. The two go hand in hand as a prediagramming system.

2. Fill in the following chart with the correct subject pronouns.

Subject Pronouns

	Singular	Plural
First Person	I	we
Second Person	you	you
Third Person	he, she, it	they

3. Make the following words into *contractions*.

   a. I am: I'm

   b. you are: you're

   c. they are: they're

   d. he is: he's

   e. it is: it's

   f. we are: we're

4. Rewrite sentence *b* from exercise 1 to make it a declarative sentence. Choose a different subject pronoun as well.

   They are getting a new puppy.

5. Imagine you are playing with a brown puppy, and then write an interrogative sentence about it using a *helping verb* and a *subject pronoun*.

   Will you feed the brown puppy?

Well-Ordered Notes B

Review It

Review the following:

What is a noun?
What is a pronoun?
What is a direct object?
What are the subject pronouns?

Practice It

Lead the students in What Is Missing? to reinforce their understanding of contractions composed from the verbs *will* and *would*. Write the following chart on the board, leaving blanks for the students to fill in and omitting the answers in parentheses. Ask the students for an example of a contraction for the second-person plural (e.g., *you would*). Have a student come to the board and fill in the missing contraction (e.g., *you'd*). Have the student turn to the class and ask for another contraction, naming what type of pronoun (e.g., *a third-person singular*). Have her choose a volunteer. Continue until the whole chart is filled with the appropriate contractions.

Person	Singular	Plural
First Person	I will = ________ (I'll) I would = ________ (I'd)	We will = ________ (we'll) We would = ________ (we'd)
Second Person	you will = ________ (you'll) you would = ________ (you'd)	you will = ________ (you'll) you would = ________ (you'd)
Third Person	he will = ________ (he'll) he would = ________ (he'd) she will = ________ (she'll) she would = ________ (she'd) it will = ________ (it'll) it would = ________ (it'd)	they will = ________ (they'll) they would = ________ (they'd)

Analyze It

Now, as a class, analyze the four sentences in the lesson. Here is the script for the first one to help you lead the choral analysis and model the markings on the board. The words in parentheses are like stage directions to guide you and are not to be spoken. The words in gray and enclosed in quotation marks are for you and the students to speak in chorus.

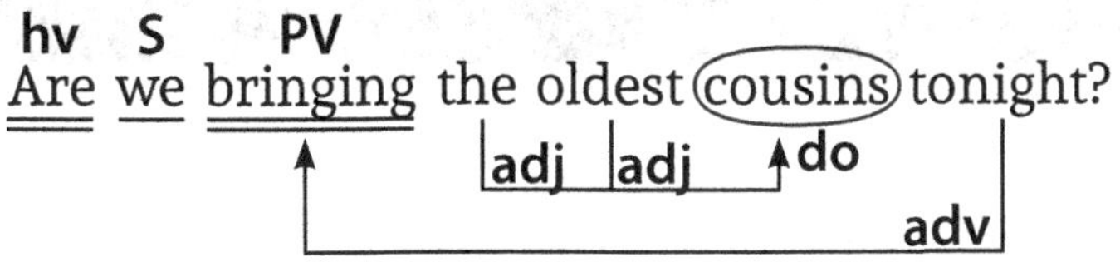

a. (First, read the sentence aloud.) "Are we bringing the oldest cousins tonight?"

b. "This is a sentence and it is interrogative."

c. "This sentence is about *we*." (Underline the subject.) "So, *we* is the subject because it is what the sentence is about." (Place a capital letter *S* above the subject.)

d. "This sentence tells us that we *are bringing*." (Double underline the predicate.) "So, *are bringing* is the predicate because it is what the sentence tells us about *we*." (Place a capital letter *P* above the action verb.) "It is a predicate verb because it shows action. There is no linking verb because predicate verbs do not need linking verbs." (Place a capital letter *V* to the right of the *P*.) "*Are* is the helping verb because it helps the verb." (Place lowercase *hv* above the helping verb.)

e. "*Cousins* tells us *whom* we are bringing." (Draw a circle around the word.) "So, *cousins* is an objective element because it completes the meaning of the action verb. It is a direct object because it tells us *whom* we are bringing." (Write *do* in lowercase letters underneath the direct object.)

f. "*Tonight* tells us *when* we are bringing." (Draw a straight line down from the adverb, then a horizontal line toward the word that it modifies, and then a straight line with an arrow pointing to the word it modifies.) "So, *tonight* is an adverbial element because it modifies a verb. It is an adverb." (Write *adv* in lowercase letters in the elbow opposite the line with the arrow.)

g. "*Oldest* tells us *what kind* of cousins." (Draw a straight line down from the adjective, then a horizontal line toward the word that it modifies, and then a straight line with an arrow pointing to the word it modifies.) "So, *oldest* is an adjectival element because it modifies a noun. It is an adjective." (Write *adj* in lowercase letters in the elbow opposite the line with the arrow.)

h. "*The* tells us *which* cousins." (Draw a straight line down from the adjective, then a horizontal line toward the word that it modifies and connect this modifier line with the modifier line for *oldest* since these adjectival elements are modifying *cousins*.) "So, *the* is an adjectival element because it modifies a noun. It is an adjective." (Write *adj* in lowercase letters in the elbow opposite the line with the arrow.)

Lesson to Learn
Interrogative Sentences

B

1. Analyze the following sentences.

   hv S PV
   a. Are we bringing the oldest (cousins) tonight?
   adj adj do adv

   hv S PV
   b. May she come along too?
   adv adv

   hv S PV
   c. Will they watch the basketball (game) tomorrow?
   adj adj do adv

   hv S PV
   d. Would you really leave the youngest two (boys) alone?
   adv adj adj adj do adv

2. Fill in the following chart with the correct subject pronouns.

Subject Pronouns

	Singular	Plural
First Person	I	we
Second Person	you	you
Third Person	he, she, it	they

3. Make the following words into *contractions*.

   a. she will: she'll

   b. they would: they'd

   c. I will: I'll

   d. we would: we'd

   e. he will: he'll

   f. you would: you'd

4. Rewrite sentence *c* from exercise 1 to make it a declarative sentence. Choose a different subject pronoun as well.

   We will watch the basketball game tomorrow.

5. Imagine your cousins or good friends are coming over to your house tonight, and then write an interrogative sentence about it using a *helping verb* and a *subject pronoun*.

   Will they come over for dinner?

Well-Ordered Notes C

Review It

Review the following:

What is a verb?
What is a transitive verb?
What are the twenty-three helping verbs?
What is an intransitive verb?
What is a direct object?

Practice It

Lead the students in Clap It Back to reinforce their understanding of contractions composed from the verbs *have* and *has*. This is a rapid-response review. Write the following chart on the board as a reference. As you speak aloud a pronoun and a verb, simultaneously clap for each word (e.g., *I have* = clap clap). Ask the students to say back in unison the appropriate contraction, clapping once as they speak the word (e.g., *I've* = clap). As you work your way through the whole chart, be sure you and your students clap once simultaneously for each word spoken.

After identifying all the contractions, flip the order. Now, say and clap a contraction (e.g., *they've* = clap) and have the students say and clap the two words that make up the contraction (e.g., *they have* = clap clap).

Example:
Teacher: "I have." (clap clap)
Students: "I've." (clap)

	Singular	Plural
First Person	I have (I've) I had (I'd)	we have (we've) we had (we'd)
Second Person	you have (you've) you had (you'd)	you have (you've) you had (you'd)
Third Person	he has (he's) he had (he'd) she has (she's) she had (she'd) it has (it's) it had (it'd)	they have (they've) they had (they'd)

Analyze It

Now, as a class, analyze the four sentences in the lesson. Here is the script for the first one to help you lead the choral analysis and model the markings on the board. The words in parentheses are like stage directions to guide you and are not to be spoken. The words in gray and enclosed in quotation marks are for you and the students to speak in chorus.

hv S PV
Please, would you grab those wet towels?
adv adj adj do

a. (First, read the sentence aloud.) "Please, would you grab those wet towels?"

b. "This is a sentence and it is interrogative."

c. "This sentence is about *you*." (Underline the subject.) "So, *you* is the subject because it is what the sentence is about." (Place a capital letter *S* above the subject.)

d. "This sentence tells us that you *would grab*." (Double underline the predicate.) "So, *would grab* is the predicate because it is what the sentence tells us about *you*." (Place a capital letter *P* above the action verb.) "It is a predicate verb because it shows action. There is no linking verb because predicate verbs do not need linking verbs." (Place a capital letter *V* to the right of the *P*.) "*Would* is a helping verb because it helps the verb." (Place a lowercase *hv* above the helping verb.)

e. "*Towels* tells us *what* you would grab." (Draw a circle around the word.) "So, *towels* is an objective element because it completes the meaning of the action verb. It is a direct object because it tells us *what* you would grab." (Write *do* in lowercase letters underneath the direct object.)

f. "*Wet* tells us *what kind* of towels." (Draw a straight line down from the adjective, then a horizontal line toward the word that it modifies, and then a straight line with an arrow pointing to the word it modifies.) "So, *wet* is an adjectival element because it modifies a noun. It is an adjective." (Write *adj* in lowercase letters in the elbow opposite the line with the arrow.)

g. "*Those* tells us *which* towels." (Draw a straight line down from the adjective, then a horizontal line toward the word that it modifies, and connect this modifier line with the modifier line for *wet* since both adjectival elements are modifying *towels*.) "So, *those* is an adjectival element because it modifies a noun. It is an adjective." (Write *adj* in lowercase letters in the elbow opposite the line with the arrow.)

h. "*Please* tells us *how* you would grab." (Draw a straight line down from the adverb, then a horizontal line toward the word that it modifies, and then a straight line with an arrow pointing to the word it modifies.) "So, *please* is an adverbial element because it modifies a verb. It is an adverb." (Write *adv* in lowercase letters in the elbow opposite the line with the arrow.)

Lesson to Learn
Interrogative Sentences

C

1. Analyze the following sentences.

a. Please, would you grab those wet towels?

hv: would; S: you; PV: grab; adv: Please (→ grab); adj: those, wet (→ towels); do: towels

b. Should they be hauling the dirty clothes downstairs?

hv: Should; S: they; hv: be; PV: hauling; adj: the, dirty (→ clothes); do: clothes; adv: downstairs (→ hauling)

c. Do I carry the laundry basket too?

hv: Do; S: I; PV: carry; adj: the, laundry (→ basket); do: basket; adv: too (→ carry)

d. Later, will he wash the extra sheets?

hv: will; S: he; PV: wash; adv: Later (→ wash); adj: the, extra (→ sheets); do: sheets

2. Fill in the following chart with the correct subject pronouns.

Subject Pronouns

	Singular	Plural
First Person	I	we
Second Person	you	you
Third Person	he, she, it	they

3. Make the following words into *contractions.*

   a. we have: we've

   b. he has: he's

   c. you had: you'd

   d. she had: she'd

   e. they have: they've

   f. I had: I'd

4. Rewrite sentence *b* from exercise 1 to make it a declarative sentence. Choose a different subject pronoun as well.

   He should be hauling the dirty clothes downstairs.

5. Imagine you are helping with laundry, and then write an interrogative sentence about it using a *helping verb* and a *subject pronoun.*

   Did you wash the socks too?

Well-Ordered Notes D

Review It

Review the following:

What is a sentence?
What is a noun?
What is a direct object?
What are the four kinds of sentences?
What are the principal elements?

Practice It

Lead the students in Make It a Sentence. Write out the following negative contractions on index cards. Distribute one card to each student. Have the students use the given negative contraction to construct a sentence either on scrap paper or orally. To help generate ideas, suggest the topic of places to go for a family day trip (e.g., a museum, a sporting event, a nature park).

Fewer than Five: Have the student(s) make a set of negative contraction cards on index cards using the provided list. Mix up the cards and put them in a basket. Have the student(s) select one card (e.g., *won't*) and orally give a sentence with that negative contraction (e.g., I *won't* have cheese on my sandwich). Have each student write at least one of his sentences on the board.

Example:

isn't: My friend *isn't* coming with us to the pioneer museum.

isn't
aren't
wasn't
weren't
haven't
hasn't
hadn't
won't
wouldn't
don't
doesn't
didn't
can't
couldn't
shouldn't

Analyze It

Now, as a class, analyze the four sentences in the lesson. Here is the script for the first one to help you lead the choral analysis and model the markings on the board. The words in parentheses are like stage directions to guide you and are not to be spoken. The words in gray and enclosed in quotation marks are for you and the students to speak in chorus.

hv S hv PV
Will you not be heading westward?
adv adv

a. (First, read the sentence aloud.) "Will you not be heading westward?"

b. "This is a sentence and it is interrogative."

c. "This sentence is about *you*." (Underline the subject.) "So, *you* is the subject because it is what the sentence is about." (Place a capital letter *S* above the subject.)

d. "This sentence tells us that you *will be heading*." (Double underline the predicate.) "So, *will be heading* is the predicate because it is what the sentence tells us about *you*." (Place a capital letter *P* above the action verb.) "It is a predicate verb because it shows action. There is no linking verb because predicate verbs do not need linking verbs." (Place a capital letter *V* to the right of the *P*.) "*Will be* are the helping verbs because they help the verb." (Place a lowercase *hv* above both of the helping verbs.)

e. "*Westward* tells us *where* you will be heading." (Draw a straight line down from the adverb, then a horizontal line toward the word that it modifies, and then a straight line with an arrow pointing to the word it modifies.) "So, *westward* is an adverbial element because it modifies a verb. It is an adverb." (Write *adv* in lowercase letters in the elbow opposite the line with the arrow.)

f. "*Not* tells us *how* you will be heading." (Draw a straight line down from the adverb, then a horizontal line toward the word that it modifies, and then a straight line with an arrow pointing to the word it modifies.) "So, *not* is an adverbial element because it modifies a verb. It is an adverb." (Write *adv* in lowercase letters in the elbow opposite the line with the arrow.)

Lesson to Learn
Interrogative Sentences

D

1. Analyze the following sentences.

    a. Will you not be heading westward?
    (hv: Will; S: you; hv: be; PV: heading; adv: not; adv: westward)

    b. Tomorrow, must I leave alone?
    (hv: must; S: I; PV: leave; adv: Tomorrow; adv: alone)

    c. Did they bring the maps along too?
    (hv: Did; S: they; PV: bring; adj: the; do: maps; adv: along; adv: too)

    d. Could he not ride behind?
    (hv: Could; S: he; PV: ride; adv: not; adv: behind)

2. Fill in the following chart with the correct subject pronouns.

Subject Pronouns

	Singular	Plural
First Person	I	we
Second Person	you	you
Third Person	he, she, it	they

3. Make the following words into *contractions*.

   a. has not: **hasn't**

   b. will not: **won't**

   c. is not: **isn't**

   d. were not: **weren't**

   e. are not: **aren't**

   f. would not: **wouldn't**

4. Rewrite sentence *b* from exercise 1 to make it a declarative sentence. Choose a different subject pronoun as well.

   Tomorrow, she must leave alone.

5. Imagine your family is going on a day trip and you want to bring a friend, and then write an interrogative sentence about it using a *helping verb* and a *subject pronoun*.

   Can I invite a friend?

Sentences for Practice
Interrogative Sentences

Analyze the following sentences.

hv S PV
1. May they play inside today?
adv adv

hv S PV
2. Did she not close the front (door) again?
adv adj adj do
adv

hv S PV
3. Quickly, could you grab the (dog)?
adv adj do

hv S PV
4. Does he always run away?
adv adv

hv S PV
5. Can you find that naughty (dog) alone?
adj adj do
adv

hv S PV
6. Must I also search?
adv

hv S PV
7. Will we wander the neighborhood together?
adj do
adv

hv S PV
8. Should she not call the police now?
adv adj do
adv

hv S PV
9. Did you find the frisky fellow?
adj adj do

hv S PV
10. Was he secretly hiding underneath?
adv adv

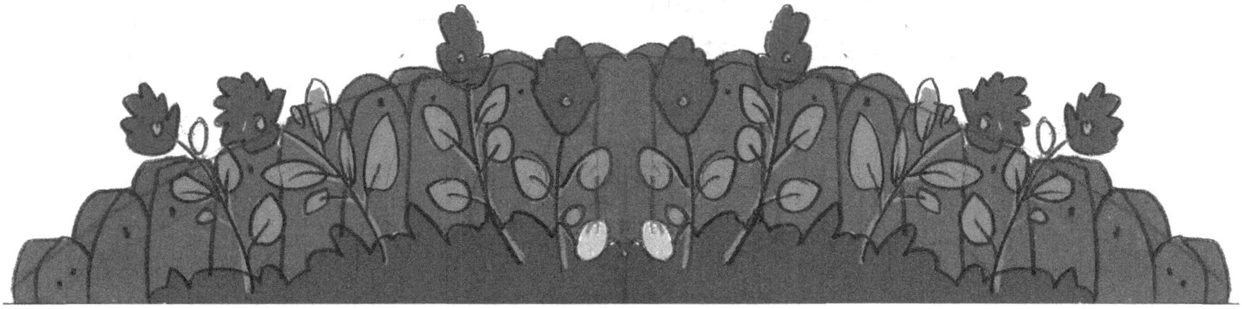

Lesson to Enjoy—Poem
Interrogative Sentences

Have you ever cracked an egg? If so, could you put it back into its shell? Usually questions are meant to have an answer, but sometimes an answer isn't expected—the questions are meant simply to make you think and wonder. Such questions are called rhetorical questions. In a way, that is what poetry does as well: it makes you ponder unusual points of view. Kate Lawrence's poem "Questions" is a sonnet (a fourteen-line rhyming poem) that strings together a number of rhetorical questions about things that can't be undone once they've been done. Read the poem carefully to note what word begins each of her interrogative sentences.

From the Sideline: Have the students reread the introductory paragraph and identify the three contractions that are used: isn't (is not), can't (cannot), they've (they have).

Questions

Kate Lawrence (n.d.)

Can you put the spider's web back in its place,
  that once has been swept away?
Can you put the apple again on the bough,
  which fell at our feet to-day?
Can you put the lily-cup back on the stem,
  and cause it to live and grow?
Can you mend the butterfly's broken wing,
  that you crushed with a hasty blow?
Can you put the bloom again on the grape,
  or the grape again on the vine?
Can you put the dewdrops back on the flowers,
  and make them sparkle and shine?
Can you put the petals back on the rose?
  If you could, would it smell as sweet?
Can you put the flour again in the husk,
  and show me the ripened wheat?

Can you put the kernel back in the nut,
  or the broken egg in its shell?
Can you put the honey back in the comb,
  and cover with wax each cell?
Can you put the perfume back in the vase,
  when once it has sped away?
Can you put the corn-silk back on the corn,
  or the down on the catkins—say?
You think my questions are trifling, dear?
  Let me ask you another one:
Can a hasty word ever be unsaid, or a deed unkind, undone?[2]

corn-silk: the long, silky threads that grow on an ear of corn
catkins: a tree with dangling, downy spikes like a pussy willow
trifling: of little importance, trivial

Questions to Ponder

1. What does it mean to put a "lily-cup back on the stem"?
2. What line in the poem summarizes or explains why Lawrence wrote all these questions?
3. Can you think of a time when you used hasty words?

2. Kate Lawrence, "Questions," *Wide Awake* 16, no. 1 (December 1882), ed. Charles Trowbridge Pratt, Chautauqua Young Folks' Reading Union (Boston: D. Lothrop & Company, 1883), 91. Available at https://books.google.com/books?id=dNnNAAAAMAAJ.

Well-Ordered Notes—Poem

Read

- Read the poem slowly first, stopping after each line so the students can picture what is being described. If it is possible, bring in props to demonstrate the impossibility of undoing each action described. For example, demonstrate lines 2, 5, or 9 with an apple still attached to a branch, a bunch of grapes, or an egg.
- Assign fourteen students to read the poem aloud, standing for their individual lines and then being seated when completed. Have the first student read the first line, the second student read the second line, and so forth.

Retell

- Use the Questions to Ponder as discussion starters:

  1. **What does it mean to put a "lily-cup back on the stem"?**
     The flower of a lily plant is shaped a bit like a cup, which you can demonstrate to the students clearly by showing them pictures of a calla lily, a trumpet lily, or a lily of the valley. In ordinary speech, one might say such plants have "cup-shaped flowers," but the poet creates a condensed expression with "lily-cup." Once that flower is picked, it's separated from the stem permanently and will no longer "live and grow."
  2. **What line in the poem summarizes or explains why Lawrence wrote all these questions?**
     The last line explains the point of the poem. It is introduced and emphasized by the line that immediately precedes it. All of the images from nature in the first twelve lines of the poem turn out to be analogies for the idea in the last line: If people speak or act without consideration for others, they can't undo the damage. Like many sonnets, this poem provides in the last two lines a sort of resolution to a problem laid out in the first twelve lines.
  3. **Can you think of a time when you used hasty words?**
     Answers will vary. Allow the students to think and share, and then ask them which of the images from nature in the poem best represents their experience of saying something they wish they hadn't.

- Modify lines of the poem so students can analyze them either as a group or individually.

  Example:
  Can you mend the torn web?
  Can you reattach an apple?
  Can you glue back a lily-cup?

Record

- Have the students write in their copybook their favorite line or two from the poem and draw a picture to go with their sentences.
- Using the following template, write a class poem similar to "Questions." Have the children brainstorm nouns that would work in the blanks. The answers provided are suggestions.

Can You Put the Oak Leaf Back?

by Tammy Peters

Can you put the ___oak leaf___ back on its branch so fair?
Can you put the ___pumpkin___ back on the vine? It's rare!
Can you put the ___song notes___ back in a lark now gone?
Can you put the ___color___ back, once December dawns?
Can you put the ___cinnamon___, once sprinkled, in its jar?
Can you put the ___apple slices___ back to make a star*?
Can you put the ___milkweed seed___ back into its shell?
Can you put the ___fire___ back once it's snuffed out well?
Can you put the ___pinecones___ back once timbers shake?
Can you put the ___crumbs___ together back into a cake?
Can you put the ___river___ back, once gushed, among the rocks?
Can you put the ___minutes___ back once they've ticked on clocks?
My questions may seem silly, friend. Let me ask another:
Can hasty words be unsaid, or unkind deeds recovered?

*A star is hidden in the center of an apple. If you cut an apple across the middle (east to west), you'll find the seeds in a star-shape pattern.

Review
Interrogative Sentences
ANSWERS

1. Analyze the following sentences.

    hv S PV
    a. Do you want these squishy apples?
    adj adj do

    hv S PV
    b. May I have the last good apple?
    adj adj adj do

    hv S PV
    c. Will she make an apple pie?
    adj adj do

    hv S PV
    d. Could we make applesauce instead?
    do adv

2. Fill in the following chart with the correct subject pronouns.

Subject Pronouns

	Singular	Plural
First Person	I	we
Second Person	you	you
Third Person	he, she, it	they

3. Make the following words into *contractions.*

   a. they are: they're

   b. had not: hadn't

   c. you will: you'll

   d. will not: won't

   e. I have: I've

   f. it is: it's

4. Rewrite sentence *c* from exercise 1 to make it a declarative sentence. Choose a different subject pronoun as well.

   They will make an apple pie.

5. Imagine you are gathering apples to make an apple pie, and then write an interrogative sentence about it using a *helping verb* and a *subject pronoun.*

   Do you use the green apples?

Quiz
Interrogative Sentences

ANSWERS

1. Analyze the following sentences.

   hv S PV
   a. Are you doing (chores) today?
   do adv

   hv S PV
   b. Will he load the heavy (box) alone?
   adj adj do
   adv

   hv S PV
   c. Did they chop some (wood) earlier?
   adj do
   adv

   hv S PV
   d. Should we scrub underneath too?
   adv adv

2. Fill in the following chart with the correct subject pronouns.

Subject Pronouns

	Singular	Plural
First Person	I	we
Second Person	you	you
Third Person	he, she, it	they

3. Make the following words into *contractions.*

   a. I am: I'm

   b. they are: they're

   c. she is: she's

   d. you would: you'd

   e. is not: isn't

   f. we will: we'll

4. Rewrite sentence *b* from exercise 1 to make it a declarative sentence. Choose a different subject pronoun as well.

   I will load the heavy box alone.

5. Imagine you are doing chores on the weekend, and then write an interrogative sentence about it using a *helping verb* and a *subject pronoun.*

   Will you sweep the garage?

Sentences for Practice—Fable
Interrogative Sentences

Analyze the following sentences.

> **From the Sideline:** These extra practice sentences are a synopsis of the fable "The Donkey and His Driver." The fable and the extended lesson notes are on the following pages.

hv S PV
1. Can I follow the leader afterward?
adj do
adv

hv S PV
2. Has he stubbornly not moved yet?
adv adv adv

hv S PV
3. Should he watch the Master?
adj do

hv S PV
4. Might you listen?

hv S PV
5. Does he not realize the distance?
adv adj do

hv S PV
6. Finally, would he pull the cart forward too?
adv adj do
adv adv

Sentences for Practice—Fable
Interrogative Sentences

hv S PV
7. Does he understand?

hv S PV
8. Could you stop that animal?
adj do

hv S PV
9. Was he pulling away?
adv

hv S PV
10. Did he not learn the moral?
adv adj do

Lesson to Enjoy—Fable
Interrogative Sentences

Have you ever been so stubborn that you didn't listen to the good sense or wisdom of another? In this next fable by Aesop, a donkey decides he knows best. His reward for his stubbornness is his own demise, that is, his death. What do you think of his idea?

The Donkey and His Driver

by Aesop

A Donkey was being driven along a road leading down the mountainside, and the animal suddenly took it in his silly head to choose his own path. He could see his barn at the foot of the mountain. To him, the quickest way down seemed to be over the edge off the nearest cliff. Just as he was about to leap over, his Master caught him by the tail and tried to pull him back.

"Stop!" cried the Master. "Stop or you will surely break your neck!"

yield: give up

The stubborn Donkey would not yield and pulled with all his might.

willful: stubborn

"Very well," said his Master, "go your way, you willful beast, and see where it leads you."

With that he let go, and the foolish Donkey tumbled head over heels down the mountainside.

misfortune: bad luck

Moral: They who refuse to listen to good reason and advice deserve their misfortune.[1]

1. Aesop, "The Ass and His Driver," from *Writing & Rhetoric Book 1: Fable* by Paul Kortepeter (Camp Hill, PA: Classical Academic Press, 2013), 48.

Questions to Ponder

1. What was the crazy idea the Donkey had?
2. What does "the quickest way down seemed to be over the edge" mean?
3. What does the Master do when the Donkey continues to pull "with all his might"?

Well-Ordered Notes—Fable

Read

- Read the fable aloud while listening to a piece of classical music, such as *The Donkey and the Driver*, op. 61 by Steven Isserlis with Thomas Ades (available at http://capress.link/wol1arev0801).
- Have students sing the definition of a fable (audio track 1–14; see page 194 for lyrics).

Retell

- Use the Questions to Ponder as discussion starters:
    1. **What was the crazy idea the Donkey had?**
    The Donkey thought he should be able to decide which way to go. He should have known that the Master would make a wiser choice.
    2. **What does "the quickest way down seemed to be over the edge" mean?**
    The Donkey thought following a straight line would be the quickest way to travel from one point to another. But that straight line was straight down!
    3. **What does the Master do when the Donkey continues to pull "with all his might"?**
    The Master lets go of the Donkey's tail. He figures the Donkey deserves what he gets because of his stubborn foolishness. He gives up trying to change the donkey's mind. Ask the students if they have ever been like the Donkey or the Master.
- Have students act out the fable. Add characters—the Master's family or friends—who try to make other arguments to convince the Donkey to stop trying to go over the edge.

Record

- Have the students rewrite the moral in fewer words, such as "Stubborn fools deserve their destruction." Then, have the students draw a picture of the poem using their moral.
- Have the students make a diorama of the fable using shoeboxes.

Notes

Sentence Bank

These four additional sentences are for extra practice if needed. The scripts are provided for your reference as you model the marking on the board while the students analyze the sentences aloud.

hv S PV
Are they working together?
adv

a. (First, read the sentence aloud.) "Are they working together?"

b. "This is a sentence because it is a group of words that expresses a complete thought. It is an interrogative sentence because it asks a question."

c. "This sentence is about *they*." (Underline the subject.) "So, *they* is the subject because it is what the sentence is about." (Place a capital letter *S* above the subject.)

d. "This sentence tells us that they *are working*." (Double underline the helping verb and the predicate verb.) "So, *are working* is the predicate because it is what the sentence tells us about *they*." (Place a capital letter *P* above the action verb.) "It is a predicate verb because it shows action." (Place a capital letter *V* to the right of the *P*.) "There is no linking verb because predicate verbs do not need linking verbs. *Are* is the helping verb." (Place the lowercase letters *hv* above the helping verb.)

e. "*Together* tells us *how* they are working." (Draw a straight line down from the adverb, then a horizontal line toward the word that it modifies, and then a straight line with an arrow pointing to the word it modifies.) "So, *together* is an adverbial element because it modifies a verb. It is an adverb." (Write *adv* in lowercase letters in the elbow opposite the line with the arrow.)

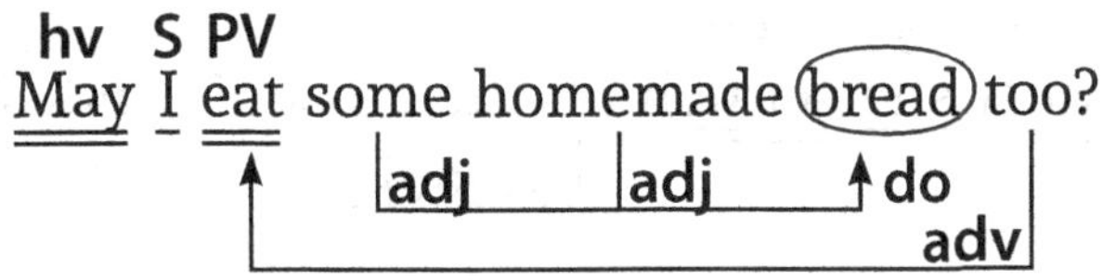

a. (First, read the sentence aloud.) "May I eat some homemade bread too?"

b. "This is a sentence because it is a group of words that expresses a complete thought. It is an interrogative sentence because it asks a question."

c. "This sentence is about *I*." (Underline the subject.) "So, *I* is the subject because it is what the sentence is about." (Place a capital letter *S* above the subject.)

d. "This sentence tells us that I *may eat*." (Double underline the helping verb and predicate verb.) "So, *may eat* is the predicate because it is what the sentence tells us about *I*." (Place a capital letter *P* above the action verb.) "It is a predicate verb because it shows action." (Place a capital letter *V* to the right of the *P*.) "There is no linking verb because predicate verbs do not need linking verbs. *May* is the helping verb because it helps the verb." (Place a lowercase *hv* above the helping verb.)

e. "*Bread* tells us *what* I may eat." (Draw a circle around the word.) "So, *bread* is an objective element because it completes the meaning of the action verb. It is a direct object because it tells *what* I may eat." (Write *do* in lowercase letters beneath the direct object.)

f. "*Too* tells us *how* I may eat." (Draw a straight line down from the adverb, then a horizontal line toward the word that it modifies, and then a straight line with an arrow pointing to the word it modifies.) "So, *too* is an adverbial element because it modifies a verb. It is an adverb." (Write *adv* in lowercase letters in the elbow opposite the line with the arrow.)

g. "*Homemade* tells us *what kind* of bread." (Draw a straight line down from the adjective, then a horizontal line toward the word that it modifies, and then a straight line with an arrow pointing to the word it modifies.) "So, *homemade* is an adjectival element because it modifies a noun. It is an adjective." (Write *adj* in lowercase letters in the elbow opposite the line with the arrow.)

h. "*Some* tells us *how much* bread." (Draw a straight line down from the adjective, then a horizontal line toward the word that it modifies and connect the line to the modifying line of the word *homemade*. The two modifying lines are joined and point, with a straight line, toward the word they modify.) "So, *some* is an adjectival element because it modifies a noun. It is an adjective." (Write *adj* in lowercase letters in the elbow opposite the line with the arrow.)

hv S PV
Must she scratch all the mosquito (bites?)
adj adj adj do

a. (First, read the sentence aloud.) "Must she scratch all the mosquito bites?"

b. "This is a sentence because it is a group of words that expresses a complete thought. It is an interrogative sentence because it asks a question."

c. "This sentence is about *she*." (Underline the subject.) "So, *she* is the subject because it is what the sentence is about." (Place a capital letter *S* above the subject.)

d. "This sentence tells us that she *must scratch*." (Double underline the helping verb and predicate verb.) "So, *must scratch* is the predicate because it is what the sentence tells us about *she*." (Place a capital letter *P* above the action verb.) "It is a predicate verb because it shows action." (Place a capital letter *V* to the right of the *P*.) "There is no linking verb because predicate verbs do not need linking verbs. *Must* is the helping verb." (Place a lowercase *hv* above the helping verb.)

e. "*Bites* tells us *what* she must scratch." (Draw a circle around the word.) "So, *bites* is an objective element because it completes the meaning of the action verb. It is a direct object because it tells *what* she must scratch." (Write *do* in lowercase letters beneath the direct object.)

f. "*Mosquito* tells us *what kind* of bites." (Draw a straight line down from the adjective, then a horizontal line toward the word that it modifies, and then a straight line with an arrow pointing to the word it modifies.) "So, *mosquito* is an adjectival element because it modifies a noun. It is an adjective." (Write *adj* in lowercase letters in the elbow opposite the line with the arrow.)

g. "*The* tells us *which* bites." (Draw a straight line down from the adjective, then a horizontal line toward the word that it modifies and connect the line to the modifying line of the word *mosquito*. The two modifying lines are joined and point, with a straight line, toward the word they modify.) "So, *the* is an adjectival element because it modifies a noun. It is an adjective." (Write *adj* in lowercase letters in the elbow opposite the line with the arrow.)

h. "*All* tells us *how many* bites." (Draw a straight line down from the adjective, then a horizontal line toward the word that it modifies and connect the line to the modifying line of the words *the* and *mosquito*. The three modifying lines are joined and point, with a straight line, toward the word they modify.) "So, *all* is an adjectival element because it modifies a noun. It is an adjective." (Write *adj* in lowercase letters in the elbow opposite the line with the arrow.)

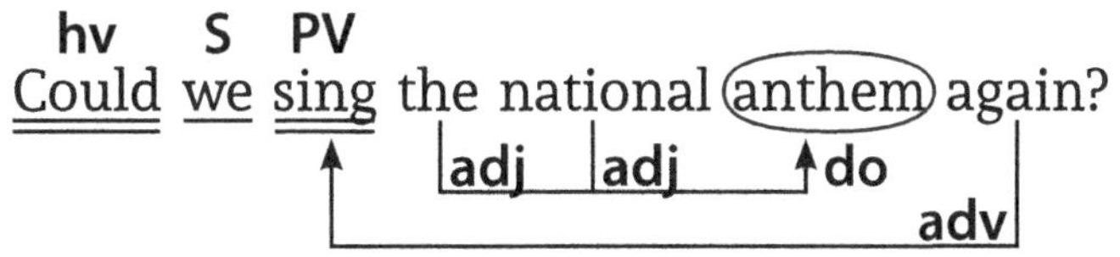

a. (First, read the sentence aloud.) "Could we sing the national anthem again?"

b. "This is a sentence because it is a group of words that expresses a complete thought. It is an interrogative sentence because it asks a question."

c. "This sentence is about *we*." (Underline the subject.) "So, *we* is the subject because it is what the sentence is about." (Place a capital letter *S* above the subject.)

d. "This sentence tells us that we *could sing*." (Double underline the predicate.) "So, *could sing* is the predicate because it is what the sentence tells us about *we*." (Place a capital letter *P* above the action verb.) "It is a predicate verb because it shows action." (Place a capital letter *V* to the right of the *P*.) "There is no linking verb because predicate verbs do not need linking verbs. *Could* is the helping verb because it helps the verb." (Place a lowercase *hv* above the helping verb.)

e. "*Anthem* tells us *what* we could sing." (Draw a circle around the word.) "So, *anthem* is an objective element because it completes the meaning of the action verb. It is a direct object because it tells *what* we could sing." (Write *do* in lowercase letters beneath the direct object.)

f. "*Again* tells us *how* we could sing." (Draw a straight line down from the adverb, then a horizontal line toward the word that it modifies, and then a straight line with an arrow pointing to the word it modifies.) "So, *again* is an adverbial element because it modifies a verb. It is an adverb." (Write *adv* in lowercase letters in the elbow opposite the line with the arrow.)

g. "*National* tells us *what kind* of anthem." (Draw a straight line down from the adjective, then a horizontal line toward the word that it modifies, and then a straight line with an arrow pointing to the word it modifies.) "So, *national* is an adjectival element because it modifies a noun. It is an adjective." (Write *adj* in lowercase letters in the elbow opposite the line with the arrow.)

h. "*The* tells us *which* anthem." (Draw a straight line down from the adjective, then a horizontal line toward the word that it modifies and connect the line to the modifying line of the word *national*. The two modifying lines are joined and point, with a straight line, toward the word they modify.) "So, *the* is an adjectival element because it modifies a noun. It is an adjective." (Write *adj* in lowercase letters in the elbow opposite the line with the arrow.)

The Curious Child 's Literary Appendix

In each chapter, we have used a classic poem or excerpt from a classic book to illustrate the grammatical principles taught in that chapter. Reading just a few lines from a fine piece of literature is like getting a small sample of something savory (delicious) at the grocery store. That is called "whetting your appetite." If you want more, you beg to be allowed to buy what you only tasted.

Have you been tantalized by any of the literary samples? If so, you can find the fuller feast here in this appendix. All the poems are presented in their entirety. All the excerpts from fiction are presented in more detail to whet (sharpen) your appetite for the whole book from which they are taken.

Of course, you can really treat yourself to a banquet at the library, where you can check out and read the novels or entire collections of poetry. *Bon appétit!* (Enjoy!)

From the Sideline: The passages in bold text in this appendix indicate the excerpts that are included in the chapters. You and your students will be able to see at a glance how the portions of text you've already studied fit into the larger context of the stories or poems.

Chapter 1

What O'Clock?

by Edith Nesbit (1858–1924)

What o'clock is it, children dear?
Ask of the dandelions here!
Blow, blow, blow, and away they go—
But they do not tell us the time you know!

what o'clock: a poetic way of asking someone what time it is; in England, a fluffy dandelion gone to seed is called a "clock"

Say, what month is it, children dear?
We think it is August because we hear
The swing of the sickle, restless and slow,
And that's a sign of the month, you know.

sickle: a curved blade with a handle; used to cut grain or grass.

Where are you going, children dear?
Where the lane winds deep and the stream runs clear—
There are plenty of beautiful ways to go—
But only one way that two only know.

Where are *we* going, children dear?
To a beautiful country that's very near,
Hand in hand is the way to go
Up into fairyland you know.[1]

1. E. Nesbit and Saretta Nesbit (aka Caris Brooke), *All Round the Year* (London: Von Portheim & Co.), last modified January 20, 2007, http://tinyurl.com/ocao7gy.

Chapter 2

At the Back of the North Wind

From Chapter 4, "North Wind"
by George MacDonald (1824–1905)

"What will you do, then?" asked Diamond.

"Move on," she answered.

"Where?"

"Oh, anywheres. Bless you, I'm used to it."

"Hadn't you better come home with me, then?"

"That's a good joke, when you don't know where it is. Come on."

"But where?"

"Oh, nowheres in particular. Come on."

Diamond obeyed. The wind had now fallen considerably. They wandered on and on, turning in this direction and that, without any reason for one way more than another, until they had got out of the thick of the houses into a waste kind of place. By this time they were both very tired. Diamond felt a good deal inclined to cry, and thought he had been very silly to get down from the back of the North Wind; not that he would have minded it if he had done the girl any good; but he thought he had been of no use to her. He was mistaken there, for she was far happier for having Diamond with her than if she had been wandering about alone. She did not seem so tired as he was.[2]

inclined: willing to

2. George MacDonald, *At the Back of the North Wind* (Philadelphia, PA: Lippincott Company, 1909), 42.

Chapter 3

Song of the Brook

by Alfred, Lord Tennyson (1809–1892)

I come from haunts of coot and hern,[3]
I make a sudden sally,
And sparkle out among the fern,
To bicker down a valley.

haunts: frequently visited places
coot: a type of water bird with a white spot on its forehead
hern: heron
sally: rushing action
bicker: flow down with a lot of noise

By thirty hills I hurry down,
Or slip between the ridges,
By twenty thorps, a little town,
And half a hundred bridges.

thorps: a type of village

Till last by Philip's farm I flow
To join the brimming river,
For men may come and men may go,
But I go on for ever.

brimming: water spilling over

I chatter over stony ways,
In little sharps and trebles,
I bubble into eddying bays,
I babble on the pebbles.

sharps: above true or normal pitch
trebles: high-pitched tune
eddying: swirling

With many a curve my banks I fret
By many a field and fallow,
And many a fairy foreland set
With willow-weed and mallow.

fret: to trouble or erode
fallow: land left uncultivated
foreland: piece of land that extends into the sea
mallow: plant with hairy stems and leaves and pink, white, or purple flowers

I chatter, chatter, as I flow
To join the brimming river,
For men may come and men may go,
But I go on for ever.

3. Marginal definitions taken from http://www.english-for-students.com/The-Brook.html.

I wind about, and in and out,
With here a blossom sailing,
And here and there a lusty trout,
And here and there a grayling,

lusty trout: a big, freshwater fish
grayling: another type of fish

And here and there a foamy flake
Upon me, as I travel
With many a silvery waterbreak
Above the golden gravel,

waterbreak: a ripple

And draw them all along, and flow
To join the brimming river,
For men may come and men may go,
But I go on for ever.

I steal by lawns and grassy plots,
I slide by hazel covers;
I move the sweet forget-me-nots
That grow for happy lovers.

steal: flow very quietly
covers: hazel thickets that hide game
forget-me-nots: a type of flower

I slip, I slide, I gloom, I glance,
Among my skimming swallows;
I make the netted sunbeam dance
Against my sandy shallows.

gloom: frown
glance: flash or sparkle
skimming swallows: birds flying close to the water surface

I murmur under moon and stars
In brambly wildernesses;
I linger by my shingly bars;
I loiter round my cresses;

brambly: prickly
shingly bars: patches of loose gravel
loiter: not move on
cresses: strong-smelling plants

And out again I curve and flow
To join the brimming river,
For men may come and men may go,
But I go on forever.[4]

4. Lord Tennyson Alfred, "Song of the Brook," ed. Edna Johnson, Carrie E. Scott, and Evelyn R. Sickels, *Anthology of Children's Literature* (Cambridge, Massachusetts: Houghton Mifflin Company, 1948), 924–925.

Chapter 4

The Kitten Playing with the Falling Leaves

by William Wordsworth (1770–1850)

See the Kitten on the wall
Sporting with the leaves that fall!
Withered leaves, one, two, and three,
From the lofty elder-tree.
Through the calm and frosty air
Of this morning bright and fair
Eddying round and round they sink
Softly, slowly.—One might think,
From the motions that are made,
Every little leaf conveyed
Some small fairy, hither tending,
To this lower world descending.
—But the Kitten, how she starts!
Crouches, stretches, paws, and darts:
First at one, and then its fellow,
Just as light, and just as yellow;
There are many now—now one—
Now they stop and there are none.
What intentness of desire
In her up-turned eye of fire!
With a tiger-leap half way
Now she meets the coming prey.
Lets it go at last, and then
Has it in her power again.[5]

lofty: very high

eddying: moving in a circular way

hither: toward
tending: in a direction

prey: something that is hunted

5. William Wordsworth, "The Kitten Playing with the Falling Leaves," in *The Golden Treasury of Poetry*, ed. Louis Untermeyer (New York: Golden Press, 1998), 44.

Chapter 5

The House at Pooh Corner

From Chapter 7, "Tigger Is Unbounced"
by A.A. Milne (1882–1956)

"No," said Pooh. "But there are twelve pots of honey in my cupboard, and they've been calling to me for hours. I couldn't hear them properly before, because Rabbit *would* talk, but if nobody says anything except those twelve pots, I *think*, Piglet, I shall know where they're calling from. Come on."

They walked off together; and for a long time Piglet said nothing, so as not to interrupt the pots; and then suddenly he made a squeaky noise . . . and an oo-noise . . . because now he began to know where he was; but he still didn't dare to say so out loud, in case he wasn't. **And just when he was getting so sure of himself that it didn't matter whether the pots went on calling or not, there was a shout from in front of them, and out of the mist came Christopher Robin.**

"Oh, there you are," said Christopher Robin carelessly, trying to pretend that he hadn't been Anxious.

"Here we are," said Pooh.

"Where's Rabbit?"

"I don't know," said Pooh.

"Oh—well, I expect Tigger will find him. He's sort of looking for you all."

"Well," said Pooh, "I've got to go home for something, and so has Piglet, because we haven't had it yet, and—"

"I'll come and watch you," said Christopher Robin.

So he went home with Pooh, and watched him for quite a long time . . . and all the time he was watching, **Tigger was tearing round the Forest making loud yapping noises for Rabbit. And at last a very Small and Sorry Rabbit heard him. And the Small and Sorry Rabbit rushed through the mist at the noise, and it suddenly turned into Tigger; a Friendly Tigger, a Grand Tigger, a Large and Helpful Tigger, a Tigger who bounced, if he bounced at all, in just the beautiful way a Tigger ought to bounce.**

"Oh, Tigger, I *am* glad to see you," cried Rabbit.[6]

6. A.A. Milne, *The House at Pooh Corner* (New York: Dell Publishing Inc., Co. 1956), 124–127.

Chapter 6

Of a Spider

by Wilfrid Thorley (1878–1963)

The spider weaves his silver wire
Between the cherry and the brier.

He runs along and sees the thread
Well-fastened on each hawser-head.

And then within his wheel he dozes
Hung on a thorny stem of roses,

While fairies ride the silver ferry
Between the rose-bud and the cherry.[7]

brier: prickly bush

hawser-head: the top of a small cable (spider thread)

dozes: naps

ferry: a ship that carries people or things across a body of water; here, fairies ride the silver spider web

7. Wilfrid Thorley, "Of a Spider," in *Favorite Poems Old and New*, ed. Helen Ferris, (New York: Doubleday & Company, Inc., 1957), 141–142.

Chapter 7

The Cricket in Times Square

From Chapter 4, "Harry Cat"
by George Selden Thompson (1929–1989)

"Yes," said Chester. "These wings aren't much good for flying, but I prefer music anyhow." He made three rapid chirps.

Tucker Mouse and Harry Cat smiled at each other. "It makes me want to purr to hear it," said Harry.

"Some people say a cricket goes 'chee chee chee,'" explained Chester. "And others say, 'treet treet treet,' but we crickets don't think it sounds like either one of those."

"It sounds to me as if you were going 'crik crik crik,'" said Harry.

"Maybe that's why they call him a 'cricket,'" said Tucker.

They all laughed. Tucker had a squeaky laugh that sounded as if he were hiccupping. Chester was feeling much happier now. The future did not seem nearly as gloomy as it had over in the pile of dirt in the corner.

"Are you going to stay a while in New York?" asked Tucker.

"I guess I'll have to," said Chester. "I don't know how to get home."

"Well, we could always take you to Grand Central Station and put you on a train going back to Connecticut," said Tucker. "But why don't you give the city a try. Meet new people—see new things. Mario likes you very much."[8]

8. George Selden Thompson, *The Cricket in Times Square* (New York: A Yearling Book, 1960), 30.

Chapter 8

Peter Pan

From Chapter 11, "Wendy's Story"
by J.M. Barrie (1860–1937)

"Little less noise there," Peter called out, determined that she should have fair play, however beastly a story it might be in his opinion.

beastly: very unpleasant

"The gentleman's name," Wendy continued, "was Mr. Darling, and her name was Mrs. Darling."

"I knew them," John said, to annoy the others.

"I think I knew them," said Michael rather doubtfully.

"They were married, you know," explained Wendy, "and what do you think they had?"

"White rats," cried Nibs, inspired.

"No."

"It's awfully puzzling," said Tootles, who knew the story by heart.

puzzling: confusing

"Quiet, Tootles. They had three descendants."

descendants: children

"What is descendants?"

"Well, you are one, Twin."

"**Did you hear that, John?** I am a descendant."

"Descendants are only children," said John.

"Oh dear, oh dear," sighed Wendy. "Now these three children had a faithful nurse called Nana; but Mr. Darling was angry with her and chained her up in the yard, and so all the children flew away."

"It's an awfully good story," said Nibs.

"They flew away," Wendy continued, "to the Neverland, where the lost children are."

"I just thought they did," Curly broke in excitedly. "I don't know how it is, but I just thought they did!"

"O Wendy," cried Tootles, "was one of the lost children called Tootles?"

"Yes, he was."

"I am in a story. Hurrah, I am in a story, Nibs."

hurrah: used to express joy or approval

"Hush. Now I want you to consider the feelings of the unhappy parents with all their children flown away."

"Oo!" they all moaned, though they were not really considering the feelings of the unhappy parents one jot.

jot: a very small amount

"Think of the empty beds!"

"Oo!"

"It's awfully sad," the first twin said cheerfully.

"I don't see how it can have a happy ending," said the second twin. "Do you, Nibs?"

"I'm frightfully anxious."

"If you knew how great is a mother's love," Wendy told them triumphantly, "you would have no fear." She had now come to the part that Peter hated.

"I do like a mother's love," said Tootles, hitting Nibs with a pillow. **"Do you like a mother's love, Nibs?"**

"I do just," said Nibs, hitting back.

"You see," Wendy said complacently, "our heroine knew that the mother would always leave the window open for her children to fly back by; so they stayed away for years and had a lovely time."[9]

heroine: a female hero or noble character in a story

9. J.M. Barrie, *Peter Pan* (New York: Dover Publications, Inc., 1999), 94–95.

The Curious Child 's Literary Appendix

Understanding Poetry

While the poetry in Well-Ordered Language is provided primarily as enrichment, supplementing the teaching of grammar, you may want to use the poems we have selected as part of your literature curriculum as well. To that end, as you have seen, the literary appendix includes either the full text or a longer excerpt of each poem that is used in a chapter to demonstrate a grammatical principle. In addition, the poems that are included in Lessons to Enjoy at the ends of chapters are followed by Questions to Ponder and by suggested activities in the teacher's pages.

In order to help make poetry as meaningful and enjoyable as possible for both you and your students, we offer the following discussion prompts, adapted from *The Art of Poetry* by Christine Perrin, which you can tailor to your particular students' needs.

Poetic Elements

The following are definitions of common poetic elements that can be identified in almost any poem.

Alliteration: repeated beginning sounds of words

Form: the shape of the poem or the way it is organized on the page, often with a prescribed number of lines, number of beats per line, and rhyme scheme; also referred to as *shape*

Image: a concrete detail that speaks to the senses

Metaphor: a comparison between two things that are unlike; a resemblance forged in the mind of the poet between two unlike things; also referred to as "word pictures"

Rhyme: when words repeat or echo the same ending sound

Rhyme scheme: the pattern in which rhymes appear in a poem or stanza (e.g., *abab cdcd*)

Rhythm: the beat of the words together; the recurrence of movement and sound; the way sounds move; the rise and fall of words together

Speaker: the voice in the poem, sometimes the poet but often the voice assumed by the poet as a character

Symbol: use of a person, object, image, word, or event to evoke a range of meaning beyond the thing itself; an important image in a poem that has multiple, unspecified meanings and suggestions in its use

Tone: the attitude of the poem, of the poet toward the subject of the poem; the emotional atmosphere of the poem

Questions for Discussion

The following are more specific prompts for leading your students in the reading and study of a poem. As you discuss the poem, encourage students to think about the ways the various elements of a poem combine to create beauty and meaning.

1. **Poem title and expectation:** What does the title tell you about the poem? What do you expect the poem to be about? Does the poem surprise you?

2. **Clarifying the literal meaning of the poem:** What words are unfamiliar or curious to you? Have students use a dictionary or the vocabulary guide on the side margins to help with words they don't know. Can you put the poem into your own words? Note to students that paying attention to grammatical structures in the poem, rather than line breaks, can help.

3. **Characters in the poem:** Who is speaking and to whom? Is the speaker of the poem the poet, or is the speaker a character? What is the speaker's point of view? What is the speaker's attitude toward the subject of the poem?

4. **Setting of the poem:** Where does the poem take place? When does the poem take place? Was the poem written for a particular reason or occasion? Does the place, time, or occasion matter in the poem?

5. **Images in the poem:** What are the concrete details that make you imagine a sight, smell, sound, taste, or texture? What in the poem sparks your imagination? Are there words that affect your senses? Have you ever seen or felt in your life the things described in the poem?

6. **Sound and rhythm in the poem:** Are there rhymes at the ends of lines? If so, label them with lowercase letters of the alphabet to identify rhyme scheme, such as *abab* or *abba*. Are there repeated sounds or alliteration within lines? Do you want to tap your foot or giggle at the string of sounds? Or do you feel sad or solemn because of the sound patterns? Does the sound of the poem when you read it out loud suggest the meaning of the poem?

7. **Summarizing the poem's meaning:** What is the poem about? What is its theme or central idea? How do poetic elements, such as images, symbols, and metaphors, lead you to understand the poem?

8. **Personal response to the poem:** Do you like the poem? Have you ever thought or felt the way the poem expresses? Or is the poem different from what you already know or feel? Do you agree with the ideas expressed in the poem?

9. **Biographical, cultural, and literary context:** What do you know about the poet? Learn the basic biography of the poet (see Biographies: Meet the Authors for biographies of the authors featured in the Lessons to Enjoy sections of the book), and share something of this with your students. Do you think readers of the poem when it was first published would have understood it differently from you? Consider learning something about the time period in which this poem was written. Does the poem follow a particular form that is traditional, such as sonnet (a poem of fourteen lines in iambic pentameter with varying rhyme schemes) or ballad (a narrative poem originally meant to be sung with a regular rhyming stanza) form, or does it break literary convention?

Notes

Biographies
Meet the Authors

written by Marie Kramb Campbell

Aesop *(c. 620–564 BC)*

Everything we know about the ancient Greek fable teller Aesop is speculation. His life story itself may be a fable. That makes Aesop legendary. According to tradition, he lived in the sixth century BC and told his animal stories orally. The story goes that Aesop was a slave who was extremely ugly, even misshapen, but who was also extraordinarily clever. He was able to win his freedom through his wit, revealing to his master surprising truths beneath the surface of everyday life. In the end, he became an advisor to kings. Aesop's fables were passed down through generations of storytellers until finally, about 300 years after he told them, the fables were written down in a collection. The fables, such as "The Tortoise and the Hare," feature tales of animals who behave like humans and demonstrate moral lessons through their folly. (See chapters 1–8, Lesson to Enjoy—Fable.)

Alfred, Lord Tennyson *(1809–1892)*

Good looking, funny, clever—Alfred Tennyson drew to himself many good friends throughout his life, among them Albert, the husband of Queen Victoria, who named Tennyson a baron. That's why he's called Alfred, *Lord* Tennyson. Born in 1809 into a family that struggled with poverty, Tennyson made up verses as a youth while he was busy walking or doing other things, memorizing them in order to write them down later. He suffered the loss of a number of loved ones to early death, and he feared the insanity that seemed to run in his family. Perhaps because of such troubles, some of his poems are mournful. His first great success is a book of poetry entitled *In Memoriam*, which was written after his best friend died unexpectedly, but he also reworked in poetic form the legends of King Arthur and the Knights of the Round Table in his epic poem *The Idylls of the King*. The first prominent poet in the age of modern science and industrialization, Tennyson reflected in his work the Victorian people's strong moral values as well as their doubts about their rapidly changing world. With imagination, compassion, and extraordinary language skills, Tennyson created a poetic harmony that Victorians found appealing. After William Wordsworth died, Tennyson was named Poet Laureate, and was considered by his many readers to be the eminent poet of the nation. Tennyson died in 1892 with his family around him. He was buried with the copy of the Shakespeare play that he was reading when he died. (See chapter 3, Ideas to Understand; The Curious Child's Literary Appendix.)

Allingham, William *(1824–1889)*

William Allingham turned to poetry to stimulate his intellect and artistic spirit, possibly as a result of disappointment at having to leave school and go to work as a bank clerk when he was only thirteen. Allingham was born in 1824 on the west coast of Ireland. Like many Irish people, he was devoted to poetry and music. He is said to have roamed around in the evenings, listening to the townspeople singing folk ballads in their homes, collecting the songs in his memory and turning them into poetry. Later, after he took a job in a customs house, he published a book of poetry called *Day and Night Songs*. His work attracted the attention of established poets, such as Alfred, Lord Tennyson and Dante Gabriel Rossetti, with whom he became friends. His success led him at last to being the editor of a London literary magazine, where he met and fell in love with the accomplished watercolor painter, Helen Paterson, who later became his wife. He died in 1889, having published a number of volumes of poetry and having influenced a number of Irish poets. (See chapter 1, Lesson to Enjoy—Poem.)

Barrie, J.M. *(1860–1937)*

Best remembered for his play-turned-novel, *Peter Pan*, James Matthew Barrie had a long and successful career as a dramatist. He wrote forty plays over the course of fifty years, often basing his characters on real people in his life. He said the character of Peter Pan is a combination of five boys—the Davies brothers—whom he befriended and for whom he was guardian after their parents died. Like Peter, Barrie himself lost his mother when he was young, though he remained devoted to her throughout his life. He wrote *Peter Pan* with an adult audience in mind and did not consider it a children's play. In one scene, the members of the audience must clap in order to revive Tinker Bell. That kind of interaction between the actors and the audience was an original dramatic technique that had not been tried before. Because of the play's success, the name *Wendy*, which had rarely been given to baby girls previously, became a popular name. Barrie bequeathed the rights to the play and the novel to a children's hospital in England, so for many years every time it was produced or published, that hospital received a portion of its sales. At the same time children around the world enjoyed the story of Peter Pan, sick children were benefiting from its profits. (See chapter 8, Ideas to Understand; The Curious Child's Literary Appendix.)

Cary, Alice *(1820–1871)*

Born in 1820 near Cincinnati on a farm called Clovernook, Alice Cary was considered something of a frontierswoman because Ohio was still part of the West at that time. Everyone in her large family had to work hard, but Cary's father used to sing and recite poetry while he labored, and Cary's mother encouraged her to love literature and to write poetry. Sadly, after her mother died, Cary's father remarried and her stepmother frowned upon poetry and would not allow her to waste candles for light so that she could write in the evenings. With her sister Phoebe, young Alice would write in secret, fashioning a makeshift candle with lard oil in a saucer and a rolled-up rag for a wick. When they grew up, the sisters were able to support themselves in New York City with their practiced and polished writing, and Alice's poetry and short stories were highly regarded. Supporters of freedom for slaves and voting rights for women, the two sisters made their home a gathering spot for New York's artistic and socially active citizens. Cary's beliefs, her writing talent, and her charm drew people to her. When she died in 1871, circus founder P.T. Barnum and *New York Tribune* editor Horace Greeley were two of her pallbearers. She may have come a long way from that Ohio farm, but one of her most popular books was based on her experiences there: *Clovernook, or Recollections of Our Neighborhood in the West.* (See chapter 3, Lesson to Enjoy—Poem.)

Cooper, George *(1840–1927)*

An ordinary life might not get much attention in biographies, but that does not mean it can't lead to extraordinary poetry that inspires generations of readers. Not much is recorded about George Cooper's life, but his poetry and music have not been forgotten. We know that he was born in New York City in 1840, and he died in 1927. Even as a boy, he loved to wander away from the city into the woods and fields. Nature is a theme in much of his poetry. He studied to be a lawyer and was admitted to the bar, but he walked away from that profession in order to follow his passion for language and devote himself to writing. He wrote many hymns and also translated many foreign hymns into English verse. Cooper was devoted to his own family, and was pleased by the fact that schoolchildren of his time memorized his poems. History books record him as a close friend of Stephen Foster, who is acclaimed as the "father" of American music. Cooper wrote the lyrics for a number of songs set to music by Foster, particularly Civil War songs. (See chapter 2, Lesson to Enjoy—Poems in the downloadable PDF.)

Lawrence, Kate *(n.d.)*

When we took our question "Who was Kate Lawrence, writer of the poem 'Questions'?" to the library, we couldn't find an answer, not even when the librarian helped us. We may not be able to tell you where Kate Lawrence was born, how she lived, or when she died, but we can guess that she approved of the magazine in which she published her poem in 1882. In fact, that popular children's magazine, *Wide Awake*, has a sort of life story of its own. Published in the United States between 1875 and 1893, *Wide Awake* brought to young people countless illustrated stories, poems, puzzles, and nonfiction articles, also including letters from its readers. In addition, it serialized longer fiction, which meant a story would start in one issue and continue through a number of issues. Prominent writers and illustrators, as well as beginning ones, were featured in its pages. Ultimately, the magazine merged with another popular magazine of the era, *St. Nicholas*. Before the days of television and comic books, the internet and social media, *Wide Awake* and other such innovative magazines were the cutting-edge media that kept young people connected to each other and the world around them. The magazine's founder, Daniel Lothrop, and its original editor, Ella Farman, were determined to bring to young people a "new school" of children's literature that aimed to be "bright and sparkling without being foolish; humorous and nonsensical, even, without being silly; fanciful without being senseless; descriptive without being dry, and absorbing without being sensational."[1] Do you think Kate Lawrence's "Questions" fits that description? (See chapter 8, Lesson to Enjoy—Poem, "Questions.")

MacDonald, George *(1824–1905)*

Before there were The Chronicles of Narnia by C.S. Lewis and *The Hobbit* and *The Lord of the Rings* by J.R.R. Tolkien, there was *At the Back of the North Wind* by the nineteenth-century Scottish writer George MacDonald. He was a pioneer in writing fantasy, a type of story featuring imaginary worlds where magical creatures are common and where the forces of good battle with and defeat the forces of evil. All his life MacDonald loved fairy tales and regarded them as profoundly interesting. He was raised in the hills near Aberdeen, Scotland, in an area that could itself be a scene from a fairy tale, with the ruins of a castle, a river running through rolling hills, and a stately manor house surrounded by tall trees. Deeply religious, MacDonald became a minister as an adult and

1. "The Story of Wide Awake." Wide Awake: an Illustrated Magazine 37, no. 3 (August 1893). Boston: Lothrop & Co., 193-197. Available at https://babel.hathitrust.org/cgi/pt?id=hvd.hxp1sg&view=1up&seq=17.

often was invited to preach or lecture. However, he devoted his life to his wife and thirteen children and to writing Christian allegories, tales of fantasy with characters and events that symbolize deeper religious truths. He authored more than fifty volumes of poetry, fiction, and sermons, and both Lewis and Tolkien named him as a significant influence on their own work. (See chapter 2, Ideas to Understand; The Curious Child's Literary Appendix.)

M

McLeod, Irene Rutherford *(1891–1968)*

Australian born, Irene Rutherford McLeod lived most of her life in England, where her husband, Aubrey de Selincourt, was a teacher, classics scholar, and writer. She was a sister-in-law of A.A. Milne, who had married de Selincourt's sister. In fact, McLeod's daughter Lesley grew up to marry Milne's son, Christopher Robin. Aside from her famous relatives, McLeod is best known for the often anthologized poem "Lone Dog." She published several volumes of poetry, such as *Before Dawn* and *Songs to Save a Soul*, and she also wrote novels and plays. (See chapter 5, Lesson to Enjoy—Poem.)

Milne, A.A. *(1882–1965)*

It seems that nearly everybody has heard of Winnie the Pooh. That "bear of very little brain" is one of the most widely known and loved characters in all of children's literature. What many people don't realize, though, is that his creator, Alan Alexander Milne, had a very successful career as a writer of poetry, short stories, novels, screenplays, and especially plays. He was born in London in 1882 and returned there after his education to make his living with his pen. Later, he would move with his wife and young son, the real-life Christopher Robin, to a farm in Sussex. There he would write two collections of stories for children—*Winnie the Pooh* and *The House at Pooh Corner*—basing the characters on his son and his stuffed animals. By the time Milne died in 1965, he was a bit disappointed that his fame was based mostly on Pooh, wishing his other works to endure as well. When he grew up, Christopher Milne donated the original stuffed animals and they now reside in New York Public Library in New York City; however, Pooh and Piglet, Tigger, Kanga and Roo, and dear old melancholy Eeyore reside forever in the imaginations of their fans, both children and adults. (See chapter 5, Ideas to Understand; chapter 7, Lesson to Enjoy—Poem.)

Nesbit, Edith *(1858–1924)*

Beloved for her novel *The Railway Children*, among other novels for children, English author and poet Edith Nesbit is praised as one of the first modern writers of children's literature because her characters seem realistic, like ordinary children, even though they are confronted with extraordinary, magical events. In this way, her work has influenced the writers of The Chronicles of Narnia, *Mary Poppins*, and even the Harry Potter series. Several sites around England feature walkways or trails named after Nesbit's railway novel. Made into two television serials, a movie, and a made-for-TV movie, *The Railway Children* has never been out of print. In it, two sisters and a brother seek to get their unjustly imprisoned father pardoned. Nesbit herself, born in 1858 in London, had lost her father when she was only four, and her novels often feature children searching for their father. She published more than sixty books for children, including *The Story of the Treasure Seekers* and *The Wouldbegoods*. Children love not only Nesbit's appealing characters but also the inventive plots and the engaging style of the language in her books. (See chapter 1, Ideas to Understand; The Curious Child's Literary Appendix.)

Rossetti, Christina *(1830–1894)*

Considered one of the most important English poets of her time, Christina Rossetti wrote in a broad range of styles and about many different topics: both children's and adult literature; both fantastic and religious works; both lighthearted, humorous poems and dark, brooding ones. Born in 1830, she grew into a beautiful young woman and was a model for her brother, Dante Gabriel Rossetti, who was a famous painter, poet, illustrator, and translator. She was high spirited and passionate and worked hard her whole life to control her temper. Relying on a deep faith in God, she considered spiritual beauty, rather than physical beauty, more important, so she devoted herself to writing and to the people she loved. She died in London in 1894. In the midst of all her accomplishments, one of her children's books stands out as particularly musical and witty. *Sing-Song: A Nursery Rhyme Book* includes some poems that teach children virtues such as patience, some that help children remember a lesson such as the order of the months, and some with playful rhymes and rhythms that are just plain fun for children. (See chapter 6, Lesson to Enjoy—Poem.)

Scott, Sir Walter *(1771–1832)*

When Walter Scott was a baby, he suffered a disease that left his right leg crippled. Yet all his life he loved to hike around the countryside of his beloved Scotland. Because he so enjoyed being outdoors, especially if his rambling took him near the ruins of a medieval castle or church, he learned to overcome his limp. Though he was educated as a lawyer and even eventually became sheriff of a region in Scotland bordering England, his deeper education came through his encounters in the countryside with ordinary Scottish people. He collected their stories and their songs, and voraciously read books about Scottish history. That's what prepared him for huge success as a writer of novels such as *Ivanhoe* and *Rob Roy*. He was an international literary celebrity, and in 1819 the Prince Regent of England named him a baronet, a hereditary title of nobility, which is why he is called "Sir." Perhaps his greatest contribution to literature is his invention of the historical novel, which is a fictional story about real events in the past. He wrote long novels very quickly, and, unlike most writers, he rarely took time for revision. His was a genius at vividly depicting characters who were ordinary people, not just the famous ones recorded in history books. (See chapter 4, Lesson to Enjoy—Poem in the downloadable PDF.)

T

Thompson, George Selden *(1929–1989)*

Just like his beloved character, Chester the Cricket, George Selden Thompson was born and raised in Connecticut. He always knew he wanted to be a writer, so he majored in English and classical studies when he went to Yale. He was awarded a prestigious Fulbright scholarship to Italy, and spent an entire year touring Europe. When he returned to the United States, he was determined to succeed in a writing career and took up residence in New York City. After several failed plays and mediocre novels, he suddenly got the inspiration for his Newberry Medal–winning modern classic, *A Cricket in Times Square*. He told the story like this: "One night I was coming home on the subway, and I did hear a cricket chirp in the Times Square subway station. The story formed in my mind within minutes. An author is very thankful for minutes like those, although they happen all too infrequently."[2] By the time he died at the age of sixty in 1989, Thompson, who wrote under the pen name George Selden, had written seven books about Chester and his friends. His animal characters, like those of A.A. Milne and Kenneth Grahame, are distinctly human in the complexity of their emotions and interactions. They teach their human readers a lot about being human. They show that no matter if our differences are wide, friendship and compassion can carry us through the difficulties of life. (See chapter 7, Ideas to Understand; The Curious Child's Literary Appendix.)

2. "George Selden," *MacMillan Publishers Website*, accessed December 3, 2015, http://us.macmillan.com/author/georgeselden.

Thorley, Wilfrid *(1878–1963)*

Wilfrid Thorley was born in Lancashire, England, in 1878. During his lifetime, Thorley became not only a poet but also a translator who published more than fifteen books. He specialized in teaching English to foreign students around Europe in the years before World War I, and wrote his own textbooks for them. He wrote a biography of nineteenth-century French poet Paul Verlaine that was considered one of the best biographies published in 1914. One reviewer comments on his "sympathetic clarity" and his "subtlety and insight." Well, a spider hardly rates the same attention as a French poet, but haven't we seen how Thorley applied his insight and sympathetic clarity to that silver wire–weaving creature in "Of a Spider"? (See chapter 6, Ideas to Understand; The Curious Child's Literary Appendix.)

Wordsworth, William *(1770–1850)*

Many of William Wordsworth's readers in his own day thought his poetry was bad. They criticized the poet for using ordinary words, for dwelling on scenes from everyday life, and for writing about his own personal experiences, thoughts, and emotions. However, for those very reasons, today's readers consider Wordsworth one of the most important writers of his day, one of the founders of an artistic movement called Romanticism. It wasn't just Wordsworth's poetry that was fresh and innovative; he himself was unconventional. He was born in 1770 in the Lake District of England and enjoyed a comfortable home life until he was orphaned at the age of thirteen. Thrown into poverty, he relied on the goodness of relatives and his own passion for life. After completing his education, he became involved with the radical politics of the French Revolution and put himself in danger traveling back and forth to France. He loved beauty and nature and took long walking tours through parts of England and abroad. He always returned to his beloved Lake District, which was the inspiration for much of his poetry. He considered poetry an essential part of life—more important than wealth. Toward the end of his life, he started writing more conventionally. Then, more accepted by his contemporaries, he was made Poet Laureate of England (the officially recognized leading poet of the country) until his death in 1850. (See chapter 4, Ideas to Understand; The Curious Child's Literary Appendix.)

Works Referenced for Author Biographies

"Alfred, Lord Tennyson." In *Authors and Artists for Young Adults*. Vol. 50. Detroit: Gale, 2003.

"Alfred, Lord Tennyson Biography." *Cliffs Notes: Idylls of the King*. Accessed December 3, 2015. http://www.cliffsnotes.com/literature/i/idylls-of-the-king/alfred-lord-tennyson-biography.

"Biography: A.A. Milne." Teachers Site. Scholastic.com. Accessed December 3, 2015. http://www.scholastic.com/teachers/contributor/milne.

Chase, Gilbert. "America's Minstrel." In *America's Music, from the Pilgrims to the Present*. Chicago: University of Illinois Press, 1992.

"Christina (Georgina) Rossetti." In *Major Authors and Illustrators for Children and Young Adults*. Detroit: Gale, 2002.

Columbia Daily Spectator, 58, no. 46, November 14, 1914. Columbia University Libraries Information Services. Accessed December 3, 2015. http://spectatorarchive.library.columbia.edu/cgi-bin/columbia?a=d&d=cs19141114-01.2.22.

Concise Dictionary of British Literary Biography. Vol. 5. Detroit: Gale, 1991.

Dictionary of American Biography. New York: Charles Scribner's Sons, 1936.

Edwards, June. "The Cary Sisters." In *Dictionary of Unitarian & Universalist Biography*. Article published March 20, 2003. uudb.org/articles/carysisters.html.

Encyclopedia Britannica, http://www.britannica.com.

Fitzgerald, Thomas W. "William Allingham." In *Ireland and Her People: a Library of Irish Biography*. Ireland: Fitzgerald Book Co., 1910. Digitized June 10, 2010. http://bit.ly/1OWlOZ0.

Gardner, Lyn. "Golden Age." *The Guardian*. March 25, 2005. http://www.theguardian.com/stage/2005/mar/26/theatre.booksforchildrenandteenagers.

"George MacDonald." In *Contemporary Authors Online*. Detroit: Gale, 2003. *Biography in Context*. Web. November 17, 2015.

"George Selden." *MacMillan Publishers*. Accessed December 3, 2015. http://us.macmillan.com/author/georgeselden.

"George Selden Papers." *De Grummond Children's Literature Collection*. Accessed December 3, 2015. http://www.lib.usm.edu/legacy/degrum/public_html/html/research/findaids/DG0978.html.

"George Selden Thompson." In *Major Authors and Illustrators for Children and Young Adults*. Detroit: Gale, 2002.

"Irene Rutherford McLeod." *Answers.google.com*. Accessed December 3, 2015. http://answers.google.com/answers/threadview?id=249465.

Kettler, Sara. "J. M. Barrie & Peter Pan: From Fantasy to Dark Realities." Biography.com. Article published December 2, 2014. http://www.biography.com/news/peter-pan-jm-barrie-facts-biography.

Moulton, Charles Wells. "George Cooper." *The Magazine of Poetry*, 3, issues 1–4 (January 1891). http://bit.ly/1Yl7haY.

"The New Adventures of the Real Winnie-the-Pooh." *Treasures of the New York Public Library*. NYPL.org. Accessed December 3, 2015. https://www.nypl.org/about/locations/schwarzman/childrens-center-42nd-street/pooh.

Pringle, David., ed. "A(lan) A(lexander) Milne." In *St. James Guide to Fantasy Writers*. New York: St. James Press, 1996.

———. "E(dith) Nesbit." In *St. James Guide to Fantasy Writers*. New York: St. James Press, 1996.

Stableford, Brian. "J.M. Barrie: Overview." In *St. James Guide to Fantasy Writers*. Edited by David Pringle. New York: St. James Press, 1996.

"Steamboats, Viaducts and Railways." *The Writer's Almanac with Garrison Keillor*. April 7, 2015. http://writersalmanac.org/episodes/20150407/.

"The Story of *Wide Awake*." *Wide Awake: an Illustrated Magazine*. 37, no. 3 (August 1893). Boston: Lothrop & Co., 193–197. Available at https://babel.hathitrust.org/cgi/pt?id=hvd.hxp1sg&view=1up&seq=17.

Venable, William Henry. *Beginnings of Literary Culture in the Ohio Valley: Historical and Biographical Sketches*. Cincinnati: Robert Clarke & Co., 1891. Accessed November 19, 2015. http://bit.ly/1Yl44YL.

"Walter Scott." In *Authors and Artists for Young Adults*. Vol. 22. Detroit: Gale, 1997.

"Wilfrid Thorley." *Wikipedia: The Free Encyclopedia*. Wikipedia Foundation, Inc. August 10, 2015. https://en.wikipedia.org/wiki/Wilfrid_Thorley.

"William Allingham." *AllPoetry.com*. Accessed November 19, 2015. http://allpoetry.com/William-Allingham.

"William Wordsworth." In *Authors and Artists for Young Adults*. Vol. 70. Detroit: Gale, 2006.

Bibliography
Seek the Sources

Aesop. 'Two Travelers and the Bear." *The Book of Fables*. Edited by Ernest Griset, Samuel Croxall, Jean de La Fontaine, and Roger L'Estrange. New York: American Book Exchange, 1880. https://books.google.com/books?id=msEqAAAAYAAJ.

———. "The Ass and His Driver." In *Writing & Rhetoric Book 1: Fable*. Written by Paul Kortepeter. Camp Hill, PA: Classical Academic Press, 2013.

———. "The Crow and the Pitcher." In *Writing & Rhetoric Book 1: Fable*. Written by Paul Kortepeter. Camp Hill, PA: Classical Academic Press, 2013.

———. "The Fox and the Grapes." In *Writing & Rhetoric Book 1: Fable*. Written by Paul Kortepeter. Camp Hill, PA: Classical Academic Press, 2013.

———. "The Hunter and the Doves." In *Writing & Rhetoric Book 1: Fable*. Written by Paul Kortepeter. Camp Hill, PA: Classical Academic Press, 2013.

———. "The Jay and the Peacock." In *The Fables of Aesop*. Edited by Joseph Jacobs. London and New York: Macmillan and Company, 1917.

———. "The Lion and the Mouse." In *Writing & Rhetoric Book 1: Fable*. Written by Paul Kortepeter. Camp Hill, PA: Classical Academic Press, 2013.

———. "Three Young Bulls and a Lion." In *Writing & Rhetoric Book 1: Fable*. Written by Paul Kortepeter. Camp Hill, PA: Classical Academic Press, 2013.

Allingham, William. "Robin Redbreast." *Anthology of Children's Literature*. Edited by Edna Johnson, Carrie Scott, and Evelyn Sickels. Cambridge, MA: Houghton Mifflin Company, 1948.

"Baa Baa, Black Sheep." *The Children's Mother Goose*. Illustrated by William Donahey. Chicago: The Reilly & Lee Co., 1921.

Barrie, J.M. *Peter Pan*. New York: Dover Publications, Inc., 1999.

"Cackle, Cackle Madam Goose." *The Children's Mother Goose*. Illustrated by William Donahey. Chicago: The Reilly & Lee Co., 1921.

Cary, Alice. "To a Honey-Bee." *Ballads for Little Folks*. Boston and New York: Houghton Mifflin Co., 1873. https://books.google.com/books?id=D3dPAAAAYAAJ.

Cooper, George. "October's Party." *The Home Book of Verse: American and English 1580–1912*. Edited by Burton Egbert Stevenson. New York: Henry Holt and Company, 1915.

Lawrence, Kate. "Questions." *Wide Awake* 16, no. 1 (December 1882). Edited by Charles Trowbridge Pratt, Chautauqua Young Folks' Reading Union. Boston: D. Lothrop & Company, 1883. Available at https://books.google.com/books?id=dNnNAAAAMAAJ.

MacDonald, George. *At the Back of the North Wind*. Philadelphia, PA: Lippincott Company, 1909.

McLeod, Irene Rutherford. "Lone Dog." *Favorite Poems Old and New*. Edited by Helen Ferris. New York: Doubleday & Company, Inc., 1957.

Milne, A.A. "Us Two." *There's Always Pooh and Me*. New York: Dutton Children's Books, 1998.

Milne, A.A. *The House at Pooh Corner*. New York: Dell Publishing, Inc., Co. , 1956.

Nesbit, E. and Saretta Nesbit (aka Caris Brooke). *All Round the Year*. London: Von Portheim & Co. Last modified January 20, 2007. http://tinyurl.com/ocao7gy.

"Robert Barns, Fellow Fine." *The Children's Mother Goose*. Illustrated by William Donahey. Chicago: The Reilly & Lee Co., 1921.

Rossetti, Christina G. "A Pin." *Rossetti Poems*. New York: Alfred A. Knoff, 1995.

Scott, Sir Walter. "Hunter's Song." *Select Works of the British Poets*. Edited by John Aikin. Philadelphia: Thomas Wardle, 1838. https://books.google.com/books?id=PKgcAAAAMAAJ.

Tennyson, Lord Alfred. "Song of the Brook." *Anthology of Children's Literature*. Edited by Edna Johnson, Carrie E. Scott, and Evelyn R. Sickels. Cambridge, Massachusetts: Houghton Mifflin Company, 1948.

Thompson, George Selden. *The Cricket in Times Square*. New York: A Yearling Book, 1960.

Thorley, Wilfrid. "Of a Spider." *Favorite Poems Old and New*. Edited by Helen Ferris. New York: Doubleday & Company, Inc., 1957.

Wordsworth, William. "The Kitten Playing with the Falling Leaves." *The Golden Treasury of Poetry*. Edited by Louis Untermeyer. New York: Golden Press, 1998.

Glossary of Terms

	Chapter
A	
Action Verb: An action verb, also known as a predicate verb, shows what the subject does. *See also* predicate verb.	3
Adjectival Element: A word (or a group of words) that modifies nouns or pronouns.	5
Adjective: An adjective is a part of speech. It's used to describe or define the meaning of a noun or pronoun (*see also* noun, pronoun). It answers the questions *how many*, *whose*, *which one*, or *what kind*. It modifies a noun or pronoun.	5
Adverb: An adverb is a part of speech. It modifies a verb, an adjective, or adverb. It answers the questions *how*, *when*, or *where*. An adverb is a part of speech.	4
Adverbial Element: A word (or a group of words) that modifies verbs, adjectives, and adverbs.	4
Antecedent: The antecedent is a noun, clause, or phrase to which a pronoun refers. If the antecedent is singular, then the pronoun is singular too. But if the noun, clause, or phrase is plural, then the pronoun must be plural too. The antecedent determines which pronoun is used.	7
Auxiliary Verb: *See* helping verb.	3
C	
Clause: A clause is a group of words containing a subject and a predicate, behaving like one part of speech.	4
Conjunction: A part of speech that joins words, phrases, or clauses. Conjunctions indicate the relation between the elements that they join.	1

	Chapter
Consonant: A letter of the alphabet that represents a constricted speech sound. The indefinite article "a" is used before words beginning with consonants: *b, c, d, f, g, h, j, k, l, m, n, p, q, r, s, t, v, w, x, y,* and z. *See also* vowel.	5
Contraction: A shortened form of two words that uses an apostrophe in place of the letters and spaces left out.	8

D

Declarative Sentence: One of the four kinds of sentences. It makes a statement and ends with a period.	1
Definite Article: The adjective *the*. It identifies a particular noun and is placed before nouns or adjectives. *See also* indefinite article.	5
Direct Object: A direct object is an objective element that tells what the subject is acting on. It's a noun or pronoun after a transitive verb. It answers the question *what* or *whom* after the verb and is labeled *do*.	6

E

Eight Parts of Speech: The eight parts of speech are classes of words with the same kind of meaning and use. And they are nouns, verbs, adjectives, adverbs, prepositions, pronouns, conjunctions, and interjections.	1
Exclamatory Sentence: One of the four kinds of sentences. It expresses strong feeling and ends with an exclamation point.	1

F

First Person: A grammatical category of pronouns used by the speaker to refer to himself or herself (i.e., the subject pronouns *I* or *we* and the object pronouns *me* or *us*). *See also* person.	7

H

Helping Verb: A verb that helps another verb express its meaning. It is placed alongside a transitive, linking, or intransitive verb to form a verb phrase. Both words work together as one action. The helping verbs are *am, is, are, was, were, be, being, been, have, has, had, do, did, does, may, might, must, should, would, could, shall, will, can.*	3

	Chapter
I	
Imperative Sentence: One of the four kinds of sentences. It gives a command and ends with a period or exclamation point.	1
Implied Subject: A subject that does not appear in the sentence but is indirectly expressed or suggested. *See also* subject.	1
Indefinite Article: The adjective *a* or *an*. It is placed before nonspecific nouns and identifies them as being singular; *a* is used before nouns or adjectives beginning with a consonant, and *an* is used before nouns or adjectives beginning with a vowel sound. *See also* definite article.	5
Interjection: A part of speech that is a word or short phrase that expresses strong emotion. It is inserted into a sentence or stands alone.	1
Interrogative Sentence: One of the four kinds of sentences. It asks a question and ends with a question mark.	1
Intransitive Verb: A verb that does not take an objective element or join the subject to the predicate.	6
L	
Linking Verb: A verb that joins the subject to the predicate. In other words, it is the glue that joins the subject either to a noun that renames the subject or to an adjective that describes the subject. Linking verbs express a state of being.	3
M	
Modifier: A word (or a group of words) that modifies or changes the meaning of a word. Adjectives modify nouns and pronouns; adverbs usually modify verbs, but adverbs also can modify adjectives and other adverbs.	4
N	
Negative Adverb: An adverb such as *no, not,* and *never* that modifies a verb by negating it or making its meaning the opposite.	4
Nominative Case: The grammatical term indicating that a noun or pronoun is the subject in a sentence or a clause. *See also* subjective case.	7

	Chapter
Noun: A noun is a part of speech. It names a person, place, or thing. A noun names a quality or an idea. A noun is a part of speech. It names a person, place, or thing. A noun may be singular or plural.	2
Number: A property of a noun or pronoun that tells how many. Singular in number means only one, and plural in number means more than one.	7

O

Object: A word that names the person or thing that directly receives the action of the verb.	6
Objective Case: The grammatical term indicating that a noun or pronoun is the object in a sentence, phrase, or clause.	7
Objective Element: A word or group of words that completes the meaning of the action verb. *See also* direct object. Objective elements can also include indirect objects or the objects of prepositions.[1]	6
Object Pronoun: A personal pronoun that is used as a direct object or the object of the preposition (i.e., *me, us, you, him, her, it, them*).	7
Ordinal Numbers: An adjective that denotes what place an object is in an order, such as *first, second, third,* or *fourth.*	5

P

Person: A property of a noun or pronoun that distinguishes between speaker, addressee, and others. There are three persons: first person (the one speaking); second person (the one being spoken to); and third person (the one being spoken about).	7
Personal Pronoun: A pronoun that takes different forms depending on the person of its antecedent (i.e., first, second, or third person). *See also* pronoun, object pronoun, subject pronoun.	7
Phrase: A group of words behaving like one part of speech. A phrase does not contain a subject and a predicate.	4
Plural: A grammatical category for nouns, pronouns, and verbs that refer to more than one thing.	2
Predicate: One of the principal elements in a sentence. It tells something about the subject, like what it is doing or being.	2

1. You'll learn about indirect objects and objects of the preposition in later books in the WOL series.

	Chapter
Predicate Verb: An action verb showing what the subject does. If it is a transitive verb, it takes a direct object. If it is an intransitive verb, it does not. *See also* action verb, intransitive verb, transitive verb.	3
Prefix: A group of letters added to the beginning of a root word to form a different word, but usually not a different part of speech. *See also* root word.	2
Principal Elements: Principal elements are the parts of the sentence that are needed for the sentence to be completed. Subject and predicate are those parts.	2
Pronoun: A pronoun is a part of speech used in place of a noun or of more than one noun. A pronoun is a part of speech.	7

R

Root Word: A word without any elements added either to its beginning (prefix) or to its end (suffix). *See also* prefix, suffix.	2

S

Second Person: A grammatical category for pronouns used by the speaker to refer to the person being spoken *to* (i.e., *you* as either a singular or plural subject pronoun or a singular or plural object pronoun). *See also* person.	7
Sentence: A sentence is a group of words expressing a complete thought. There are four kinds of them: Declarative Sentence – Makes a statement. Interrogative Sentence – Asks a question. Imperative Sentence – Gives a command. Exclamatory Sentence – Expresses strong feeling.	1
Simple Predicate: The main word or words, not including modifiers, that tell what the subject is doing or being.	4
Simple Subject: The main word or words, not including modifiers, that tell what the sentence is about.	4
Singular: A grammatical category for nouns, pronouns, and verbs that refer to only one thing.	2
Stanza: A group of lines in a poem.	3
Subject: One of the principal elements in a sentence. It is a noun or pronoun and is what the sentence is about.	2
Subjective Case: The grammatical term indicating that a noun or pronoun is the subject in a sentence or a clause. *See also* nominative case.	7

	Chapter
Subject Pronoun: A personal pronoun that is used as the subject in a sentence (i.e., *I, we, you, he, she, it, they*).	7
Subject-Verb Agreement: A correct sentence structure in which the subject and verb agree in person (first, second, or third person) and in number (singular or plural).	3
Subordinate Element: A word (or a group of words) that change(s) or limit(s) the meaning of the principal elements. Also known as modifiers.	4
Suffix: A group of letters added to the end of a root word to form a different word, usually a different part of speech	2
Syntax: Word order. It is the way in which words are combined to form phrases, clauses, or sentences.	2

T

Tense: A form of a verb that is used to show time or when an action occurs, as in past, present, and future.	3
Third Person: A grammatical category for pronouns used by the speaker to refer to anyone or anything being spoken about that is not the speaker or the one addressed (i.e., the subject pronouns *he, she, it,* or *they* and the object pronouns *him, her,* or *them*). *See also* person.	7
Transitive Verb: A verb that takes an objective element (i.e., a direct object). It transitions from the subject to the direct object.	6

V

Verb: A part of speech that shows action or a state of being.	2
Verb Phrase: A helping verb together with either an action verb or a linking verb.	3
Vowel: A letter of the alphabet that represents a voiced speech sound. The indefinite article *an* is used before words beginning with vowels: *a, e, i, o, u*. *See also* consonant.	5

Song Lyrics

Eight Parts of Speech *(1–1)*

The eight parts of speech are classes of words
with the same kind of meaning and use.
They are: nouns, verbs, adjectives, adverbs,
prepositions, pronouns, conjunctions, interjections.
These are the eight parts of speech,
classes of words with the same kind of meaning and use. *(Repeat.)*

Sentence *(1–2)*

A sentence is a group of words expressing a complete thought.
There are four kinds of sentences:
Declarative sentence—makes a statement.
Interrogative sentence—asks a question.
Imperative sentence—gives a command.
Exclamatory sentence—expresses strong feelings.
A sentence is a group of words expressing a complete thought.
There are four kinds of sentences. *(Repeat.)*

Principal Elements *(1–3)*

Principal elements are the parts of the sentence
that are needed for the sentence to be completed.
Subject and predicate are those two parts.

From the Sideline: The numbers in parentheses for each of these songs and chants refer to the audio tracks available at ClassicalAcademicPress.com.

When you see *(Repeat.)* at the end of a song, it means that all of the song lyrics are sung through once and then repeated. If *(repeat)* appears at the end of one or more lines in the song, it means that those specific lines are repeated. For songs that have the notation *(echo)* at the end of a line, you may want to split your class into two groups and have one group echo the other group as they sing the song.

Subject and Predicate *(1–4)*

A subject, a subject is a noun or a pronoun
and is what the sentence is about *(clap, clap).*
A predicate, a predicate tells us something about the subject
like what it is doing or being *(clap, clap).*

Noun *(1–5)*

A noun is a part of speech.
It names a person, place, or thing.
A noun names a quality or an idea.
A noun is a part of speech.
It names a person, place, or thing.
A noun may be singular *(clap)* or plural *(clap clap clap). (Repeat.)*

Verb and Helping Verb *(1–6)*

A verb is a part of speech. *(echo)*
A verb shows action or a state of being. *(echo)*
A verb is a part of speech. *(echo)*
A verb shows action or a state of being. *(echo)*
A helping verb helps another verb to express its meaning.
A helping verb stands near the verb.
It is called an auxiliary.
Am, is, are, was, were, be, being, been, has, have, had, do, does,
did, may, might, must, should, could, would, shall, will, and *can.*
A helping verb stands near the verb and is called an auxiliary.
A helping verb stands near the verb. It is called an auxiliary.

Adverb *(1–7)*

An adverb is a part of speech.
It modifies a verb or another adverb.
It can also modify an adjective
and answers three questions: *how? when?* or *where?*
It answers three questions: *how? when?* or *where?*

Adjective *(1–8)*

An adjective is a part of speech
used to describe or define
the meaning of a noun or pronoun.
It answers the questions:
How many? (echo)
Whose? (echo)
Which one? (echo)
or *What kind? (echo)*
It modifies a noun or pronoun.
It modifies a noun or pronoun.

Direct Object *(1–9)*

d-o, d-o
A direct object is an objective element
that tells what the subject is acting on.
d-o, d-o
It's a noun or pronoun after a transitive verb.
d-o, d-o
It answers the question *what* or *whom* after the verb
and is labeled *do*.

Four Classes of Verbs *(1–10)*

These are the four classes of verbs:
The four classes of verbs are transitive verbs, linking verbs,
intransitive verbs, and helping verbs.
These are the four classes of verbs.
A transitive verb takes an objective element.
A linking verb joins a subject to a predicate.
An intransitive verb does not take an objective element
or join a subject to a predicate.
A helping verb helps another verb express its meaning.
A helping verb helps another verb express its meaning.
These are the four classes of verbs.
These are the four classes of verbs.

Pronoun *(1–11)*

A pronoun is a part of speech
used in place of a noun or nouns.
A pronoun is a part of speech
used in place of a noun or nouns.
A pronoun is a part of speech.

Subject Pronouns *(1–12)*

Subject pronouns are in the nominative case:
I, you, he, she, it, we, you, they *(repeat)*.
Subject pronouns are in the nominative case:
I, you, he, she, it, we, you, they *(repeat)*.

Antecedent *(1–13)*

The antecedent is a noun, clause, or phrase
to which a pronoun refers.
If the antecedent is singular,
then the pronoun is singular too.
But if the noun, clause, or phrase is plural,
then the pronoun must be plural too.
The antecedent determines which pronoun is used.

Fable *(1–14)*

A fable *(echo)*
is a moral tale.
A fable *(echo)*
is not a fairy tale.
A fable is short, direct, and clear.
Animals are characters sneaky or sincere.
Teaching lessons not to be deceived,
fables warn us not to be naive.

About the Title

The title of this series was inspired by a passage in a small book by Josef Pieper titled *Abuse of Language—Abuse of Power*. In the book, Pieper writes:

> [T]he well-ordered human existence, including especially its social dimension, is essentially based on the well-ordered language employed. A well-ordered language here does not primarily mean its formal perfection, even though I agree . . . that every correctly placed comma is decisive. No, a language is well ordered when its words express reality with as little omission as possible.[1]

Language is the means by which we make sense of reality. It is the medium by which we perceive truth. Therefore, a well-ordered language—one that best represents reality with as little distortion as possible—would provide the best access to truth. Language education, then, should be focused on developing as complete and accurate an understanding of language as possible.

While the pursuit of truth through language involves careful thinking (logic) and eloquent expression (rhetoric), the youngest students must first acquire a solid foundation in the structure and function of the language itself (grammar). Mirroring the well-ordered nature of language, effective educators employ an approach to language instruction that is itself well-ordered, structured, and disciplined. Critics of a well-organized and disciplined approach often confuse its form with the disposition of those who employ it. The disciplined approach to language study can be employed through intimidation and aggression, but it can just as easily be administered with love and compassion. The disciplined approach—often mischaracterized as "drill-and-kill"—actually respects the humanity of the student because it acknowledges that children learn differently than mature adults do.

For children to feast upon the rich cuisine of that which is good, true, and beautiful, they should first be shown how to taste, savor, and digest what they encounter. Without proper instruction that will cultivate their taste, students may turn from the "feast" in disgust, reject further sustenance, and perhaps never return. By acquiring a well-ordered language,

1. Josef Pieper, *Abuse of Language—Abuse of Power* (San Francisco: Ignatius Press, 1992), 36.

students will also acquire that taste for language that will lead them to the great feast that awaits. To impart this taste is to avoid one of the greatest errors of modern educational theory, which is the assumption that children can learn without first acquiring those tools of learning that we call the language arts.

Notes

adjectives
CONJUNCTIONS
prepositions
verbs
interjections

Notes

adjectives
CONJUNCTIONS
prepositions
verbs
interjections

Notes

adjectives
CONJUNCTIONS
prepositions
verbs
interjections

Notes

adjectives
CONJUNCTIONS
prepositions
verbs
interjections